Preface Books

A series of scholarly and critical studies of major writers intended for those needing modern and authoritative guidance through the characteristic difficulties of their work to reach an intelligent understanding and enjoyment of it.

General Editor: MAURICE HUSSEY

Marble bust of Alexander Pope, 1740, by Louis François Roubiliac

A Preface to Pope

Second Edition

I.R.F. Gordon

Longman, London and New York.

Longman Group UK Limited,
Longman House, Burnt Mill,
Harlow, Essex CM20 2JE, England
and Associated Companies throughout the world.

*Published in the United States of America
by Longman Publishing, New York*

First published 1976
Second Edition 1993

ISBN 0 582 08927 1

British Library Cataloguing-in-Publication Data

A catalogue record for this book is
available from the British Library

Library of Congress Cataloging-in-Publication Data

Gordon, I. R. F.
    A Preface to Pope / I. R. F. Gordon. – 2nd ed.
        p. cm. – (Preface books)
    Includes bibliographical references and indexes.
    ISBN 0-582-08927-1
    1. Pope, Alexander, 1688–1744–Criticism and interpretation.
    I. Title.
    PR3634.G67   1993
    821'.5 - dc20   93-10076
CIP

Set in Linotron 202 10/11 Baskerville by 150

Printed in Malaysia by PMS

Contents

Contents

PART TWO: CRITICAL SURVEY

PART THREE: REFERENCE SECTION

List of illustrations

The *cover* reproduces an oil portrait of Alexander Pope painted by
his friend Charles Jervas. The painting shows the poet in reflective
mood with a lady, possibly Martha, 'Patty', Blount replacing a book
on a shelf behind him. If it is Martha then her shadowy background
position may be intended to suggest that she is the subject of his
reverie.

Acknowledgements

My indebtedness to the many colleagues and students at Anglia Polytechnic University who have shared my enthusiasm for Pope's poetry is too extensive to list in full. They have contributed to my appreciation and understanding of Pope, over more than quarter of a century, and it gives me pleasure to warmly acknowledge their help and support. I should also like to thank Mike Salmon, Vice-Chancellor of the University, and Steve Marshall, Dean of the Faculty of Humanities, Arts and Education for granting me a term's study leave to complete this second edition of *A Preface to Pope*.

Carol Rigglesford has unstintingly given of her time to supplement the inadequacies of my word processing skills and Alysoun Owen, the literature editor at Longman, has been the most helpful and constructive of editors with whom to work. My particular thanks, however, go to Felicia Gordon, to whom this book is dedicated, who painstakingly endured the various drafts of my revision. She read nothing that she did not sharpen or improve and helped me, like the poet I admire, to make precision my study and aim. Needless to say the faults that remain are my own.

We are grateful to the following for permission to reproduce illustrations and photographs:

D. Baxter (page 25); The British Library (pages 50, 56 and 167); British Museum (page 74); The Syndics of Cambridge University Library (pages 38-9, from John Stow, *A Survey of Cities of London and Wetstminster* Volume I, Book I, London, 1720, p. 1; pages 67 *bottom*, 76; frontispiece from W. K. Wimsatt, *The Portraits of Alexander Pope*, Yale University Press, New Haven and London, 1965, p. 238); J. J. Eyston and the Tate Gallery (page 17); I. R. F. Gordon (page 67 *top*); The Huntington Library, San Marino, California (page 199); The Mansell Collection (page 245).

Foreword to the First Edition

Alexander Pope, unquestionably the leading English poet of the first half of the eighteenth century, was an intriguing and paradoxical character: a man of wrath, full of recrimination and accusation, and at the same time a poet of the virtues of friendship, reasonableness, good sense and social responsibility. Ian Gordon's *Preface* pulls out, one by one, the strands in that artistic and social temperament, and offers a biographical and intellectual portrait of a man, cultivating his famous grotto and garden down by the Twickenham riverside, who remained at the centre of metropolitan culture and wit: a man whom the Whigs reviled and the Tories admired, both to an exorbitant degree.

That other arts than literature should play a large part in a survey such as this will occasion no remark, but the reader unfamiliar with its subject may be surprised by the importance attached in literature between the times of Pope and Jane Austen to landscape gardening. In this pursuit lies the blend of the aesthetic with the practical, an art much lower than architecture but ideally planned together with it in the same perspective. As we discover from pp. 181-8 Pope accused the landlord figure he calls Timon of exceeding all good taste, not least in the size of his operations that 'brings all Brobdignag before your thought'. Yet, on the other hand, he supports the planning projects, also vast, of his friend Burlington:

> Let his plantations stretch from down to down,
> First shade a Country, and then raise a Town.
> > (*Epistle to Burlington*, 189-90)

He goes further and imagines whole navies, harbours, temples, the entire solid texture of a community. The distinction between these two men is important. What Timon's building lacks is an ideal dimension, an attempt to reduce the wildness of nature to provide the context for a civilized city. Such a vision is at the core of Pope's art as a way of stemming the onrush of dulness, madness, corruption and universal darkness which were his obsessions in the years when he was completing *The Dunciad*. Such an art, replete with social responsibility, provides the modern searcher with a perfect model of a literary art in close touch with the ultimate problems of its day, a relevance, and a justification.

As expressed in his *Essay on Man*, which Dr Gordon analyses in chapter 5, Pope's ideas assumed a more systematic though not original form. He can always produce the epigrammatic statement and build a series of them into a credible, if encapsulated, species of dogma. To hold an entire poetic structure in our imagination and respond to it adequately, so as to appreciate the overall design, may be for some readers a most demanding activity, especially where the freer forms and more glowing images of romantic poetry still cling to the mind. Yet it is, as Dr Gordon's readers will discover, a poetic vision, much crisper though less emotionally intense, and probably no less exciting when we come across such a couplet as:

> The spider's touch, how exquisitely fine!
> Feels at each thread, and lives along the line;
>
> (*Essay on Man*, I, 217–18)

The poems and passages chosen for the Critical Survey are examined in depth as all Pope's verse should be. A single canto or epistle at a time is as much as the new reader should undertake. Here, informed by the author's experience in teaching Pope's poetry to several types of student, readers are equipped with the ideas and skills desirable to promote their own expanding enjoyment of a major poet.

MAURICE HUSSEY
General Editor
(1975)

Maurice Hussey died suddenly in June 1991. The Publishers and author would like to pay tribute to his wisdom, inspiration and friendship as Editor of Preface Books. He will be sadly missed.

Introduction to the Second Edition

This book, first published in 1976, has been substantially re-written for this new edition. I have taken account of the considerable body of Pope scholarship and criticism that has been published since I first wrote it nearly twenty years ago, in particular of Maynard Mack's masterly life of Pope.[1] In addition I have taken the opportunity to correct errors that have been pointed out to me by reviewers and readers, and to revise and expand sections where my views of what I wrote then have changed. The most substantial additions are to Part Two, where I have included short introductory essays to a selection of Pope's major poems.

In Part One, which places Pope in his own time and attempts to give the reader a sense of the historical, intellectual and cultural climate in which his poetry developed, each chapter has been updated and references have been provided. Chapter 1 is a short biography that pays special attention to those bonds of friendship and duty that shaped Pope's life. Chapter 2 deals with his responses to the city and the country and the ways in which those responses take on allusive and metaphoric significance at the same time as they establish a concrete reality for his poetry. Chapter 3 shows how an understanding of Pope's relationship to the kindred arts of his day enriches our appreciation of his work, while chapter 4 deals with literary criteria and expectations that eighteenth-century readers took for granted but that we in the twentieth century no longer do. Chapter 5 considers the intellectual context of Pope's thought and the way it affected his writing.

Part Two offers brief introductory essays, together with close readings of some key passages, on a selection of Pope's major poems chosen to represent the range of his achievement and the development of his art. Part Three is a reference section intended as a tool to help those readers who may feel discouraged by the frequent naming of contemporary persons and places in Pope's poetry. Though we can never entirely regain the full trenchancy of a poetry much of which was written to be topical, we can go a long way towards doing so as we extend our knowledge of early eighteenth-century social and political history.

Few English poets have led a life so completely devoted to poetry as Pope. Keats is another who springs to mind, but then his life was cut even more tragically short than Pope's, and there is no knowing how it might have developed had it run a fuller course. By saying that Pope led a life completely devoted to poetry I mean that it was everything, or very nearly everything, to him. He lived almost entirely for poetry, not just reading and writing, but also translating and editing it. Except for a brief flirtation with painting, he was never really tempted to follow any other pursuit. He had other interests and pastimes of course, especially landscape gardening and his loving construction of the elaborately decorated grotto that became his private retreat, but from his earliest days it was poetry that was his abiding love and passion. As he puts it in *An Epistle to Dr Arbuthnot*:

> As yet a Child, nor yet a Fool to Fame,
> I lisp'd in Numbers for the Numbers came.
> I left no Calling for this idle trade,
> No duty broke, no Father dis-obey'd.[2]   (127–30)

The playfully light-hearted tone here appears to dismiss poetry as an 'idle trade', in contrast to the high-minded 'Calling' attributed to other professions, but one feels that the coded thrust behind the ironic self-deprecation is that it is poetry that involves the true 'Calling' and other professions that are mere 'idle trades'.

Pope is, above all else, an ideological[3] and idealistic poet who, if his whole life makes him aware of the pains and pressures of everyday reality, nevertheless clings to one especial idea and one great ideal: the idea that the poet has a central moral role to play in society and the ideal of a well-run society as a reasonable human aspiration. He sees himself in his earlier poetry, and especially in *Windsor-Forest*, as a defender of the ideal of the decently ordered state and a promoter of the fame of 'Albion's Golden Days' (424); while in his later poetry, particularly in the *Imitations of Horace* and *The Dunciad*, the various spokespersons he creates become public prosecutors of all those who seek to disregard, subvert or destroy this ideal.

One of his most passionate utterances in this respect comes in the *Epilogue to the Satires: Dialogue II*, written towards the end of his life, where he casts himself in the role of a divinely appointed public watchman forced to take the law into his own hands, brandishing his satiric pen to stir into wakefulness those who should be guarding the well-being of the state:

> O sacred Weapon! left for Truth's defence,
> Sole Dread of Folly, Vice, and Insolence!
> To all but Heav'n-directed hands deny'd,
> The Muse may give thee! but the Gods must guide.
> Rev'rent I touch thee! but with honest zeal;
> To rouze the Watchmen of the Public Weal,
> To Virtue's Work provoke the tardy Hall,
> And goad the Prelate slumb'ring in the Stall   (212–19)

A strong religious quality, general rather than specifically Christian, imbues the language of these lines. Satire is a 'sacred' weapon placed in the poet's hands at 'Heaven's' direction. The poet may be inspired by the Muse but he relies for guidance on the 'Gods'. Satire is a weapon that is seen as the last defence of Truth and only handled by the poet with due 'reverence'. It is a weapon used, as the verbs in particular indicate, for active, even militant, combat; to 'rouze', 'provoke' and 'goad'. Thirty lines further on the metaphor of the pen as a sword becomes even more explicit as the satirist proudly, if somewhat self-consciously, pulls it from its scabbard:

> Yes, the last Pen for Freedom let me draw,
> When Truth stands trembling on the edge of Law   (248–9)

It is an heroic, even epic, concept of the satirist's role, infused with high moral and prophetic purpose, that Pope puts forward here.

Such a position undoubtedly presents today's readers with difficulties. It can seem an unconscionably complacent, even pious, role to adopt. Who is Pope, a modern reader might well say, to assume that his satirist's hands are Heaven-directed and guided by the Gods? A similar objection might be made to the poet's rousing injunction in *An Essay on Man*:

> Know then thyself, presume not God to scan;
> The proper study of mankind is Man.   (II, 1–2)

Who is Pope to tell us what we should, or should not, know, and what is, or is not, the proper study of mankind? The voice of rational exhortation presumes as much as that of passionate conviction, and the modern reader, reared in a culture constructed around the sanctity of individual freedom, is not used to being told so peremptorily what he or she should, or should not, do.

And yet this is exactly the point. Pope lived at a time when the poet was held in such high esteem in educated society that it was accepted that he had a right to assume such a voice. The poet was invested with privilege through the very nature of his being a poet. This privilege had been proclaimed and elaborated by the great English Renaissance apologists for poetry – Sidney, Ben Jonson, Milton and Dryden – who preceded Pope, so that he and his Augustan contemporaries inherited an accepted belief in the poet's important place within the state's moral, civilized and hierarchical structure. 'Now therein of all sciences', says Sir Philip Sidney in his *Defence of Poesie*, first published in 1595, 'is our poet the monarch'.[4] 'The study of it [Poesy]', says Ben Jonson in *Timber, Or Discoveries*, written some thirty or forty years later, 'offers to mankind a certain rule, and pattern of living well, and happily; disposing us to all civil offices of society.'[5] Note the inclusive 'all'. The authority for the assumed weight and grandeur of so many of the voices that Pope adopts in his poems had been clearly established by the major English poet-critics of the preceding period.

Pope's poety attracts our admiration in a variety of different ways. Sometimes it is the wit and sweep of its rhetorical and imaginative structures that strike us most forcefully; at other times it is the ease and eloquence of its numbers; and on still other occasions it is the cutting compactness of its language that has the strongest effect. But above all, for this reader, it is the poet's passionate concern for the state of society and his undying commitment to a moral order in civilized life that compel continuing respect and attention. Pope's pointed couplets and poised rhythms confront his readers with critical choices that require them to re-examine their own position with regard to the world they live in. As Dr Johnson says in his *Life of Pope*, 'he did not court the candour, but dared the judgment of his reader'.[6]

IAN GORDON
August 1992

Notes

1. Maynard Mack, *Alexander Pope: A Life* (Yale University Press, New Haven, 1985).
2. All quotations from Pope are taken from the Twickenham Edition of *The Poems of Alexander Pope*, ed., John Butt *et al.*, 11 vols (Methuen, London, 1938–68). Where the particular poem referred to is named in the text the line numbers alone are given in parentheses at the end of the quote; where the poem is not named in the text the name is given in parentheses, together with the line numbes, at the end of the quote.
3. For a fuller discussion of this somewhat neglected aspect of Pope's poetry see Brean Hammond's stimulating study *Pope* (The Harvester Press, Brighton, 1986).
4. Sir Philip Sidney, *The Defence of Poesie* (1595; A Scolar Press Facsimile, Menston, 1968).
5. Ben Jonson, *Timber, Or Discoveries* (1641); ed. G. B. Harrison (Edinburgh University Press, Edinburgh, 1966), p. 90.
6. Samuel Johnson, 'Pope' in *Lives of the English Poets* (1779–81), ed. G. B. Hill, 3 vols (Clarendon Press, Oxford, 1905), Vol. III, p. 221.

For Felicia

Part One
The Poet in his Setting

Chronological table

	MAIN EVENTS OF POPE'S LIFE	RELATED HISTORICAL AND LITERARY EVENTS
1688	(May 21) Pope born, Lombard St., London.	'The Glorious Revolution' William of Orange becomes King of England. James II flees to France.
c.1696	At school in a Catholic seminary, at Twyford, Hants.	
c.1700	Pope's family moves to Binfield in Windsor Forest.	Death of Dryden.
1702		Death of William III. Accession of Queen Anne. Declaration of war on France.
c.1705	Becomes acquainted with Wycherley, Walsh, and other literary persons.	
1709	*Pastorals*	Peace negotiations.
1710	Beginning of friendship with Caryll.	Fall of Whigs. Tory Ministry formed under Robert Harley, later Lord Oxford.
1711	*An Essay on Criticism.* Friendly with Addison and Steele.	Swift's *Conduct of the Allies.*
1712	*The Rape of the Lock* (2 Canto version). First meets Swift, Gay, Arbuthnot, Parnell and Oxford. Beginning of Scriblerus Club.	
1713	*Windsor-Forest.* Proposals issued for translation of the *Iliad*. Painting lessons from Jervas.	Peace of Utrecht. Harley and Bolingbroke struggle for power within Tory party.

2

1714	Enlarged (5 Canto) version of *The Rape of the Lock*. Scriblerus Club breaks up on death of Queen Anne.	Death of Queen Anne. Accesion of George I. Tories fall from power. Swift sent to Ireland.
1715	*The Temple of Fame. Iliad*, Vol. I (Books I–IV). Friendship with Lady Mary Wortley Montagu begins.	Impeachment of Oxford and Bolingbroke. Oxford put in Tower, Bolingbroke flees to France. Jacobite rebellion.
1716	*Iliad*, Vol. II (Books V–VIII). Family move to Chiswick.	Septennial Act.
1717	*Iliad*, Vol. III (Books IX–XII). Pope's *Works* including *Eloisa to Abelard* and *The Elegy to the Memory of an Unfortunate Lady*. (October) Death of Pope's father.	
1718	*Iliad*, Vol. IV (Books XIII–XVI).	Death of Parnell.
1719	Pope and his mother move to Twickenham	Death of Addison. Defoe's *Robinson Crusoe*.
1720	*Iliad*, Vols. V and VI (Books XVII–XXIV).	South Sea Bubble.
1721	Pope's edition of Parnell's *Poems* with 'Epistle to Oxford' as preface. Begins work on edition of Shakespeare.	Robert Walpole becomes Lord Treasurer.
1722	Begins work on translation of the *Odyssey* with Fenton and Broome.	Atterbury charged with complicity in a plot to reinstate the Pretender.
1723	Pope's edition of Buckingham's *Works*, seized by Government on suspicion of Jacobite passages. Pope appears before House of Lords as witness at Atterbury's trial.	Atterbury found guilty of Jacobitism and exiled. Bolingbroke pardoned and returns for brief stay.

3

1725	Pope's edition of Shakespeare in 6 volumes. *Odyssey* Vols I–III (with Fenton and Broome).	Bolingbroke returns from exile and settles near Pope at Dawlay Farm.
1726	*Odyssey* IV–V. Swift visits Pope. Friendship with Spence begins.	Bolingbroke begins *The Craftsman*. Theobald's *Shakespeare Restored*. Swift's *Gulliver's Travels*.
1727	Pope–Swift *Miscellanies*, I–II. Swift's second visit to Pope.	Death of George I. Accession of George II.
1728	Pope–Swift *Miscellanies*, III, including *Peri Bathous*. *The Dunciad*, in 3 Books, with Theobald as hero.	Gay's *Beggar's Opera*. The War with the Dunces reaches a peak.
1729	*The Dunciad Variorum*.	Swift's *Modest Proposal*.
1731	*Epistle to Burlington*.	
1732	Pope–Swift *Miscellanies*, IV.	Death of Gay. Hogarth's prints of *The Harlot's Progress*.
1733	*Epistle to Bathurst. Imitation of Horace, Satire II, i. An Essay on Man*, Epistles I–III. (June) Death of Pope's mother. Pope becomes more committed to the Patriot opposition.	Walpole's Excise Scheme defeated. Bolingbroke's 'Dissertation upon Parties' appears in *The Craftsman*.
1734	*Epistle to Cobham. An Essay on Man*, Epistle IV. *Imitation of Horace, Satire II, ii*.	
1735	*An Epistle to Dr Arbuthnot. Epistle to a Lady*. Pope's *Works*, Vol. II. Curll's edition of Pope's letters. Prince of Wales visits Pope at Twickenham.	Death of Arbuthnot and Lord Peterborough. Bolingbroke returns to France. Hogarth's prints of *The Rake's Progress*.
1737	*Imitation of Horace, Epistle II, ii*. Authorized edition of Pope's letters. *Imitation of Horace, Epistle II, i*.	Death of Queen Caroline. Prince of Wales heads Patriot opposition. Crousaz attacks *An Essay on Man*.

1738	*Imitation of Horace, Epistle I, vi. Imitation of Horace, Epistle I, i. Epilogue to the Satires.*	Bolingbroke returns from France and stays with Pope at Twickenham. Dr Johnson's *London.*
1739	Spends winter with Ralph Allen at Prior Park near Bath.	Warburton's *Vindication of the Essay on Man* defends Pope against Crousaz.
1740	First meets Warburton. Refurbishes his grotto.	Cibber's *Apology for his Life.*
1741	Publishes *Memoirs of Martinus Scriblerus.* Works closely with Warburton on revised edition of his poems.	
1742	*The New Dunciad* (i.e. Book IV).	Walpole resigns. Handel's *Messiah* receives its first performance, in Dublin. Cibber's *A letter from Mr Cibber to Mr Pope.*
1743	*The Dunciad, in Four Books,* with Cibber replacing Theobald as hero. Pope's health deteriorates.	
1744	(May 30) Pope dies at Twickenham.	

1 Alexander Pope, the man and his life

Lord Bolingbroke's usual health after dinner is 'Amicitiae et Libertati'. I should like to have it for a motto to my door, with an 's' added after it.　　　　　　　　　　　　　　(Pope to Spence, April 1742)[1]

> I believe, if any one, early in his life should contemplate the dangerous fate of authors, he would scarce be of their number on any consideration. The life of a Wit is a warfare upon earth; and the present spirit of the learned world is such, that to attempt to serve it (any way) one must have the constancy of a martyr, and a resolution to suffer for its sake.

When Pope wrote these words in the Preface to the first edition of his collected *Works* in 1717 he was not overdramatizing the vulnerability of the poet's position, nor was he exaggerating the degree of forbearance necessary to serve the learned world. 'The life of a Wit', in post-Restoration England, truly was 'a warfare upon earth'. Dryden had received similar, if not as savage, treatment a generation earlier, and both Swift and Gay had to come to terms with it during Pope's own time. Each of these writers found themselves attacked for reasons that only too often had little or nothing to do with their published work. The Augustan man of letters' private life became a public concern, much as a politician's does in our own day. Any scandal that could be dredged up, whether fictional or factual hardly mattered, was useful ammunition in the continual warfare that attended the Augustan literary scene. As a result contemporary accounts of early eighteenth-century writers' lives were frequently deliberately distorted or confused. Swift, we are told, was mad, whereas Pope was seen as having a warped mind in a warped body. Such impressions, however partisan they may originally have been, tend, like mud, to stick, and we can find Pope described as recently as 1925 and by Lytton Strachey as a 'fiendish monkey' ladling out 'spoonfuls of boiling oil' at an upstairs window 'upon such of the passers-by whom the wretch had a grudge against'.[2]

Furthermore the beginning of the eighteenth century was a period in which political parties were establishing themselves in England, and literature found itself closely connected with such a development. Writers were in heavy demand as purveyors of propaganda and, even if an author managed to avoid becoming a paid party hack, the author's duty to the public was sufficiently strongly felt that he was more or less forced to commit himself to either a Whig or Tory position.[3] Either way the author was bound to make enemies as well as friends, and although Pope strove hard for a number of years to maintain a posture of Party independence his essential Tory sympathies were bound to create enemies for him. Such persons leapt at the slightest chance to vilify him (see chapter 2), and though his conduct was by no means spotless (he was certainly capable of giving at least as good, and generally better, than he got) it was far more attractive and praiseworthy than common literary lore has, until comparatively recent times, held it to be. It seems to be worthwhile, therefore, beginning this introduction to his work with a brief account of the major events of his life.[4]

Early life and education, 1688–1708

Alexander Pope was born, of Catholic parents, in Plough Court, off Lombard Street in the City of London on 21 May 1688. He was the only child of his parents' marriage and was born when his mother was already forty-six and his father forty-two. His lifelong devotion to his elderly parents, whom he cared for till the time of their respective deaths, is one of the most moving and significant aspects of his life. This admiration and love is poignantly expressed in the final forty lines of *An Epistle to Dr Arbuthnot*, composed just before his mother's death in 1733, where he celebrates his parents' 'unspotted names' and in particular their virtue, gentleness, honesty and independence.

The Pope family lived in Lombard Street until Alexander was five years old. By all accounts he was a very healthy and happy child of a particularly sweet temper who showed no signs of the illness that later disfigured him. Spence tells us that a portrait of him painted when he was about ten years old shows his face as 'round, plump, pretty, and of a fresh complexion. I have often heard Mrs Pope say that he was then exactly like that picture . . . and that it was the perpetual application he fell into about two years afterwards that changed his form and ruined his constitution.' (9).

His father had been a successful linen merchant for almost twenty years prior to his son's birth, but had been forced to retire early in life owing to the anti-Catholic laws passed after the arrival of William III. In the same year as Alexander was born an Act of Parliament came into being which prohibited Catholics from living within ten miles of the City of London. This Act, which received renewed prominence from royal proclamations issued in 1696, 1715 and 1744, became a major factor in determining the course of Pope's life. We do not know for certain where the Pope family lived from the time they left Lombard Street in 1693 to the time they moved to Binfield in Berkshire about 1700. There is some indication they lived at Hammersmith, which although not far enough out of the city of London legally to satisfy the anti-Catholic laws, would probably have been far enough out to indicate the right intention.

Pope received his first education when he was about eight years old from a priest named Edward Taverner who instructed him in Latin and Greek. He then went to Twyford School, near Winchester, which was one of the best schools available for Catholic boys at the end of the seventeenth century. He only stayed there for one year, however, being expelled at the end of that time for writing a satire on one of the masters – an omen, perhaps, of things to come. When Pope was twelve his father complied with the anti-Catholic legislation and moved his family from London. He purchased Whitehill House, together with nineteen acres of land in Windsor Forest, at Binfield in Berkshire.

The move to Binfield brought Pope's formal education to a close and henceforth he largely educated himself. In June 1739 he told Spence that:

> When I had done with my priests I took to reading by myself, for which I had a very great eagerness and enthusiasm, especially for poetry. In a few years I had dipped into a great number of the English, French, Italian, Latin and Greek poets. This I did without any design but that of pleasing myself, and got the languages by hunting after the stories in the several poets I read, rather than read the books to get the languages. I followed everywhere as my fancy led me, and was like a boy gathering flowers in the woods and fields just as they fall in his way. I still look upon these five or six years as the happiest part of my life.
>
> (24)

They may have seemed in retrospect the happiest years of his life but they were also the years that saw the beginning of what he later referred to, in *An Epistle to Dr Arbuthnot*, as 'this long Disease, my Life'. Until the move to Binfield Pope was a perfectly healthy child, but about the age of twelve he contracted a tubercular disease of the bone which became known later as Pott's disease (after Dr Percival Pott, 1714–88, whose observation and treatment of it were famous in the eighteenth century). This disease, which was contracted through milk and was widespread in the days before pasteurization, gradually reduced Pope to a humpbacked condition and dwarfed his growth, so that at his most fully grown he never attained a height greater than four foot six. It finally left him a permanent cripple in need, as Dr Johnson tells us, of wearing stays in order to be able to stand.

Marjorie Nicolson and G. S. Rousseau, who have made a detailed study of Pope's illness, point out in *This Long Disease, My Life* that as a result of this weakness 'he felt the cold severely, and wore three pairs of hose and heavy under garments, sometimes of fur'.[5] Pope remained a chronic invalid and eventually required constant attention from maid-servants in dressing and undressing. The fragility of his 'little, tender, and crazy carcase', as William Wycherley affectionately referred to it, brought other weaknesses with it. Pope suffered continually from severe headaches, coughing, and fevers, and, towards the close of his life, from a whole series of compound illnesses.

But it would be a mistake to end this discussion of Pope's health with the impression that his illness affected his life in a totally negative way. It is true that he could never escape it, and true that occasionally it reduced him to a state of intense gloom, but one of the most striking things that any reader of Pope's *Correspondence*[6] must feel is the power of his struggle to overcome these difficulties and his determination to travel as much as he could and lead as full a life as possible within the limitations forced on him by his body.

About 1704, when Pope was sixteen and already suffering from the tubercular affliction just described, his perpetual application to his studies began to reduce him to so bad a state of health that he believed he was going to die. He sat down and wrote last farewells to his friends, including the Abbé Southcote. The Abbé immediately went to Dr John Radcliffe, the most eminent physician of his time, told him about Pope's illness, and then rode down to Binfield with Radcliffe's directions. The chief part of Radcliffe's advice was that Pope should take more exercise and should ride every day. This advice not only restored him but seems to have been the origin of the horseback rambles through Windsor Forest which he took with his father's neighbour, Sir William Trumbull.

Sir William was a retired Secretary of State with a great interest in literature, and was over sixty years old when Pope first knew him. Pope was only sixteen or seventeen at the time, but the two men, despite these disparities in age, felt immediate respect for one another. They rode through the Forest together, while the older man listened with great patience to the early efforts of the young poet. As Pope says in the opening lines of his *Pastorals*, written in 1704:

> First in these Fields I try the Sylvan Strains
> Nor blush to sport on *Wintsor's* blissful Plains. (1–2)

The *Pastorals* were Pope's first published poems, but he had been experimenting in poetry long before their publication in 1709. There is perhaps some slight exaggeration in the claim which he later made in *An Epistle to Dr Arbuthnot* that,

> As yet a Child, nor yet a Fool to Fame,
> I lisp'd in Numbers, for the Numbers came.   (127–8)

but only the most literal minded would object. It is quite clear that he began being interested in poetry at a very early age: he told Spence in March 1743 that 'I began writing verses of my own invention farther back than I can remember' (32). His mother gave Spence similar testimony:

> Mr. Pope's father . . . was no poet, but he used to set him to make English verses when very young. He was pretty difficult in being pleased and used often to send him back to new turn them. 'These are not good rhymes' he would say, for that was my husband's word for verses.   (11)

Pope's precocity in poetry is perhaps best illustrated by his attempt to write an epic poem when he was only twelve. The subject was Alcander, Prince of Rhodes, and he later told Spence that he wrote four books towards it, of about one thousand verses each.

During these years of growing up at Binfield, the young poet was not only extending his reading and trying out his poetry, he was also developing his literary acquaintance. At a remarkably early age he got to know the literary wits at Will's Coffee House, who had formed Dryden's circle. There is even a record of Pope being taken, when he was only twelve years old, to see Dryden. The particular members of the Will's group that Pope got to know apart from Trumbull, who has already been mentioned, were the critic William Walsh; the poet Samuel Garth; the dramatists William Wycherley and William Congreve; and the actor Thomas Betterton. These were all older and distinguished literary men by the time Pope knew them and it was obviously not mere coincidence that they should all share an enthusiasm for the young man's ability and company. There is certainly something a little self-conscious in the correspondence Pope wrote to these worldly men of letters, but that is hardly surprising in a young man anxious to make a good impression.

With Wycherley and Walsh Pope struck up particularly close friendships. He helped the old playwright prepare his verse for publication and maintained a long correspondence with him. He visited Walsh at his seat at Abberley in Worcestershire in 1707 and it was from him that he received the famous advice to make correctness his study and aim:

> When about fifteen, I got acquainted with Mr Walsh. He encouraged me much, and used to tell me that there was one way left of excelling, for though we had had several great poets, we never had any one great poet that was correct – and he desired me to make that my study and aim.   (73)

The eighteenth-century notion of correctness as a literary virtue is improperly understood today. It is by no means the same thing as correction. The first involves the principle of proper literary decorum (see chapter 4), while the second involves the more mechanical matter of revision. Both Pope and Walsh were only too well aware of the dangers of too much of the latter, and I shall end this account of the first phase of Pope's life by quoting from a letter he wrote to Walsh on 2 July 1706 saying just this:

> I am convinc'd as well as you, that one may correct too much; for in Poetry as in Painting, a Man may lay colours one upon another, till they Stiffen and deaden the Piece. Besides to bestow heightening on every part is monstrous; Some parts ought to be lower than the rest; and nothing looks more ridiculous, than a Work, where the Thoughts, however different in their own nature, seem all on a level: 'Tis like a Meadow newly mown, where Weeds, Grass, and Flowers are all laid even, and appear undistinguish'd. I believe too that sometimes our first Thoughts are the best as the first squeezing of the Grapes makes the finest and richest Wine.   (I, 18–19)

The experimenting poet, 1709–1717

The eight years from the time of Pope's first published work, the *Pastorals* (May 1709), to the time of the first edition of his collected *Works* (June 1717), form a fairly cohesive unit in his life. This was a period of extraordinary poetic activity which he later described as wandering in 'Fancy's Maze' (*Epistle to Dr Arbuthnot*, 340). In these eight years he tried his hand at half a dozen different 'kinds' of poetry (see chapter 4), ranging from pastoral and georgic (*Windsor-Forest*), to didactic (*Essay on Criticism*), to elegiac (*The Elegy to the Memory of an Unfortunate Lady*), to heroic (*Eloisa to Abelard*), to mock-epic (*The Rape of the Lock*), to actual epic (the translation of the *Iliad*). To say he tried his hand is perhaps to suggest an unfinished, or trial, state totally inappropriate to these highly finished and successful poems. The phrase is used here to indicate the sense in which Pope was feeling for his strength during these years and trying out different possibilities. The wide range of his success is a mark of his versatility.

These years were also a time of great expansion in his personal and social life. They mark a period during which Pope spent more time in London than at any other stage in his life, at the same time as he continued to visit his Catholic acquaintances around Binfield. They include the making of the lasting and major friendships with Gay, Swift, Arbuthnot, Bolingbroke and Oxford among his literary and political friends, and with the Carylls, Englefields, Dancastles and Blounts among his Catholic friends.

The family's move from Binfield to Chiswick in 1716 and the sudden death of his father on 23 October 1717 brought this period, which was so much freer of sober responsibility than most of his life, to a close. There is a strong element of carefree gaiety about the poetry written during these years that is in marked contrast to the more overtly moral mood of his later work:

> Soft were my Numbers, Who could take offence
> While pure Description held the place of Sense ?
> Like gentle *Fanny's* was my flow'ry Theme,
> A painted Mistress, or a purling Stream.
>
> (*Epistle to Dr Arbuthnot,* 147–50)

Such an element is undoubtedly linked to the relative freedom he enjoyed at the time, though with the death of his father he became solely responsible for his seventy-five-year-old mother.

The period begins with the publication of the *Pastorals*. While these were greatly admired by Pope's Tory friends at Will's, they immediately brought him into conflict with London's rival literary group, Addison's 'little Senate' of Whig writers who met at Buttons' coffee-house. Pope's poems were published in a volume of Tonson's *Miscellanies* that also included the *Pastorals* of Addison's friend Ambrose ('Namby Pamby') Philips. Philips was a third-rate poet and his *Pastorals* were clearly inferior to the young Pope's, but Addison's friends Welsted, Tickell and Gildon all highly praised Philips's *Pastorals* in the current periodicals at various times during the next few years, whilst totally ignoring Pope's. Pope was not so much angry as annoyed and when, in 1713, the *Guardian* ran a series of articles on pastoral poetry in general and set Philips along-side Theocritus, Virgil and Spenser, he took the opportunity to expose such critical claptrap for what it was. He anonymously wrote an ironic essay (*Guardian,* no. 40) to conclude the series in which he continued the pattern of praising Philips but, this time, for patently absurd reasons. Philips was furious and threatened to beat Pope with a rod if he ever came near Buttons'. Pope had not only demonstrated an early knack with irony, but had shown that he was quite capable of looking after himself in the eighteenth-century literary jungle. Since Pope's friend Gay further ridiculed Philips's *Pastorals* in his mock-pastoral poem, *The Shepherd's Week,* published a year later in April 1714, scores had been more than evened.

The conflict with Philips and the Buttons' group is told in some detail here in order to give an idea of the sort of jostling for literary standing that was part and parcel of the literary scene in the early part of the eighteenth century. Nearly every publication of Pope's was attended with this sort of critical and personal dispute and the

fracas surrounding the publication of the *Pastorals* was mere skirmish-
ing compared with the warfare that was to surround many of his
later publications.

Pope's second major publication was *An Essay on Criticism*, first
published in 1711 though mostly written at least two years earlier.
It was an ambitious undertaking for a young man for in it Pope
hoped to compress and refine the wisdom of all past ages concerning
criticism and poetry. Such a conception was quintessentially neoclassical, and the poem is consequently a key starting point for
anyone wanting to understand eighteenth-century assumptions about
literature (see chapter 4). Its reception was quiet at first but then,
quite suddenly, a storm broke loose as the critic John Dennis
savagely attacked Pope in his *Reflections Critical and Satyrical, upon
a late Rhapsody, Call'd, An Essay Upon Criticism*. Dennis's attack was full
of the most vitriolic and personal abuse imaginable: 'As there is no
creature so venomous, there is nothing so stupid and impotent as a
hunch-back'd Toad'.[7] Pope was sensible enough to ignore Dennis's
vituperation for the time being, but it was a searing experience and
as Maynard Mack so tellingly comments, 'The hiss of the branding
iron enters the soul'.[8] He retired to friends in the country and
particularly to the solace of his older Catholic friend, John Caryll,
who lived at Ladyholt, near West Harting in Sussex.

It was during this period that Caryll suggested the subject matter
for that most delightful of all Pope's poems, *The Rape of the Lock*. The
poem was written, as Pope later told Spence, to 'make a jest' of the
estrangement between two Catholic families, the Fermors and the
Petres, and 'to laugh them together again'. The incident that Pope was
making fun of was the cutting off of a lock of Arabella Fermor's hair
by Caryll's cousin the young Lord Petre. Pope brilliantly ridiculed
this episode by giving the events a mock-solemn epic inflation
clearly out of all proportion to their trivial significance. The poem
was published in its first form, that is without the addition of the
epic *Machinery* of Sylphs, Gnomes, Nymphs and Salamanders, in
Lintot's collection of *Miscellaneous Poems* of May 1712.

In the following year Pope moved back to London, where he
found himself drawn more and more strongly into the circle of
writers supporting the Tory Government. His poem, *Windsor-Forest*,
published in March 1713 to celebrate the Treaty of Utrecht, was
taken by many as a statement of his party commitment despite his
proclaimed attempts to maintain neutrality,

> In Moderation placing all my Glory,
> While Tories call me Whig, and Whigs a Tory. (67–8)

as he later put it in his *Imitations of Horace, Satire II, i*. For most of the
year, however, he lived with the Whig painter Jervas, who had been

a pupil of the famous portrait painter Sir Godfrey Kneller. During this year Pope studied painting more closely than at any other time in his life and this had a formative effect on his poetry (see chapter 3).

The following spring Pope became involved with the Scriblerus Club. This was a group of five persons – Swift, Parnell, Pope, Gay, and Arbuthnot – occasionally joined by a sixth, Robert Harley, Lord Oxford, who met over dinner once a week to joke and talk about literature. They had in common a philosophic belief in conserving the best from the past coupled with a scorn for the leaden weight of much modern learning. The past must be preserved not as a dead but as a living thing. Accordingly they planned to produce the *Memoirs of Martinus Scriblerus* which would burlesque the overpedantic works of contemporary scholars and antiquaries such as Dr Woodward, a well-known geologist and physician. Various members of the Club wrote different chapters, but the whole thing was brought to an abrupt halt with the dissolution of the Club that resulted from the death of Queen Anne on 1 August 1714. With the Whigs' return to power Arbuthnot was replaced as Court physician, Swift left for his voluntary exile in Ireland, and Oxford was put in the Tower. Pope, by retiring to the country, survived the change of Government with nothing worse than the separation of his friends. The *Memoirs* were not published till 1741.[9] The Club is even more important, however, for the many other literary projects which were first discussed at these meetings but which only came to fruition much later.

In the summer of 1713 Pope had found, two years after the event, the opportunity to get even with Dennis for his attack on *An Essay on Criticism* in a way that his Scriblerian friends would doubtless have approved. Under the guise of defending Addison, whose play *Cato* Dennis had just attacked, Pope published *The Narrative of Dr Robert Norris*. He invented a fictive episode in Dennis's life in which a Dr Norris was called to cure him of his lunacy. The piece is full of farcical high jinks that completely destroy Dennis, although not in the malignantly vindictive way in which he had attacked Pope.

In October 1713 Pope published his proposals to translate the *Iliad*, and, after the fall of the Tory Ministry in the following summer and his own subsequent fall from a position of political influence, he turned his attention almost entirely to Homer. This was to be the major literary occupation of his next six years. It was difficult and sometimes tedious work, but it shaped his genius and ensured his financial independence. At first he had grave doubts about his ability to complete such an undertaking. He told Spence, years later, that 'In the beginning of my translating the *Iliad* I

15

wished anybody would hang me, a hundred times. It sat so heavily on my mind at first that I often used to dream of it, and so do sometimes still'. Spence tells us further that 'he used to dream that he was engaged in a long journey, puzzled which way to take, and full of fears that he should never get to the end of it' (197). But by June 1715 the first four books, in one volume, were published, and from this time forward he proceeded with his task at the rate of four books a year until the poem was completed in May 1720.

The success of the translation of the *Iliad*, both from a literary and financial point of view, marked something of a milestone in Pope's life. Not only did its critical reception establish him as indisputably the pre-eminent English poet of the day, but its financial success established him as a person of independent means for the rest of his life. The publication demonstrated that not only was Pope a literary genius, but he also possessed sharp business acumen, inherited no doubt from his father who had operated so successfully as a linen merchant that he was able to retire, worth ten thousand pounds, on the birth of his son, in 1688, when he was only forty-two. Pope's contract with Lintot gave him 200 guineas for each of the six volumes, plus 750 copies of each volume, which he sold to the subscribers for a guinea a volume, or six guineas a set. Thus the whole contract was worth five thousand seven hundred guineas, or very nearly six thousand pounds. It is difficult to give an equivalency in today's terms, but even at a conservatively low conversion rate of one hundred to one Pope earned well over the equivalent of half a million pounds, in our terms, for his contract.[10]

One of the most important aspects of Pope's life during the years we are dealing with here was his growing acquaintance with Teresa and Martha Blount. Pope and Teresa were the same age, and two years older than Martha, known as 'Patty' to all her friends. Pope was initially attracted to the more striking looks and flirtatious spirit of the elder sister, but over a period of time his feelings towards her waned and it was to the gentler, more modest, diffident and good humoured Patty that he gradually developed a love and affection which grew stronger as he grew older and endured till his death. 'Patty belonged to the same world of Catholic piety as his mother, and could like her be idealized as one who despised public glamour and lived a quiet life devoted to friendship,' says Valerie Rumbold in her fine study of women's place in Pope's world.[11] 'I love you upon unalterable Principles,' he wrote in his last letter to Patty before he died, and the phrase resonantly encapsulates the fusion of constancy and idealism that shaped his feeling for her. When, during the night of 23 October 1717, his father suddenly died, it was to Patty that he wrote next day: 'My poor father dyed last night. Believe, since I don't forget you this moment, I never shall.' As his

Martha and Teresa Blount, by Charles Jervas, c. 1716

will shows, in which he left her all his goods and chattels, and the income from his estate for life, he never did.

The significance of his father's death as an event in Pope's life cannot be too strongly stressed. Five days later he wrote to Caryll saying:

> You have humanity enough to believe I can be in no disposition to write to anybody, or have one thought that can be entertaining, when I acquaint you that I lost my father five days ago. My poor mother is so afflicted that it would be barbarity to leave this winter, which is the only and true reason that I am not now at Ladyholt. (I, 448)

17

For the next sixteen years the conduct of his life was to be largely shaped by the need to look after his aged and beloved mother who could not be left alone for long periods of time.

Translator and editor, 1718–1725

Various changes in Pope's life ensued from his father's death. The elder Pope had left Binfield in 1716, probably to avoid the increased land taxes which were being levied on Catholics, and had moved to Chiswick. But now Pope was himself the head of the family and, whether it was to get away from the place of his father's death, or because the size of the house was no longer suitable, or for some other reason, he moved in March 1719 with his mother into a small villa which he leased on the bank of the Thames at Twickenham. Except for occasional expeditions into the surrounding countryside, the last twenty-five years of his life were spent at 'Twitnam', as he affectionately called it. The improvements that he wrought on his house, garden and grotto here became his chief relaxation in life as well as an integral part of his art (see chapter 3). He set out to establish his small estate at Twickenham as a symbol of those cultural and civilized values – literacy, honesty, generosity and hospitality – which he so profoundly believed in and which he gradually came to feel were crumbling all about him in Hanoverian England.

His life now took on a much quieter aspect. At first he was fully engrossed in finishing his translation of the *Iliad*. However, when in 1720 that was completed he did not go back, as one might have expected, to writing poetry, but turned instead to editing. He wrote to Caryll in October 1722 saying: 'I must again sincerely protest to you that I have wholly given over scribbling, at least anything of my own, but am become by due gradation of dulness, from a poet a translator, and from a translator a mere editor' (II, 140). We might feel that anyone who has the attitude to his work that the words 'dulness' and 'mere' here indicate is unlikely to be very successful at it, and we would not be far from wrong. By modern standards Pope was not a particularly good editor, tending to correct and improve rather than restore and preserve.

His main editorial project was an edition of Shakespeare that would supersede Rowe's, but he also worked on a posthumous edition of his friend Parnell's *Poems* (which was published in 1721), and of the Duke of Buckingham's *Works* (which was published on 24 January 1723 but was seized by the Government three days later on suspicion of Jacobite tendencies in some passages). The Shakespeare edition, in six volumes, finally appeared in March 1725, and though the preface was lively and penetrating the text itself was hastily collated and emended. A year later the leading Shakespearean scholar of the day, Lewis Theobald, published his *Shakespeare Restored, or, a Specimen of the Many Errors Committed . . . by Mr Pope*. Theobald's book was an accurate, if pedantic, explication of Pope's mistakes and was to have consequences for the author more far-reaching than he can possibly have imagined.

The other major piece of work belonging to these years was the translation of the *Odyssey*. Pope was led into this by the huge success of his translation of the *Iliad*. But his heart was no longer in translation and it was undertaken largely as a business venture. He therefore engaged two collaborators, Broome and Fenton, to help him. The idea was that Broome and Fenton would do much of the translation and Pope would revise and polish it. However, the collaboration got him into all sorts of problems about how much should be admitted (the public would be far more likely to pay to read a translation by Mr Pope than to read one by Messrs Pope, Broome and Fenton), and about how much remuneration the collaborators should receive. In the end Broome translated eight books, Fenton four and Pope the remaining twelve. But Pope made over £5,000 on the venture while Broome and Fenton received £600 and £300 respectively. Unjust as this may seem they could not have made anywhere near that amount without the benefit of Pope's reputation and his tireless effort to raise a list of subscribers.

Pope's financial independence as an author was now completely assured. Henceforth he would be able to write whatever he wanted to, and not just whatever would sell best. By dint of his own hard work and inventiveness he had made himself the first English author of any kind to be able to live off his writings independently of a patron. He was fiercely proud of such independence and clung to it so tenaciously that he twice turned down offers of official Government pensions. His description of himself as 'Un-plac'd, un-pensioned, no Man's Heir, or Slave', in his *Imitation of Horace, Satire II, i*, written in 1733, best sums up this justifiable pride. Four years later still he put the same thought slightly differently in his *Imitation of Horace, Epistle II, ii*:

> But (thanks to *Homer*) since I live and thrive,
> Indebted to no Prince or Peer alive. (68–9)

The Scriblerian fruition, 1726–1733

Although no particular event occurred in 1726 to cause a sudden change in Pope's life, the completion of his projects as a translator and editor did bring a distinct change of direction in his literary career. The years of experimentation and of journeywork were now over. The poet was free to come fully into his own. Satire, a mode in which he had as yet given only a few glimpses of his genius (*Guardian* no. 40, *The Rape of the Lock*, *The Narrative of Dr Norris*), was to become for the rest of his life the vehicle for its fulfilment.

In 1725 Bolingbroke returned from exile in France and settled near Pope. Together with Swift's two visits to England in 1726 and 1727 (the first for twelve years, and the last of his life) this brought about a kind of Scriblerian revival. Bolingbroke had never been a full member of the Scriblerus Club, but as a leading member of Oxford's Ministry, and as a particular friend of Pope's, he had been closely connected with it. There were reunions at Pope's villa with Gay and Arbuthnot (Parnell had died in 1718, and Oxford in 1724), and there was a revival of spirit in the Tory Opposition with the launching, in 1726, of Bolingbroke's new anti-Walpole journal, *The Craftsman*. During the next few years the true harvest of the seeds sown at the meetings of the Scriblerus Club in 1714 was reaped. *Gulliver's Travels* was published in October 1726, *The Beggar's Opera* was first produced in January 1728, and the first *Dunciad* came out in May of the same year. In addition, there were other offshoots of the Scriblerus Club published in the four volumes of the Pope-Swift *Miscellanies*, 1727–32, including *Peri Bathous* or *The Art of Sinking in Poetry*. It was, by any standards, a vintage harvest.

The Dunciad has always been a controversial poem. It was of course written as such: Pope meant to annihilate his enemies. Many readers feel, however, that in attacking those persons who had attacked him, Pope sinks to their level. There is undeniably a strong element of personal revenge about *The Dunciad*, but it is important to recognize that the poem grew out of the most profound and deeprooted of all Pope's feelings about literature. At its base is the firmly held belief that bad literature, indeed bad art generally, is immoral, and if allowed to spread unchecked will corrupt and eventually destroy civilization. The artist's duty therefore is a moral duty. He defends the validity of the written word at a time when it is being defiled by those all about him, and in doing so he preserves the living bond between idea and language.

The first *Dunciad* consisted of three books that centred on the crowning of King Tibbald (Lewis Theobald) as King of the Dunces, and came to a climax with a vision of the future in which the Goddess of Dulness held full dominion. In 1728 this is still a vision or portent of what is to come, but by the time of the revised *Dunciad*, in four books, of 1743, the vision has become actuality. The poem is not easy to read. It is full of dense imagery, classical allusions, names of living persons and topical references. Partly to explain these, although largely to continue the fun, Pope came out in 1729 with a Variorum edition. 'The Dunciad is going to be printed in all pomp . . .', Pope wrote to Swift in June 1728; 'It will be attended with *Proeme, Prologomena, Testimonia Scriptorum, Index Authorum*, and Notes *Variorum*' (II, 503). He doesn't even mention the seven appendices. All this prefatory and reference matter is a continuation of the satire on pedantry, and if much of it is lost upon us today that is because, on the whole, most of our books are less cluttered with such padding.

All this time Pope's health had been deteriorating. In 1728 his ailments had become so bad that in August he agreed to go to Bath to see if the waters would help him. He stayed there for ten weeks but there was no appreciable improvement. 'I do not think I ever shall enjoy any health four days together, for the remaining Sand I have to run', he wrote to Bathurst on 7 November 1728; 'The Bath was tryed after all other remedies, as a last remedy, and that has proved totally ineffectual' (II, 525). The five years 1728–33 were the most painful Pope had yet had to suffer, partly because of his own weakness and partly because of his mother's failing condition. He lived daily in fear of 'that accident which I dread the most, my Mother's death'. He was afraid to leave Twickenham for more than three days at a time, and when, in the spring of 1731, he was so ill that he had to go on a diet of asses' milk, a highly esteemed cure in the eighteenth century, he travelled all the way back from Bolingbroke's home, at Dawlay Farm, to Twickenham to visit her on several occasions.

Meanwhile he was working on *An Essay on Man*. He wrote to Swift in June 1730: 'Yet am I just now writing, (or rather planning) a book, to make mankind look upon this life with comfort and pleasure, and put morality in good humour' (III, 117). But the first poem actually to be published after the *Dunciad Variorum was* the *Epistle to Burlington* in December 1731. The publication of this poem, on false taste in gardening and architecture, was attended with enough noise and recrimination to indicate to Pope that *The Dunciad*, far from destroying his enemies, had merely multiplied them. Timon was immediately identified by Grub Street as Lord Chandos, and Pope was accused of the basest ingratitude to an old friend. It was in vain that Pope protested that no particular person was intended in the portrait. Henceforth the plague of scribblers, ('They pierce my Thickets, thro' my Grot they glide'), was to accompany his every publication, and his own efforts to avoid them became correspondingly more devious.

It was for this reason that when the first three epistles of *An Essay on Man* finally appeared in February-May 1733 they did so anonymously. Pope carefully published two other poems at the same time, the *Epistle to Bathurst* in January, and the *Imitation of Horace, Satire II*, *i: To Fortescue* in February, in order to throw off suspicion of his authorship of *An Essay on Man*. His ruse was totally successful and the poem was so highly acclaimed that when he did finally admit authorship on the publication of the fourth epistle in January 1734 it was difficult for the critics to recant. They then turned to other means of attack and, taking up the cue from the Swiss theologian Jean-Pierre de Crousaz, accused him of Christian heterodoxy, Deism and even Spinozism instead. But this and the defence of his new ally William Warburton belong to the last period of his life, the years that come after the deaths, within six months of each other, of his close friend John Gay and of his dearly beloved mother.

As Pope grew older – he had turned forty in 1728 – so his life took on a mellower and more assured quality. He had no need to impress anyone now. Instead he could make friends according to his own clear beliefs. Over and over again what strikes the reader of Pope's correspondence is the importance of the role that friendship played in his life. Once he had established the bond of friendship he nursed it with almost as much care and affection as he bestowed on his ailing mother. His closest friends – Caryll, Gay, Swift, Arbuthnot, Bolingbroke, Fortescue, Bethel, and later Warburton, Allen, Spence and Marchmont – were clearly the most valuable thing in his life, and when one was ill, or when one died, his grief was immense. 'Good God!' he wrote to Swift on 5 December 1732 the morning after Gay's death, 'how often are we to die before we go quite off this stage? In every friend we lose a part of ourselves, and the best part. God keep those we have left!' (III, 335). The following day he wrote to Patty Blount in just as disturbed terms:

> The world after all is a little pitiful thing, not performing any one promise it makes us, for the future, and every day taking away and annulling the joys of the past. Let us comfort one another, and if possible, study to add as much more friendship to each other, as death has depriv'd us of in him.   (III, 336)

Over four months later he was still depressed at the remembrance of Gay's death. He wrote to Swift on 20 April 1733:

> You say truly, that death is only terrible to us as it separates us from those we love, but I really think those have the worst of it who are left by us, if we are true friends. I have felt more (I fancy) in the loss of poor Mr Gay, than I shall suffer in the thought of going away myself into a state that can feel none of this sort of losses.   (III, 365)

Six weeks after writing this letter his mother died at the age of ninety-one. Her death marked another milestone in the poet's life.

For his remaining eleven years he was free, in so far as his health would permit, to leave Twickenham for extended periods of time. A fortnight after he wrote to Caryll saying just this:

> To see you at Ladyholt was the first thought that I had upon this event, but as it is a great and new Æra of my life, and upon which the whole course of it will in a manner change, I must pause awhile to look about me. (III, 375)

The English Horace, 1733–1744

The most obvious change was the great amount of travelling Pope now undertook. He never went to the Continent, as so many eighteenth-century gentlemen did, but he travelled the breadth of southern England in more detail than most of his contemporaries. Nearly every summer and autumn during the last decade of his life was spent in rambling around his friends' country estates. We can reconstruct a typical ramble from his correspondence. In the summer of 1733, for instance, he set out from Twickenham to visit Lord Cobham in his magnificent house and gardens at Stowe, near Buckingham. From Stowe he went to John Morley's house at Halstead in Essex, and from Essex back across England to Lord Bathurst's estate at Cirencester. He then went down to visit Caryll at Ladyholt in Sussex for three weeks; from there he went to Lord Peterborough at Bevis Mount in Southampton for another three weeks. From Southampton he went to Lord Oxford's house in London for a few days before finally returning to Twickenham. We might add that invitations for such visits, and the letters show how pressing they were, bear remarkable testimony to the affection in which his friends held him.

But if Pope took a new delight in travelling during these last ten years he did not neglect his own house and garden at Twickenham. His grotto, the passage under the road that joined his house to his garden, became the special darling of his fancy and he lavished on it all the attention of his spare hours. There he could retire from the world and relax with his friends:

> Know, all the Distant Din that World can keep
> Rolls o'er my *Grotto*, and but sooths my Sleep.
> There, my Retreat the best Companions grace,
> Chiefs, out of War, and Statesmen, out of Place.
> (*Imitation of Horace, Satire II, i*, 123–6)

The example of Horace in retirement at his Sabine Farm is never far in the background. Indeed Horace is the major influence in these years that saw the full flowering of Pope's genius. Reuben Brower has said that Pope's life and literary career 'became progressively an *Imitatio Horatii*',[12] and while this is certainly true it is important to recognize the difference between an imitation and a copy. Pope adapted Horace in these last years, he did not ape him. The Horatian model of conversational ease and amiable urbanity formed a perfect counterpoint to Pope's militant indignation at the corruption which he saw resulting from Walpole's long hold over power. Every poem written after 1729, with the exception of the revised *Dunciad*, is in some way or another modelled on Horace. In his *Imitations of Horace* the model is explicitly admitted by being printed on the facing page, while in the *Moral Essays* and in *An Essay on Man*, which Pope described to Swift as 'a system of Ethics in the Horatian way', it is implicit in the manner and structure of the poems.

I do not intend to discuss all the poems written in this the richest poetic period of Pope's life, but *An Epistle to Dr Arbuthnot*, published in 1735, just two months before Arbuthnot's death, calls for special mention here because it says so much about Pope's literary career. The poem, 'begun many years since, and drawn up by snatches, as the several occasions offer'd', is perhaps the finest of all his poems in the Horatian mould. In it Pope replies to those persons who had for so many years attacked his 'Person, Morals, and Family',[13] by writing a conversational epistle that is largely an *apologia pro sua satura*. What calls for special mention, however, is the discrepancy between the character of Alexander Pope, the living man who writes the poem, and the character of Alexander Pope, the figure he creates who speaks in the poem. Out of the bare bones of his own life Pope has created a 'persona', or dramatic speaker, who is deliberately idealized for the sake of the satiric structure in which vice must be confronted with virtue. The poem is a controlled account of his literary development, but in reading it we need always to bear in mind that the whole thing is a carefully contrived piece of image building. It would be a mistake to take the figure of the virtuous poet that emerges from the poem as sole evidence for a biography, though Pope would, no doubt, be quite happy for us to do so.

The project that occupied most of Pope's time after his mother's death was the publication of his *Letters*. The printing of letters first written for private eyes became one of the most popular of literary productions in eighteenth-century England, and Pope's example had much to do with this. We have only to consider the famous letters of Lord Chesterfield, Horace Walpole, and Lady Mary Wortley Montagu, and the related vogue for epistolary novels and poems, to recognize the importance of the form. One very good reason for such popularity was that the eighteenth-century educated Englishman valued learning and urbanity more than almost anything else, and the

An etching of Pope by Jonathan Richardson, senior, for the title page of
Pope's Letters, *1737*

letter was a form perfectly suited for wearing one's learning lightly.
Pope wanted to have his letters published, but he did not want to seem to
do so. Accordingly he felt he must create an excuse for publication.
Through an elaborate series of manoeuvres, too complex to trace here,
he tricked his old enemy, Edmund Curll, into publishing an edition in
May 1735. This was the looked-for justification for publishing his own
edition and the 'Authentic' edition of his *Letters* followed two years later
in May 1737.

For the publication of his *Letters* Pope did very much what we
have already seen him doing in *An Epistle to Dr Arbuthnot*: he
carefully shaped his image for public display. Dr Johnson says that
he 'may be said to write always with his reputation in his head'. He
took the actual letters he had written to his various friends as the
basis for his published edition, but he rewrote, rearranged and
readdressed them where it suited his purposes. For example, there
were too many letters to his friend John Caryll, who was not well

25

known, and too few to Joseph Addison, who was the best-known literary figure of the first quarter of the eighteenth century. So Pope simply took some of his letters to Caryll, and, reworking them where necessary, readdressed them to Addison. Critics have been severe on Pope for this, accusing him of hypocrisy and vanity. But it is important to remember that he was using the letter as a literary form, as a vehicle for a special kind of familiar communication, not as a definitive biographical record. He was interested in using the letter form to set up the image of a cultivated and public-spirited man, not, as a twentieth-century writer might use it, to express his own psyche.

At the very least Pope was successful in winning the approval of one famous reader. Ralph Allen, who has been praised as the most benevolent man of his age, and was the original for Squire Allworthy in *Tom Jones*, was so impressed with the character of the man that emerged from Pope's *Letters* that he became a close friend. Indeed Pope's friendship with Allen was perhaps the strongest of all his male friendships during the last eight years of his life, and he spent a considerable part of these years staying with Allen at Prior Park, his country estate at Widcombe near Bath.

During the five years from 1733 to 1738 Pope wrote no fewer than fourteen imitations of Horace. He took to writing these imitations after Lord Bolingbroke came to see him once when he was ill and, happening to take up a Horace that lay on the table, observed 'how well that would hit my case, if I were to imitate it in English' (321a). Pope printed the Latin original on the left-hand page with his imitation on the facing page, allowing educated readers to compare the similarities and differences of the two versions thereby pointing up the thrust of his satiric attacks on various aspects of contemporary corruption at the same time as lending his barbs a classical authority. Pope creates a satiric spokesperson in these poems who speaks in a seemingly endless variety of voices, ranging from exasperation to composure and from poker-faced irony to genial playfulness. But behind all these voices lies the adopted character of a unified personality who cares deeply about his country's ruin and speaks urgently, when he has to, in the militant tones of a public prosecutor coupled with what the foremost commentator of our day on Pope has called a 'lordly air of serene superiority'.[14]

At the same time as he was writing these *Imitations* he became deeply involved with the Patriot Opposition to the Whig Government of Robert Walpole. In his earlier years Pope had tried to avoid a rigid party commitment, but he made no attempt at neutrality now. His close friend Bolingbroke, who was in the forefront of the battle to get rid of the 'Great Man', as Walpole was ironically called on account of both his size and position, must have influenced him strongly. Pope's own effort for the Patriot cause came to a climax with the passionate protestation that imbues the two dialogue poems known together as the *Epilogue to the Satires*, published in May and June 1738. In these two poems Pope entered as he put it, in his own words in a footnote to the poem, 'in the most plain and solemn manner he could, a sort of PROTEST against that insuperable corruption and depravity of manners, which he had been so unhappy as to live to see'. The poet's vision of his country had darkened dramatically since the euphoric days of *Windsor-Forest* but, as the last lines of *Dialogue II* make clear, though Truth stood trembling on the edge of Law, it still guarded the poet and sanctified the line. Although it was casting a giant shadow over things, universal darkness had not yet buried all.

The year 1739 was notable for the gaining of an unexpected, but not altogether desirable, ally. In 1737 Pope's *Essay on Man* had been attacked for its heterodoxy by a Swiss theologian Jean-Pierre de Crousaz,[15] and now two years later William Warburton, an ambitious clergy-man, published his *Vindication of the Essay on Man*, in which he defended Pope's Christianity as belonging to an established and orthodox tradition.[16] Warburton and Pope met for the first time in April 1740, and from this point on Warburton's influence on Pope steadily increased. He was a ponderous but aggressive man and he soon bullied himself into the role of Pope's literary executor, pushing the far more gentle and sensitive Joseph Spence into the background. In terms of literary pursuit Pope's last few years were largely spent, with one great exception, in working with Warburton on a final edition of his *Works*.

That great exception was his reworking of *The Dunciad*. In 1742 he published the fourth book of the poem under the title *The New Dunciad*. Most readers of Pope have agreed, that this is his finest sustained piece of satiric poetry. With mounting gravity he builds up to the final apocalyptic vision in which all the accumulating fears of the last decade concerning cultural, and intellectual corruption are imaginatively realized as Dulness' dread Empire, 'Chaos is restor'd; And Universal Darkness buries all'. A new fourth book was sufficient reason for revising the first three books for a complete new edition. The major change was the substitution of Colley Cibber for Lewis Theobald as King of the Dunces. Cibber was an old enemy of Pope's and had just published *A Letter from Mr Cibber to Mr Pope* (July 1742), perhaps the cruellest attack on him ever made (see chapter 2). Besides, Theobald was a friend of Warburton's. *The Dunciad* in four books with Cibber as hero came out in October 1743. It was Pope's last published work and his most awesome and searing indictment of the cultural cataclysm that he believed he had been unfortunate enough to live to see.

During the last two years of his life Pope's illnesses became critical. As early as March 1743 we find him writing to his old friend Bethel, describing alarming symptoms of weakness:

> For I have these three months or more, been advancing to an Asthmatic Complaint, (from one Cold to another, as I believe, for I saw no further cause for it). It is now at such a height that I can scarce walk, or go up a pair of Stairs, or move much in my bed, without quite losing breath; and it is attended with a difficulty of urine, which makes me fear a Dropsy . . . and a pain in the breast is join'd to it.   (IV, 445)

As the year wore on his health deteriorated more and more until in the last five months of his life nearly every letter talks about his ailments. His sense of his own fragility is poignantly described in a note he sent to Bolingbroke and Marchmont in January 1744:

> Yes, I would like to see you as long as I can see you, and then shut my eyes upon the world, as a thing worth seeing no longer. If your charity would take up a small Bird that is half dead of the frost, and set it a-chirping for half an hour, I'll jump into your hands tomorrow, at any hour you send. Two horses would be enough to draw me (and so would two dogs if you had them) but even the fly upon the chariot wheel required some bigger animal than itself to set it a-going.   (IV, 490)

In his last illness he was watched over by many friends, but especially by those most devoted to him, Bolingbroke, Marchmont, Patty Blount and Spence. He died on 30 May 1744. The next morning his friend David Mallet wrote to the Earl of Orrery describing his death:

> On Monday last I took my Everlasting Farewell of him. He was enough himself to know me, to enquire after Mrs Mallet's Health, and anxiously to hasten his Servant in getting ready my Dinner, because I came late. The same social kindness, the same friendly concern for those he loved, even in the minutest instances, that had distinguished his heart through Life, were uppermost in his Thoughts to the last.   (IV, 525)

We cannot close this account of Pope's life on a finer note than by quoting Spence's record of Bolingbroke's emotional profession of love for his dying friend. 'I never knew in my life a man that had so tender a heart for his particular friends, or a more general friendship for mankind. I have known him these thirty years; and value myself more for that man's love than . . .' sinking his head and losing his voice in tears.(652 and 653).

Epitaph

And so at the age of fifty-six Alexander Pope, the greatest poet of his day, and one of the greatest of any day, had died. The obloquy that had pursued him through life continued to pursue him in death. Until comparatively recent times – that is until Edith Sitwell's *Alexander Pope*, 1930, and George Sherburn's *Early Career of Alexander Pope*, 1934 – Pope has been harshly treated by biographers and critics alike. He has had his defenders, many of them distinguished and eloquent persons such as Samuel Johnson and Lord Byron, but his general lot has been to be cast in the role of the villain, a reputation which his physical infirmity did much to increase. I have tried to show that he did not deserve such a reputation. His behaviour was certainly not flawless, but neither was it vile, and when his character and life are impartially examined there is much to admire.

The best record of his mature physical appearance is that left by Sir Joshua Reynolds:

> He was about four feet six inches high, very humpbacked and deformed. He wore a black coat, and, according to the fashion of the time, had on a little sword. He had a large and very fine eye, and a long handsome nose; his mouth had those peculiar marks of crooked persons; and the muscles which ran across the cheek were so strongly marked that they seemed like little chords.[17]

Dr Johnson says in his *Life of Pope* that 'His stature was so low that, to bring him to a level with common tables, it was necessary to raise his seat. But his face was not displeasing, and his eyes were animated and vivid'. It is noticeable that both Reynolds and Johnson focus on his eyes. A glance at the many portraits of Pope reproduced in W. K. Wimsatt, *The Portraits of Alexander Pope*,[18] confirms the lively intelligence of his look.

One of his most attractive qualities as a person was his loyalty to his friends. I have already described his unswerving devotion to his parents and the care he took in developing and keeping a wide circle of friends. Indeed he made something of a cult of friendship. 'I have all my life from the first years of my reasoning had a disposition to a friendship with some person or other . . .' he wrote to Caryll in 1711. He said much the same thing to Gay in October 1730:

> Nature, temper, and habit from my youth made me have but one strong desire. All other ambitions, my person, education, constitution, religion etc. conspired to remove far from me. That desire was to fix and preserve a few lasting dependable friendships.

(III, 138)

We can trace this worship of the ideal of friendship in his correspondence with Swift. 'Farewell my dearest friend! ever, and upon every account that can create friendship and esteem', he wrote on 7 February 1735. A month later he wrote saying: 'I am a man of desperate fortunes, that is a man whose friends are dead: for I never aimed at any other fortune than in friends.' Swift, knowing what his correspondent most wanted to hear wrote back to Pope in the same vein a year later saying: 'I cannot properly call you my best friend, because I have not another left who deserves the name, such a havoc have Time, Death, Exile, and Oblivion made'. Such examples of the emphasis Pope attached to the value of friendship could be multiplied many times from his letters to Caryll, Gay and Patty Blount. But if, as Johnson tells us, he was 'zealous and constant in the duties of friendship', it must also be recognized that he did not forget those who offended him. He did not easily forgive an insult and he often returned attacks on his enemies years after they were first made.

His least attractive quality was his almost instinctive equivocation and deviousness. We see it in his public declarations concerning the part Broome and Fenton played in helping him to translate the *Odyssey*, and we see it again in his manipulations concerning the publication of his *Letters*. 'In all his intercourse with mankind', says Johnson, 'he had great delight in artifice, and endeavoured to attain all his purposes by indirect and unsuspected methods. He hardly drank tea without a stratagem.' In extenuation it can be argued that such equivocation was a defence mechanism developed in the face of repeated slander and attack. If he equivocated over matters of authorship, that was no more than anyone else did in the eighteenth century, and he never equivocated over matters of principle.

As numerous accounts indicate, he was most generous with his money. He gave a tenth of his yearly income to charity, and Johnson reports that 'Lord Oxford's Servant declared that in a house where her business was to answer his call, she would not ask for wages'. He was the leading spirit amongst those who tried to help the destitute poet Richard Savage, donating half of the subscription himself. Patty Blount told Spence in 1749 that Mr Pope's not being richer may be easily accounted for:

> He never had any love for money, and though he was not extravagant in anything, he always delighted when he had any sum to spare to make use of it in giving, lending, building, and gardening – for those were the ways in which he disposed of all the overplus of his income. (355)

As he grew older he placed increasing emphasis on the moral responsibility of the artist. 'It is not the worst I have written', he wrote to Caryll in January 1733 with regard to his *Epistle to Bathurst*, 'and abounds in moral example, for which reason it must be obnoxious in this age. God send it does any good! I really mean nothing else by writing at this time of my life.' He told Spence shortly before he died that: '"He has writ in the cause of virtue, and done something to mend people's morals" is the only commendation I long for'(626).

The strong moral seriousness that imbues his later poetry, even when it is most satirically playful, is directly linked to his conception of the artist's role in eighteenth-century society. Pope wrote at a time when the artist still held a place in the centre of society. He prized his financial and political independence but he felt no need to isolate himself from the main stream of life. He could appeal to a commonly accepted set of inherited, and largely Christian, values that would act as a norm against which to measure the moral and social aberrations he attacked. Such moral touchstones are not available to the artist today, when a belief in absolute values has mostly given way to a philosophy of relativism.

Literature, both documentary and imaginative, was the main means of communication in the eighteenth century, and as such it received an attention it no longer commands. If Pope seems to us over-conscious of his public reputation this is largely because he was so aware of the artist's public role. As a member of a Catholic minority during a period of bare toleration he was only too aware of the danger of his position. Indeed what is remarkable is not that he was so anxious to appear to the best advantage, but that he dared to speak out as boldly as he did.

Notes

1. Joseph Spence, *Observations, Anecdotes, and Characters of Books and Men*, ed. J. M. Osborn, 2 vols (Oxford University Press, Oxford, 1966). Anecdote 279. All future references are to this edition. The anecdote number is given in parentheses after the quotation. The 's' after the Latin toast would make the meaning 'Sacred to Friendship and Liberty'.
2. Lytton Strachey, *Pope*, The Leslie Stephen Memorial Lecture (Cambridge University Press, Cambridge, 1925), p. 2.
3. The term 'Whig' was a shortening of Whiggamore, an adherent of the Presbyterian cause in Scotland in the seventeenth century, and was the nickname applied in 1680 to the Exclusioners who opposed the succession of James, Duke of York, to the Crown, on the grounds of his being a Roman Catholic. The term 'Tory' was an Anglicized spelling of the name for an Irish outlaw, and was the nickname given by the Exclusioners to those who opposed the exclusion of James. The growth of the Whig and Tory parties was a major political development resulting from the 1688 Revolution, and is described in more detail in chapter 5.

4. The best short life of Pope is that by Samuel Johnson, op. cit., Vol. 3, pp. 82–272. The most complete and authoritative is Maynard Mack, *Alexander Pope: A Life* (Yale University Press, New Haven, 1985).

5. Marjorie Hope Nicolson and G. S. Rousseau, *This Long Disease, My Life* (Princeton University Press, Princeton, 1968), p. 19.

6. All references to Pope's correspondence are to *The Correspondence of Alexander Pope*, ed., George Sherburn, 5 vols (Clarendon Press, Oxford, 1956). The title of the edition is omitted and volume and page appear within parentheses when the reference to Pope or his correspondent is already clear.

7. J. V. Guerinot, *Pamphlet Attacks on Alexander Pope, 1711–1744: A Descriptive Bibliography* (Methuen, London, 1969), p. 3.

8. Mack, op. cit., p. 184.

9. The best modern edition is *Memoirs of the Extraordinary Life, Works, and Discoveries of Martinus Scriblerus*, ed., Charles Kerby-Miller (Yale University Press, New Haven, 1950).

10. It is difficult to give modern real-worth equivalents of eighteenth-century money. A recent English social historian has suggested however that 'multiplying eighteenth-century sums by approximately sixty will give a rough-and-ready 1982 equivalent'. Since inflation has more than doubled in the last ten years, a conversion rate of 100 seems reasonably conservative. See Roy Porter, *English Society in the Eighteenth Century* (Allen Lane, London, 1982), p. 13.

11. Valerie Rumbold, *Women's Place in Pope's World* (Cambridge University Press, Cambridge, 1989), p. 46. There has been some speculation, assisted by Pope's half-sister, Mrs Magdalen Rackett, that Pope and Patty secretly married, but it has never been proved, and both Valerie Rumbold and Maynard Mack, in *Alexander Pope: A Life*, incline against it.

12. Reuben Brower, *Alexander Pope: The Poetry of Allusion* (Clarendon, Oxford, 1959), p. 165.

13. See 'Advertisement' to *An Epistle to Dr Arbuthnot*.

14. Mack, op. cit., p. 722.

15. Jean Pierre de Crousaz, *Examen de l'Essai de M. Pope Sur l'Homme* (1737).

16. William Warburton, *A Vindication of Mr Pope's Essay on Man, from the misrepresentation of Mr De Crousaz* (London, 1739).

17. James Prior, *Life of Edmond Malone* (London, 1860), p. 429.

18. W. K. Wimsatt, *The Portraits of Alexander Pope* (Yale University Press, New Haven, 1965).

2 The urban and rural setting

> Know, all the distant Din that World can keep
> Rolls o'er my *Grotto*, and but sooths my Sleep.
> There, my Retreat the best Companions grace,
> Chiefs, out of War, and Statesmen, out of Place.
> There *St. John* mingles with my friendly Bowl,
> The Feast of Reason and the Flow of Soul.
> (*Imitation of Horace, Satire II, i*, 123–8)

Although Pope lived in the country for most of his life he was not what we would call a nature poet. He predominantly chose the society of man for his subject matter, and as a result London, in all its different aspects, played a central part in shaping the attitudes and beliefs towards society expressed in his poetry. Pope would have strongly disagreed with Dr Johnson that 'when a man is tired of London, he is tired of life; for there is in London all that life can afford'.[1] Indeed Pope believed that life afforded very much more in the retirement of the country. His attitude towards London is succinctly expressed in the opening lines of his versification of the second satire of Dr John Donne:

> Yes; thank my stars! as early as I knew
> This Town, I had the sense to hate it too.   (1–2)

But Pope would at least have agreed with Dr Johnson in recognizing the importance of London as the centre of political, social and cultural life in eighteenth-century England. No author who saw himself as the spokesman for his age could think otherwise, even if he chose to live elsewhere.

One should beware, however, of talking about London as if it were a self-contained entity. As Sir John Fielding, the half-brother of the novelist, says in his *Brief Description of the cities of London and Westminster*: 'But the name of London we use with latitude, comprehending under that denomination all Westminster and the Suburbs, with the whole range of buildings on the South side of the river from Lambeth palace to the parish of Deptford.'[2] London probably changed more during the seventeenth and early eighteenth centuries than during any other time in its long history. At the time of the accession of James I London was largely contained within its city walls, and yet by the death of Queen Anne, just over a hundred years later, London was composed of two separate cities, one borough, and numerous suburbs (see map of 1707 on pp. 38–39). The medieval walled City of London remained the business and financial centre of English life, as it does today (although the walls and gates have long since been removed), but the social centre had moved to the west end and to the fashionable City of Westminster. Between these two cities, and all around them, the great sprawl of suburban London was already springing up.

Nevertheless London was still small enough for an individual to be familiar with most of its various parts and to attach significance to them. This was certainly so with Pope. When he mentions the name of a parish, or a street, or a building, he nearly always does so because it has a particular set of associations for him, and he knows that it would do for his audience too. A few of these associations are inevitably lost to the modern reader, but the great majority can easily be retrieved with a little help. The reader who needs such help is referred to the gazetteer of place names on p. 244. In this chapter I distinguish between three main areas of London and show how these different areas call forth different sets of associations for Pope, and how they are used by him to establish different patterns of actual and metaphorical significance. As Pat Rogers says of Pope in his fascinating account of the Grub Street subculture: 'His satiric cosmology is based on the London of his day. He makes topography serve as moral symbolism.'[3] I conclude the chapter with a section that contrasts these responses to different aspects of urban topography with his response to rural retirement.

The City of London and the moneyed men

The ancient City of London was built on the northern shore of the river Thames. Its walled perimeter, which enclosed just under 380 acres, ran, according to John Strype, in something approaching the 'form of a bow', from the Fleet Ditch in the west to the Tower in the east.[4] This stone wall, which had first been erected in the time of Roman Government and had been continuously repaired since then (it is still clearly marked on the map of 1707 reproduced on pp. 38–39), was gradually dismantled during the eighteenth century. Apart from the quays and wharfs on the river front there were eight main entrances and exits to the City through Ludgate, Newgate, Aldersgate, Cripplegate, Moorgate, Bishopsgate, Aldgate and over London Bridge. The main east to west thoroughfare was Cheapside, which joined St Paul's Cathedral in the west to the busy commercial centre around Cornhill in the east. On the southern boundary of the City a series of stairs led down to the river.

Just over twenty years before Pope was born, however, this City was ravaged by one of the worst fires of all time. The Fire of London raged for four days from 2 to 5 September 1666 and consumed all save the north-eastern and extreme western parts of the City. The Royal Exchange, the Custom House, the Guildhall, the halls of forty-four of the Livery companies, St Paul's itself, and eighty-seven of the parish churches, besides about 13,200 houses, were burned down. Barely one fifth of the City was left standing. Thus the medieval City, which had changed so very little over several hundred years, had to be almost completely rebuilt.

The work of rebuilding began almost immediately, and one of the great glories of this reconstruction was the skyline that Christopher Wren created with the dome of St Paul's Cathedral and the steeples of his churches. Otherwise the main difference between the old and the new City was that, by Act of Parliament, the houses had now to be built either of brick or stone. The old timber-framed houses of Tudor times had proved hideously combustible in such a dense setting. Apart from this change in building materials, the alterations to the City were not as great as might be expected. The street pattern of the medieval City was hardly obscured, and, most important of all as far as the citizens were concerned, the new buildings in the City increased its status as a focus of commercial life in the nation.

It was this aspect of the City that most concerned Pope. The City had always been a thriving mercantile centre, proud of its guilds and livery companies. Its leading inhabitants, in contrast to those of the City of Westminster, were traditionally men who had made their wealth in business rather than men who had inherited it from landed families. Its citizens were, by and large, industrious and successful tradesmen, as Pope was only too aware, having been born the son of a linen merchant in the very heart of the business district. But towards the close of the seventeenth century a new development in mercantile growth occurred with the extraordinary increase in capitalist activity that took place. As a result the City of London became not only a trading centre but a financial stronghold. The connotation of the word 'City', to imply mysterious dealings in the world of high finance, that we intend today when we use phrases like 'City gent', or 'he does something in the City', originated in Pope's lifetime.

The Bank of England was established by Act of Parliament in 1693. Its imposing building at the end of Threadneedle Street was not built until 1734, but long before then the Bank had introduced the paper money that Pope so disliked:

> Blest paper-credit! last and best supply!
> That lends Corruption lighter wings to fly!
>
> (*Epistle to Bathurst*, 69–70)

It was the Bank's funding of the National Debt, however, that most spectacularly dramatized the new concept of living on borrowed credit. In 1688 the Debt was a mere £300,000; by 1720 it was £54 million, and by 1749 it was £80 million.

The other great factor in the capitalist expansion of the early eighteenth century was the proliferation of joint stock companies. In 1695 the amount of capital invested in joint stock companies was £4 million, by 1717 it had risen to £20 million, and by 1720 to about £50 million. The two largest and most sensational were the East India and South Sea Companies, but the rush of support to buy stock in smaller and totally unproven enterprises is perhaps a better indication of the capitalist fever that seized the country in these years. According to Isaac Kramnick's detailed study, *Bolingbroke and His Circle*:

> A list of the new companies founded in 1720 must also include the Bleaching of Hair Company, Insurance on Horses Company, a company for the Transmutation of Quicksilver, a company to insure Marriages from Divorce, and another to design an air pump for the brain. Subscriptions were opened and filled immediately for a company to plant mulberry trees and breed silk-worms in Chelsea Park. Another company would produce a cannon with the capability to discharge round and square cannon balls and bullets. The mania possessing the English that summer is best illustrated by the subscription of three thousand pounds in one day for 'a company to carry on an undertaking of great advantage but nobody to know what it is'.[5]

In such a world the financial rewards went to those most practised in devious forms of wheeling and dealing. It was the attendant parasites of the joint stock companies, the stock-jobbers, projectors, usurers, attorneys and scriveners, rather than the merchants and traders, who most profited from all this investment and who began to derive considerable influence from it. Pope and his Tory friends saw power shifting from the landed interest to the moneyed interest, from the country aristocracy to the city financiers, and they did not like it. As a recent historian has put it, the counting house had begun to replace the country house. Writing to Pope on 10 January 1721 Swift says:

> I ever abominated that scheme of politics (now about thirty years old) of setting up a money'd Interest in opposition to the landed. For, I conceived, there could not be a truer maxim in our government than this, that the possessors of the soil are the best judges of what is for the advantage of the kingdom: If others had thought the same way, Funds of Credit and South-Sea Projects would neither have been felt nor heard of.   (II, 70)

It is this moneyed interest, Whig in its politics, and Dissenting in its religion, that Pope attacks so consistently in his poems of the 1730s. Sir Charles Duncombe, a London banker who bought the Duke of Buckingham's Yorkshire estate of Helmsley for £90,000 in 1695, is a typical example. Pope describes the transaction in his *Imitation of Horace, Satire II, ii*, addressed to Hugh Bethel:

> And Helmsley once proud Buckingham's delight,
> Slides to a Scriv'ner or a City Knight. (177–8)

Here the terms 'scrivener' (a money-lender) and 'City Knight' have become almost synonymous as the moneyed interest buys what had previously been inherited, while Pope's scorn for both is compressed in the downward motion and slippery suggestion of the word 'slides'.

We must beware, however, of oversimplification. Pope hated avarice wherever it was found. 'In Soldier, Churchman, Patriot, Man in Pow'r,/'Tis Avarice all, Ambition is no more!' he says in Dialogue One of *Epilogue to the Satires* (161–2). Pope was far too intelligent to suggest that only inhabitants of the City worshipped Mammon. What we find in his poetry is a burning denunciation of the 'One Lust for Gold' that rages throughout the land in his *Imitation of Horace, Epistle I, i* (124), addressed to Lord Bolingbroke. It is London's collective voice, from St James's in Westminster to St Paul's in the City, that is imagined creating a new town cry in the poem. Rich and poor, old and young, are consumed by the same itch, so that all seem to call out in a collective voice:

> There, London's voice: 'Get Mony, Mony still'
> And then let Virtue follow, if she will. (79–80)

Nevertheless the eager desire for monetary gain does seem to be especially associated with the City in Pope's poetry. Nowhere is this more powerfully expressed than in the conclusion to the *Epistle to Lord Bathurst*. The poem is a scathing attack on avarice generally in a country 'sunk in lucre's sordid charms' (145), but it is the finely sustained closing story about Sir Balaam with its ring of Chaucerian narrative and anticipation of Hogarthian Progress that is most apposite here.

Sir Balaam originally came from the heart of the City's business district. 'A Citizen of Sober fame' (341), he dwelt near the Monument, erected on Fish Hill in memory of the fire of London, just a stone's throw from the Royal Exchange in Threadneedle Street. Indeed his worship at this temple to Mammon is equated with his worship at the temple to God: 'Constant at Church and Change; his gains were sure . . .' The telling juxtaposition of 'Church and Change' is skilfully reinforced in the pun on his spiritual and financial 'gains'. Such a portrait anticipates by almost 200 years

A New Plan of the City of London, Westminster and Southwark, c. 1720

Max Weber's celebrated thesis on the protestant roots of capitalism.[6]
The next development is for Balaam to be made a City Knight
when Satan tempts him with riches rather than poverty. The plain
good man of the opening becomes a typical moneyed man dealing
in stocks and shares:

> The Tempter saw his time; the work he ply'd;
> Stocks and Subscriptions pour on ev'ry side,
> 'Till all the Daemon makes his full descent,
> In one abundant show'r of Cent. per Cent.,
> Sinks deep within him, and possesses whole,
> Then dubs Director, and secures his soul.   (369–74)

Sir Balaam does not now even make the pretence of attending
church as well as Change. 'His Compting-house employ'd the
Sunday-morn' (380), and his wife and family represent him at
church.

The conclusion to the story leads directly into the next section of
this chapter. Having acquired financial status Sir Balaam sets out to
acquire social status. When his first wife dies he marries a nymph of
quality, 'bows at Court, and grows polite'. He rejects the City of
London for the City of Westminster:

> Leaves the dull Cits, and joins (to please the fair)
> The well-bred Cuckolds in St James's air.   (387–8)

Pope is scarcely less scathing in dealing with the Court than with
the City. Sir Balaam's family are individually ruined by their social
aspirations. His son 'drinks, whores, fights and in a duel dies'; his
daughter marries a Viscount and 'bears a Coronet and Pox for life';
and his Lady gets him into such deep debt through her gambling
that Sir Balaam takes a bribe from France and is impeached by the
House of Commons. Finally the Court forsakes him, and 'sad Sir
Balaam curses God and dies'. The move from the City to the Court
has been a move out of the frying pan into the fire.

The City of Westminster and the Court

The City of Westminster takes its name from its abbey, or minster,
situated to the west of the City of London. For centuries it was
entirely separate from the City of London. A road, running along
the edge of the Thames, and therefore appropriately called the
Strand, connected the two cities, but there were large open spaces
between them. According to John Noorthouck's *A New History of
London*, 'it long continued an insignificant, mean, unhealthy place,
remarkable for nothing but the abbey which was very unfavourably
placed in a marshy spot'.[7] It was during the reign of Henry VIII

that the City of Westminster first began to acquire the courtly and fashionable associations that it had for Pope. In 1530 Henry VIII bought York House, as it then was, from Cardinal Wolsey and converted it into his principal residence, the palace of Whitehall. He also acquired and rebuilt St James's Palace, which had formerly been a hospital for leprous maidens, and converted the ground between the two palaces into St James's Park.

From this time forward the City of Westminster continued to gain in social importance and during the early seventeenth century wealthy persons began to move their residences there from the City of London. One of the most important persons to make such a move was the Earl of Bedford who in 1631, with Inigo Jones as his architect, built the square at Covent Garden that later became the model for the development of the West End. But it was not until after the Restoration of Charles II in 1660 that a mass exodus of wealthy persons brought about a complete separation between the fashionable life in the City of Westminster and the mercantile life in the City of London.

During the reign of Charles II, the 'merry monarch', the City of Westminster became the centre of courtly and fashionable entertainment, and, although both William III and Anne led far quieter lives, the city never really lost this reputation. When the theatres reopened in 1660 the two acting companies performed at theatres situated in areas more closely associated with Westminster than London. The Duke's company produced their plays at the Duke's Theatre in Lincoln's Inn Fields, while the King's company produced theirs at the Theatre Royal in Drury Lane. Both companies moved to new theatres before the century ended, but the theatrical world remained essentially connected with the West End. Thus when an opera house was built in 1705 it was erected in the Haymarket in the heart of Westminster. These theatres catered to a small coterie audience dominated by fashion-conscious ladies and gentlemen from the town and Court who came there to meet one another as much as they did to see the play or listen to the opera. Another favourite meeting-place at this time was the coffee-house. Different coffee, or chocolate, houses appealed to different social, professional and political sections of society, so that the *beau monde*, for example, met at White's in St James's Street, while poets and critics got together at Will's near Covent Garden. A further consideration in the development of Westminster as a social centre was the building of great town houses, such as those of Lord Burlington and the Duke of Devonshire in Piccadilly, which brought with them glittering assemblies, levées and balls. Soon Westminster, like London, began to spread its influence further west so that by the beginning of the eighteenth century the adjoining villages of Kensington with its royal palace, and Chelsea with its Ranelagh pleasure gardens, were included in its social, if not in its geographical, milieu.

This is the world that Pope lightly conjures up in his *Epistle to Miss Blount* written on her leaving the Town for her country house at Mapledurham in 1714:

> She went from Op'ra, park, assembly, play
> To morning walks, and pray'rs three hours a day.
>
> (13–14)

There is a smiling ambivalence in Pope's attitude to the fashionable life of Westminster in his earlier poems. He knows that the town is traditionally to be rejected as a place of hypocrisy and affectation, and yet one cannot help sensing the young man's attraction towards its social gaiety. A distinct affection for the glitter of society lies beneath the gently satirical surface of *The Rape of the Lock*. Pope seems ready to forgive the town its vices for the same reason that he forgives Belinda her errors:

> If to her share some Female Errors fall,
> Look on her Face, and you'll forget 'em all.
>
> (II, 17–18)

This ambivalent attitude to the City of Westminster and all it represents is most clearly found in the opening line of his poem, *A Farewell to London*: 'Dear, damn'd, distracting Town, farewell!' Pope left the town in 1715, the year this poem was written, to complete his translation of the *Iliad* in the peace of the country. He was never again to write of the fashionable world as vaguely enticing: henceforth its capacity to damn takes over from its capacity to distract. He wrote to Patty Blount in October 1715 saying:

> I am growing fit, I hope, for a better world, of which the light of the sun is but a shadow: for I doubt not but God's works here, are what come nearest to his works there; and that a true relish of the beauties of nature is the most easy preparation and gentlest transition to an enjoyment of those of heaven; as on the contrary a true town life of hurry, confusion, noise, slander and dissension, is a sort of apprenticeship to hell and its furies.   (I, 319)

But it is the City of Westminster's associations with the Court that most concern Pope. The word 'Court', in this context, describes the place where the sovereign resides and holds state, attended by his retinue. It is worth briefly considering the word's etymology here, for originally it denoted a small enclosed place (cf. courtyard, or tennis court), and this root meaning helps to fix the particular sense of a narrow coterie that pertains to the word as it refers to the king and his household. This household moved around somewhat in

Pope's lifetime. Until the time of William III the main royal residence had been at Whitehall, but William found that the London fog aggravated his asthma and he therefore moved his household, first to Hampton Court, and then to Kensington Palace. Queen Anne continued to reside at Kensington, but with the arrival of George I the Court returned to Westminster. The palace of White-hall, with the fortunate exception of the magnificent banqueting hall designed by Inigo Jones had been burned down by a fire in 1697. Therefore, St James's, which Noorthouck describes as 'an irregular brick building, without one single beauty on the outside to recommend it, being at once the contempt of foreign nations, and the disgrace of our own',[8] became the principal royal palace in England until the death of George II in 1760.

Despite the great constitutional changes that had taken place in the second half of the seventeenth century, the Court still maintained great influence in eighteenth-century England. The sovereign control-led the appointment of all ambassadors and envoys abroad, and of all dignitaries and deputies at home, quite apart from the vast number of pensions and places, for example appointments connected with the revenue, throughout the country. The Court was therefore a great focus for patronage and not only for those in search of social improvement. As Derek Jarrett says in *Britain 1688–1815*:

> There was no question of a clear-cut division between men who ministered to the King's personal needs and men who helped him rule the country. For most of the eighteenth century the Lord Chamberlain, a Household officer, could attend the Cabinet Coun-cil while his counterpart among the Officers of State, the Lord Great Chamberlain, could not; and during Anne's reign it was not unusual for the Groom of the Stole (the particular title given to the first Gentleman of the Bedchamber) and even the Master of the Horse to attend Cabinet meetings. Thus courtiers were fre-quently councillors and councillors had often to practise the arts of the courtiers. Wherever the King was, there power and influ-ence were to be won.[9]

No one realized this better than Sir Robert Walpole, and his long 'reign' as First Minister was to a great extent dependent on his influence at Court and particularly on his influence with George II's Queen, Caroline of Anspach.

Pope showed two distinct attitudes to the Court at different periods in his life. During the reign of Queen Anne, when his Tory friends Robert Harley and Henry St John had controlling influence there, Pope was full of praise for it, seeing Stuart rule, in *Windsor-Forest*, 1713, as a latterday equivalent to the age of Augustus. But once the House of Hanover came to the throne and the Whigs under

Robert Walpole gained control at Court, Pope became increasingly
disillusioned, until, in the poems of the 1730s, and especially in the
Imitation of Horace, Epistle II, i: To Augustus, 1737, and the *Epilogue
to the Satires*, 1738, he delivered a sombre protest against what
he considered to be the 'insuperable corruption and depravity of
manners'[10] brought about by the Hanoverian Court.

There are few more magnificent courtly panegyrics in the
language than *Windsor-Forest*. The poem is partly glorifying myth,
with Queen Anne seen as Diana, 'The Earth's fair light, and
Empress of the Main', and partly a merging of dream and fact as
Pope celebrates the Peace of Utrecht:

> At length great ANNA said – Let Discord cease!
> She said, the World obey'd and all was *Peace*!   (327–8)

Given such a conception it is hardly surprising that the image of
London and Westminster that emerges bears little resemblance to
the description of those two cities drawn in this chapter:

> Behold! *Augusta*'s glitt'ring Spires increase,
> And Temples rise, the beauteous Works of Peace.
> I see, I see where two fair Cities bend
> Their ample Bow, a new *White-Hall* ascend!
> There mighty Nations shall inquire their Doom,
> The World's great Oracle in Times to come;
> There Kings shall sue, and Suppliant States be seen
> Once more to bend before a *British* QUEEN.   (377–84)

This is splendid visionary poetry, but put it beside the fourth book
of *The Dunciad*, published twenty years later, and it will prove as
insubstantial as Prospero's pageant in *The Tempest*.

Pope's disillusion with the Court begins with the death of Queen
Anne. This event scattered the members of the Scriblerus Club, who
had gathered round Harley to support the Tory Ministry, into
various parts of England, Ireland and France. With the accession of
George I and the return of Whig power, Pope retired from London
life to devote himself mainly to the duties of editing and translating.
By the time he came to write of the Court again, in the Satires that
followed the first *Dunciad* over a dozen years later, his attitude was
radically different. A cultural decay, which he blamed on the House
of Hanover, seemed to him to have replaced the dream of a second
Augustan age that he had associated with the House of Stuart under
Queen Anne.

Pope's most sustained denunciation of the Court is to be found in
his *The Fourth Satire of Dr. John Donne, Dean of St. Paul's, Versifyed*,
published in 1733. The poem is a good example of what it means to
be a neoclassical writer. Poets had satirized the Court long before

Pope did so, perhaps the most famous English examples being Skelton's *Why Come Ye Not to Court?*, Spenser's *Colin Clout's Come Home Again*, and John Donne's *Satires*. What Pope does in his *The Fourth Satire of Dr. John Donne, Dean of St. Paul's, Versifyed*, is to transmit this tradition and show how it is just as relevant to his own day. He assimilates the past into the present.

The figure of the satirist who speaks in the poem describes, with a solemn sense of pain, how he was heavily punished for going once to Court. No sooner had he entered than he was intercepted by a courtier, 'a Rogue so civil, whose Tongue can complement you to the Devil' (56–7). The courtier having spied him out, engages him in obliging talk, extols the virtues of travel, gossips about Court news, and so totally provokes the satirist's patience that he 'pukes' and 'nauseates'. The satirist only escapes when the courtier flies to the Minister as he comes by. When the satirist contemplates the scene afterwards he falls into a dream in which he realizes that the Court is worse than hell:

> Not Dante dreaming all th' Infernal State,
> Beheld such Scenes of Envy, Sin and Hate. (192–3)

The Court is a 'Bladder' (205) and courtiers are 'painted puppets' (208), a 'varnished race of hollow gewgaws' (209). They have no minds of their own and are mere lifeless effigies, 'stately, staring things' (210), like waxworks. Pope's main criticism of the Court is that it produces such artificial veneers. Courtiers act every part but that of themselves. They have no individuality and no self-respect. In despair the satirist concludes that '*Courts are too much for Wits so weak as mine*' (280).

Pope's poem is mainly a general attack on the courtier as a type. It would be a mistake, however, to think that Pope does not condemn individual courtiers and even the sovereign himself in his poetry. Indeed this is where he most differs from earlier English satirists. Skelton and Spenser had both been careful to praise Henry VIII and Elizabeth respectively at the same time as they attacked their Courts. Pope, on the other hand, includes numerous onslaughts on named individuals, not least George II and Queen Caroline. Perhaps the best-known, and most typical, courtier of George II's reign was John, Lord Hervey, whose *Memoirs of the Reign of George II* are now considered one of the most valuable historical records of the time. Pope's hostility to Hervey is too complex to trace in all its ramifications here, but his portrait of him as Sporus in *An Epistle to Dr Arbuthnot* is clearly relevant as being also the portrait of a typical courtier.

The portrait picks up many of the images of the Court that we have seen in *The Fourth Satire of Dr. John Donne, Dean of St. Paul's, Versifyed*, Sporus, like the impertinent courtier in the versification of

Donne, is full of extravagant show, but at the same time this artificial exterior is linked to a sordid inner reality. Thus he has 'gilded' wings, but he is a 'bug'; he is 'painted', but he is a 'child of dirt that stinks and stings'; he is 'well-bred', but he is also a 'spaniel'; and he has a 'cherub's face', but is a 'Reptile all the rest'. The courtier has been transformed into an image of Satan: the link between the Court and Vice could not be more direct.

Pope's comments on the Court expand to reveal far wider decay. This is most clearly conveyed in the *Imitation of Horace, Epistle II, i: To Augustus*, 1737, where what begins as a satire on George II develops into an attack on the degeneration of culture in Hanoverian England. The poem as a whole is no more solely about George II than *The Dunciad* is solely about Lewis Theobald or Colley Cibber. George II, as King of England, is merely the figurehead for a greater corruption, the decay of poetry and drama generally in his time.

The presentation of George in this poem is one of the most finely controlled pieces of irony in all of Pope's poetry. Horace's respectful tribute to the Emperor Augustus is converted into a mock tribute to George Augustus Hanover:

> While You, great Patron of Mankind, sustain
> The balanc'd World, and open all the Main;
> Your Country, chief, in Arms abroad defend,
> At home, with Morals, Arts and Laws amend;
> How shall the Muse, from such a Monarch, steal
> An hour, and not defraud the Publick Weal? (1–6)

George is ironically praised for being precisely what he is not – a 'great Patron' – and for doing what he does not do, 'sustain the balanced world'. He is described opening 'all the Main', as if that were praiseworthy, when he should be protecting English shipping. He defends his country abroad in the arms of Mme Walmoden (later the Countess of Yarmouth) instead of in the arms of battle; while at home he 'amends' his country with 'Morals, Arts, and Laws', with the clear implication that the amendment is for the worse rather than the better. The ironic tone ('*such* a Monarch': the italics are mine) is clearly established so that by the time we come to the climax of this opening eulogy the ambiguity is unmistakable to all except the most obtuse (i.e. George himself):

> Wonder of Kings! like whom, to mortal eyes
> None e'er has risen, and none e'er shall rise. (29–30)

I do not intend to discuss all the references to the Court in Pope's later poetry, for, as must be clear by now, there are far too many.

The interested reader who wants to follow this up should look especially at lines 101–19 of the *Imitation of Horace, Epistle I, i*, addressed to Lord Bolingbroke. I want instead to conclude this section by commenting on a poem in which the allusions to the fashionable world of Westminster are not simply contained in a certain block of lines that attack the Court but are woven into the whole texture of the poem.

The *Epilogue to the Satires* has already been mentioned as one of Pope's most powerful satires on Hanoverian corruption. One of the chief sources of its power is the dramatic tension set up in the dialogue between its two speakers, referred to in the text as *P.* (Pope) and *Fr.* (Friend). Only when we realize that the Friend is a typical courtier can we appreciate fully the various points of view put into his mouth, and the way Pope, as author, manipulates the 'Friend', as adversary. The 'Friend' (he is of course anything but a friend) approves of Horace because 'his sly, polite, insinuating stile could please at Court' (I, 19–20); he approves of Pope attacking 'some odd Old Whig' (I, 39), so long as he doesn't include the modern Whigs who support the Court; he defends 'Immortal Selkirk' (I, 92), who was a gentleman to the Bedchamber to William III, George I, and George II; he equates the Court of Hanover with the Court of Heaven (I, 97–104); he is horrified when Pope mentions the King directly (II, 51–2); and he constantly falls back on Court jargon (e.g. II, 123). These are some of the ways in which Pope realizes the courtly character of the adversary so that the reader feels the full validity of the onslaught. Thus when the courtier protests that Pope's filthy simile quite turns his stomach, the reader shares the righteous indignation of Pope's reply:

> So does Flatt'ry mine;
> And all your Courtly Civet-Cats can Vent,
> Perfume to you, to me is Excrement.   (II, 182–4)

This excremental image aptly summarizes Pope's disgust for the Court and all it stands for. It is a disgust that seems to grow stronger throughout the satires of the 1730s. Pope's response to the Court in the *Epilogue to the Satires*, 1738, is that much more indignant than his response to the Court in *The Fourth Satire of Dr. John Donne, Dean of St. Paul's, Versifyed*, 1733, and of course put beside his response to the Court in *Windsor-Forest*, 1713, it represents a complete volte-face. In the *Epilogue to the Satires* flattery, affectation, the adoption of airs and graces, false breeding and florid eloquence are merely disguised forms of obscenity. Seen from one point of view, that of the Court, such manners smell sweet, like 'perfume', but seen from another point of view, that of Pope and, hopefully, the reader, such dressings-up smell foul, like 'excrement'.

Grub Street and the war with the Dunces

Grub Street is a term that has been used over the years to cover a multitude of different meanings. It originates from the name of an actual street, in the parish of Cripplegate just outside the City walls but within the 'liberties' of the City jurisdiction, that was largely inhabited by hack writers willing to use their pens for money, whatever the assignment. Grub Street lay in the heart of one of the most depressed areas of eighteenth-century London suburbia. To the east was the notoriously dissolute area of Moorfields, bounded to the south by Bedlam, the asylum for the mad, while to the west was the polluted area of West Smithfield with its meat market. But if Grub Street was originally the name of an actual street it rapidly acquired a metaphorical meaning. The term was used, from the early eighteenth century onwards, to describe any hack writing and not just the street itself. As Dr Johnson says in his *Dictionary*, 1755, Grub Street was 'originally the name of a street in Moorfields in London, much inhabited by writers of small histories, dictionaries, and temporary poems; whence any mean production is called *grubstreet*'. It was the meanness of the production that counted: for such writers literature was a commodity to be peddled to the highest bidder.

If the City of London was inevitably associated in Pope's poetry with the moneyed interest, and the City of Westminster with the fashionable interest, the Grub Street locale brings with it a third set of associations. Grub Street, Moorfields, Smithfield, Bedlam, Newgate, the Fleet Ditch, St Giles-in-the-Fields and St Giles Cripplegate are all places that fall between the cities of London and Westminster. They are part of a great depressed region lying between and around these two symbolic centres of money and fashion. In placing the Dunces so firmly in such a setting, as he does in *The Dunciad*, Pope was again using real description as a basis for his imaginative transformation. The filth, stench and violence associated with actual slum regions in London become an objective correlative for bad writing. In the Augustan world of absolute moral standards bad art is considered to be as immoral as bad conduct. The prostitute author is an object of contempt, not pity. It was part of the change to a Romantic sensibility at the end of the century that converted the image of the Grub Street writer from an object of scorn to an object of pathos. The nineteenth-century image of the hack writer in his garret as an alienated genius in seclusion is a gross sentimentalizing of the facts of the eighteenth-century literary environment. It was these hack writers, or scribblers, as Pope most frequently called them, the tabloid press reporters of their day, who, fiercely envious of his success as a poet and of his financial independence as an author, struck at him with such fury.

I have already described (p. 13) the campaign of careful neglect that greeted the publication of Pope's *Pastorals* in 1709, and have shown Pope's ability to deal with his literary detractors quite as effectively as they had dealt with him. But such opposition appears in a kindly light when compared to the long history of obscene and personal vituperation that followed on John Dennis's *Reflections Critical and Satyrical, Upon a Late Rhapsody, Call'd, An Essay Upon Criticism*, published in 1711. This gross personal attack on Pope's disfigurement opened the floodgates to a torrent of abuse that was to be kept up with little check until his death. It is undoubtedly true to say that no poet in our literature has been vilified so persistently and so virulently as Pope. J. V. Guerinot's bibliography of *Pamphlet Attacks on Pope* lists no fewer than 158 separate pamphlets attacking him between the time of Dennis's opening blast in 1711 and the poet's death thirty-three years later.[11] Furthermore, this list deliberately excludes the multitude of passing comments to be found in the newspapers of the day.

Two particular aspects of Pope's character come in for repeated abuse. Both are linked to laboured puns on his name: his simian-like deformity is pointed up by leaving out the middle letters of his name (A.P**E), and his despised religion is attacked through the even more obvious pun on his full name. The violent scurrility of the majority of these pamphlets can be briefly indicated through a sample list of the epithets attached to him: at various times he is called an adder, a baboon, a wasp, a whore, a pimp, an insect, a croaking toad, a portentous cub, the purest Wag-prick, a specious knave, the monkey's paw of a low faction, a true son of an impudent whore of Babylon . . . etc. Such pamphlets have little literary value, but they are helpful, nevertheless, in giving us a better understanding of the conditions that at first surrounded the reception of Pope's work, and later became part of the motive behind the writing of such poems as *The Dunciad* and *An Epistle to Dr Arbuthnot.*

Since it was the conflict with Dennis that began this long warfare it is worth pausing to examine its tenor and motive more closely. Pope had been the first to strike when in six lines of *An Essay on Criticism*, published in May 1711, he wrote:

> Fear not the Anger of the Wise to raise;
> Those best can bear Reproof who merit Praise.
> 'Twere well, might Criticks still this Freedom take;
> But Appius reddens at each Word you speak,
> And stares, Tremendous! with a threat'ning Eye,
> Like some fierce Tyrant in Old Tapestry!   (582–7)

Pope refers to Dennis by the name of one of the characters in his tragedy *Appius and Virginia*, first performed two years earlier, in

49

The frontispiece of Pope Alexander's Supremacy and Infallibility
Examin'd, *1729*

February, 1709, and makes light fun of his well-known 'stare' and favourite adjective, 'tremendous'. From a young man of twenty-three there was some mild disrespect in this description of the fifty-four-year-old critic and playwright, but nothing that could be considered to justify Dennis's furious response published next month:

> As there is no Creature in Nature so venomous, there is nothing so stupid and so impotent as a hunch-back'd Toad; and a man must be very quiet and very passive, and stand still to let him fasten his Teeth and his Claws, or be surpriz'd sleeping by him, before that Animal can have any power to hurt him.
>
> (*Reflections . . . Upon . . . An Essay Upon Criticism*)[12]

This, and much more in the same vein, established the predominant tone of the writing on Pope in his lifetime. Pope was startled and hurt by the attack, but he did not reply until two years later, in 1713, when he published *The Narrative of Dr Robert Norris* (see p. 15).

This pamphlet makes open fun of Dennis, but it never descends to the vitriolic insult that is Dennis's stock in trade. In *A True Character of Mr Pope, And His Writings*, May 1716, published by Edmund Curll, Dennis writes:

> The Deformity of this Libeller, is Visible, Present, Unalterable, and Peculiar to himself. 'Tis the mark of God and Nature upon him, to give us warning that we should hold no Society with him, as a Creature not of our Original, nor of our Species . . . . They tell me, he has been lately pleas'd to say, That 'tis Doubtful if the Race of Men are the Offspring of Adam or of the Devil. But if 'tis doubtful as to the Race of Men, 'tis certain at least, that his Original is not from Adam, but from the Devil. By his constant and malicious Lying, and by that Angel Face and Form of his, 'tis plain that he wants nothing but Horns and Tayl, to be the exact Resemblance, both in Shape and Mind, of his Infernal Father.[13]

But if the conflict with Dennis, a recognized literary critic, began the long series of insults on Pope, it was the conflict with Grub Street scribblers, who frequently remained anonymous, that continued and sustained it. Edmund Curll, a bookseller who specialized in unauthorized publication and literary scandal, was the most powerful representative of these writers, and directly commissioned a great number of the attacks. Pope's conflict with Curll came to a head in 1716 after Curll had piratically published some poems, written by Lady Mary Wortley Montagu, satirizing the Court. At this stage in his life Pope was anxious to impress Lady Mary and, since he had already suffered from Curll, he took revenge by first dropping an emetic in Curll's drink and then publishing a prose account of his ensuing sickness. This was descending to a level at which Curll was a past master and was to backfire on Pope for the rest of his life. Curll never left him alone after this and when he was not publishing some scurrilous comments on him, for example Dennis's *A True Character of Mr Pope*, 1716, or Curll's own *The Curliad*, 1729, he was busily dredging up some youthful indiscretion of Pope's never intended for publication, such as *A Roman Catholick Version of the First Psalm*, 1716.

From the time of Dennis's first engagement with Pope in June 1711 to the end of 1718 there were thirty-four pamphlet attacks on Pope. After this things quieted down a bit as Pope retired from the centre of literary attention to work on his translation of Homer and edition of Shakespeare. In the eight years from 1719 to the end of 1727 there were only nineteen onslaughts, and there were never more than three in any one year. Then in May 1728 came the publication of *The Dunciad* in three books with Theobald as hero, and the War with the Dunces was on. In the next three years alone forty-two separate pamphlets against Pope were published.

The Dunciad was Pope's first poetical reply to his enemies since they had begun their campaign in 1711. This is not to say that he had suffered silently for seventeen years; as we have already seen, he had made several prose retaliations, but he had certainly received far more abuse than he had given. He was not unmoved by these feuds, however, and two years earlier on 14 December 1725 had written to Swift saying that although he did not have much anger against the great ones of the world his spleen was raised by the little rogues of it:

> It would vexe one more to be knock't o' the head by a Pisspot, than by a thunderbolt. As to great Oppressors (as you say) they are like Kites or Eagles, one expects mischief from them: But to be Squirted to Death (as poor Wycherley said to me on his deathbed) by *Potecaries Prentices*, by the under Strappers of Under Secretaries, to Secretaries, who were no Secretaries – this would provoke as dull a dog as Philips himself. (II, 350)

However, if Pope now thought he could demolish 'the little rogues' of the world by ridiculing them, he was as mistaken as when he tried to demolish Curll by playing a practical joke on him. The main outward effect of *The Dunciad* was to multiply, not decrease, the plague of insect scribblers who pestered him. As he wrote in *An Epistle to Dr Arbuthnot* a few years later:

> Who shames a Scribler? break one cobweb thro',
> He spins the slight, self-pleasing thread anew;
> Destroy his Fib, or Sophistry; in vain,
> The Creature's at his dirty work again;
> Thron'd in the Centre of his thin designs;
> Proud of a vast Extent of flimzy lines.   (89–94)

Pope had stunned the Scribblers, not shamed them. 'No creature smarts so little as a fool' (84), and these creatures, like Swift's famous spider, had 'a good plentiful store of dirt and poison' in their breasts.[14] They would recover and be themselves.

The abuse poured on Pope as a result of *The Dunciad* plumbed new depths in character assassination. *Farmer Pope and his Son*, for example, published by Curll in September 1728, and probably written by him too, describes Pope, in a fable, as:

> A little scurvy, purblind-Elf;
> Scarce like a Toad, much less himself.
> Deform'd in Shape, of Pigmy Stature:
> A proud, conceited, peevish Creature.[15]

A year later, in August 1729, Ned Ward described Pope in the dedication to *Apollo's Maggots in his Cups* as:

> A frightful indigested Lump,
> With here a Hollow, there a Hump;
> A true Epitome of Wales,
> Made up of ugly Hills and Dales.

These lines, disgusting enough in themselves, are a mere prelude to the poem which tells, according to J. V. Guerinot, of:

> a drunken feast of the gods in which Apollo visits Parnassus and proposes to the Muses that they form a satirist, a something between a monkey and a man. Having formed a body with muck, they urinate and defecate upon it. Apollo adds the brains and animates it with a bellows ... and drops him down between Thames and Isis (i.e. Twickenham), where he reigns as King of modern wits.[16]

These examples are quite sufficient to indicate the 'literary' climate of the war with the Dunces. Before we accuse Pope of sinking to unnecessary depths of indecency in *The Dunciad* we should bear in mind the standard level of pamphlet abuse in the early eighteenth century.

In 1733 his feud with Lady Mary Wortley Montagu and John, Lord Hervey came to a head. It is difficult, if not impossible, to determine which party was the instigator in this particular battle, for relations between Pope and Lady Mary and between Pope and Lord Hervey are clouded with unknown factors. Pope's attitude to Lady Mary had dramatically soured during the 1720s after his early infatuation for her. In January 1733 he produced a devastating allusion to her as Sappho in his *Imitation of Horace, Satire II, i:*

> From furious *Sappho* scarce a milder Fate
> P-x'd by her Love, or libell'd by her Hate.   (83–4)

It was in reply to this that Lady Mary and Lord Hervey collaborated to write the most skilful of all the satires on Pope, *Verses Address'd to the Imitator of the First Satire of the Second Book of Horace*, published in *The Grub-Street Journal* of 29 March 1733. The verses culminate in a vicious curse on Pope full of personal hatred and lacking any redeeming wit:

> Like the first bold Assassin's be thy Lot
> Ne'er be thy Guilt forgiven, or forgot;
> But as thou hate'st, be hated by Mankind,
> And with the Emblem of thy crooked Mind,
> Mark'd on thy Back, like *Cain*, by God's own Hand,
> Wander like him, accursed through the Land.

The controversy stirred up by these verses raged on in the pages of *The Grub-Street Journal* for the rest of the year. It undoubtedly had much to do with Pope's magnificently damning portrait of Lord Hervey as Sporus in *An Epistle to Dr Arbuthnot* published two years later in 1735. As Pope says in the 'Advertisement' to this poem:

> This Paper is a Sort of Bill of Complaint, begun many years since, and drawn up by snatches, as the several Occasions offer'd. I had no thoughts of publishing it, till it pleas'd some Persons of Rank and Fortune [John, Lord Hervey and Lady Mary Wortley Montagu] to attack in a very extraordinary manner, not only my writings (of which being publick the Publick judge) but my Person, Morals and Family, whereof to those who know me not, a truer Information may be requisite.

Pope's poem is a defence of his life and writings, but it is, of course, never purely defensive. He pummels his various enemies with far more wit than they ever displayed, metaphorically converting them into grotesque forms of comical amusement. Thus the minor poets who pester him for favour become at one time madmen who 'rave, recite, and madden round the land'(6), and at another a plague of insects who pierce his thickets and glide through his grotto. The pedantic scholars are transformed into rare ornithological specimens, 'each Word-catcher that lives on syllables'(166), while he playfully imagines that the dunces might be whistled off his hands like trained hawks. The archetypal scribbler becomes a spider:

> Thron'd in the Centre of his thin designs;
> Proud of a vast Extent of flimzy lines. (93-4)

An Epistle to Dr Arbuthnot and the various *Imitations of Horace* that followed it were more than sufficient provocation to keep the war with the Dunces going throughout the 1730s. It is only necessary to refer individually to one more of the many attacks that continued to be made on Pope right up to his death, and that is Colley Cibber's *A Letter from Mr Cibber to Mr Pope*, published in July 1742. According to Warburton's 'Advertisement to the Reader', printed with *The Dunciad in Four Books* in October 1743, the publication of Cibber's 'ridiculous book . . . furnished him [Pope] with a lucky opportunity of improving this Poem, by giving it the only thing it wanted, a more considerable Hero'. Whether Cibber's *Letter* did in fact provoke Pope into elevating Cibber to Theobald's former eminence, or merely confirmed him in making changes he had already contemplated, is something that one cannot be sure about, but there can be no doubt that it constituted yet another vicious personal attack on Pope that cried out for some sort of reply. In his *Letter* Cibber includes the notorious 'Tom-Tit' episode (see p. 56) in which he tells how he and two other wits had lured Pope to a brothel but that he, Cibber, had saved Pope from the danger of venereal infection:

> But I (forgive me all ye mortified Mortals whom his fell Satyr has since fallen upon) observing he had staid as long as without hazard of his Health he might, I 'Prick'd to it by foolish Honesty and Love' as *Shakespear* says, without Ceremony threw open the Door upon him, where I found this little hasty Hero, like a terrible *Tom Tit*, pertly perched upon the Mount of Love! But such was my Surprize that I fairly laid hold of his Heels, and actually drew him down safe and sound from his Danger.[17]

As Guerinot points out, it is extremely unlikely that Cibber's story is true, for surely Pope would not have dared to belabour him over the years if he knew Cibber had such a weapon in store. 'Prick'd to it by foolish Honesty and Love' are Iago's words to Othello (III, iii, 418) as he schemes to betray him. It is an indication of Cibber's complacency that he has unconsciously compared himself to the most jealous villian of all.

Finally, let us ask what effect all these attacks had on Pope and how they influenced his life and writing. The most obvious effect on his work is that they turned him towards writing satire. Before *The Dunciad* of 1728 Pope had only written one major poem, *The Rape of*

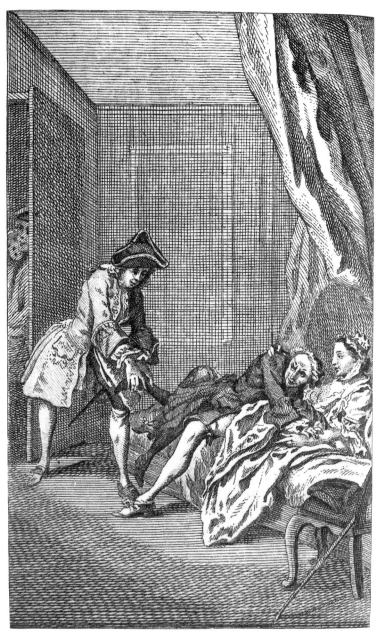

The Tom-Tit episode. Frontspiece to the third edition of A Letter from Mr Cibber to Mr Pope

the Lock, that was primarily a satiric poem and even that is in some
ways more of a comedy than a satire. After 1728 nearly everything
he wrote was strongly imbued with the satiric vein. It can of course
be argued that his strength and success as a satirist would have
emerged even if he had not been so frequently savaged, but it is far
more likely that his turning towards satire as his main mode of
expression in the latter half of his life was directly influenced by the
many attacks on him. So far as the effect of these feuds on his
personal life is concerned we can hardly do better than to conclude
this section by quoting from Guerinot, who has made the most
thorough study of them: 'To anyone who tries to read through
Popiana year by year, it is Pope's forbearance and restraint that
come to seem remarkable; the image of a poet eager to make every
one of his detractors writhe needs serious revision'.[18]

The country and retirement

Pope's rejection of the financial, fashionable and literary abuses of
London, described in the preceding sections of this chapter, are
drawn into one composite rejection of urban life in his *Imitation of
Horace, Epistle II, ii*, 1737, better known as *To a Colonel*. Near the
beginning of this poem Pope rhetorically asks the colonel whether
anyone can seriously regard London as a fit home for a poet:

> Who there his Muse, or Self, or Soul attends?
> In Crouds and Courts, Law, Business, Feasts and Friends?
>
> (90-1)

Pope, as correspondent, goes on to describe in detail the press,
anxiety and noise of London where he is besieged by lawyers,
courtiers and Grub Street writers, 'this jealous, waspish, wrong-
head, rhyming Race'(148). He only finds relief from the 'eternal
roar' of urban life when he retires to the country:

> Soon as I enter at my Country door,
> My Mind resumes the thread it dropt before;
> Thoughts, which at Hyde-Park-Corner I forgot,
> Meet and rejoin me, in the pensive Grott.
> There all alone, and Compliments apart,
> I ask these sober questions of my Heart.   (206-11)

The country has profound cultural and spiritual significance in
Pope's poetry. There the poet can attend 'his Muse, or Self, or
Soul', and ask sober questions of his Heart. The country symbolizes,
in a variety of ways all the positive values that lie behind Pope's
rejection of the city. He puts the life of rural retirement forward as

the ideal against which to measure the moral limitations and aberrations of urban life.

The country was never very far away from Pope's London. As Sir Walter Besant puts it:

> From any part of London it was possible to get into the country in a quarter of an hour. One realizes the rural surroundings of the City by considering that north of Gray's Inn was open country with fields; that Queen Square Bloomsbury, had its north side left purposely open in order that the residents might enjoy the views of the Highgate and Hampstead Hills. Within the reach of a 'short stage' the country was not only open and rural, but it was extremely beautiful.[19]

The village of Twickenham, where Pope lived for the last twenty-five years of his life, is situated on the north (Middlesex) bank of the Thames about fifteen miles upstream from London. Even in Pope's day it was not what one might call a rustic village, for it included many wealthy and noble inhabitants who lived in graceful villas on the river bank. But it was sufficiently separate from London, and surrounded by open fields and meadows, to be clearly considered part of the country in a way it certainly could not be today, having long since been swallowed up by the endless surburbia of Greater London.

It was in this gentle landscape that Pope settled down to lead a life of rural retirement. It is important to realize that such a life was, for Pope, an extension of his basically neoclassical frame of mind not a first dawning of nineteenth-century Romanticism. Its model lay clearly in the classical motif of the *beatus vir*, or happy man, found in the writings of Virgil and Horace. The retirement theme, considered as a literary tradition, is related to the pastoral tradition in seeing the country as representative of the good values in life. Both traditions give us the other side of the coin to satire, which, from Juvenal on Rome to T. S. Eliot on London, sees the city as representative of corrupt values. But there are also crucial differences between the pastoral and retirement traditions, the most important being that where the pastoral poet deliberately idealizes rural life, so that his shepherds and shepherdesses become consciously artificial figures, the retirement poet offers a realistic appreciation of country life according to stoic principles.

It is well known that Pope's earliest published poems were his *Pastorals* but it is perhaps less well known that his earliest poem 'written at about twelve years old', as he himself said, was the *Ode to Solitude*. The poem relies heavily on Horace's *Second Epode*, which is the basis of the whole retirement tradition. Pope's opening phrase, 'Happy the man', would immediately remind readers of Horace's opening words, '*Beatus ille*'. Pope's ode is a paean to the life of the rural husbandman, and ends with a plea that the poet himself might be allowed to live such a life. Thus early did the retirement ideal enter into the consciousness of the young poet.

The theme of the happy man underwent many changes in emphasis from the time of Horace to the time of Pope, but a certain core of ideals remained essentially unchanged for both poets. The happy man retired to the country, first, because it offered a physical quietness that led to peace of mind, in total contrast to the anxiety and strife of the town. Second, he could achieve in the country a degree of self-reliance, by growing his own food and supplying his own attire, that again was altogether unattainable in the town. Third, he could participate in the general harmony of nature and thereby enjoy the greater harmony of God's creation. And finally, the happy husbandman had no ambitious desires. He rejected extravagant taste in favour of a simple but healthy sufficiency; 'Content with little', says Pope in *Satire II, ii*, 'I can piddle here/On Broccoli and mutton round the year' (137–8). At the core of the retirement tradition then, lay the key values of peace, self-reliance, a harmonious relationship with nature and a healthy sufficiency. Above all, such a life offered the conditions for contemplation. 'Oft in the clear, still Mirrour of Retreat', Pope writes in the *Epilogue to the Satires: Dialogue II* (78), 'I studied Shrewsbury, the wise and great'. Retirement is 'clear' and 'still'. It offers the chance for 'study' in a way that the active life in the city does not, which is not to say, of course, that the husbandman's life is inactive. 'Contemplative life', wrote Pope to Atterbury when the bishop urged him in 1717 to join the Anglican faith and become more active, 'is not only my scene, but it is my habit too' (I,454).

The clearest examples of the happy man in Pope's poetry are the portraits of Trumbull in *Windsor-Forest* (235–58), and of the Man of Ross in the *Epistle to Bathurst* (249–90). Sir William Trumbull is praised as an example of those values noted in the previous paragraph. He is content with peace, the 'humbler joys of homefelt Quiet' (239); he is self-reliant, gathering 'Health from Herbs the Forest yields' (241); he lives in accord with Nature, 'to follow Nature' (252); and he lives a life of contemplation, 'wandering thoughtful in the silent wood' (249). The praise for John Kyrle, the Man of Ross, relies on the same set of values with added stress being given to his generosity and good works. It is significant that he too is addressed as a 'happy man' (275).

However, if the portraits of Trumbull and John Kyrle are the clearest individual examples of the 'happy man' motif in Pope's poetry, his composite portrait of himself as speaker, especially as it emerges in the satires of the 1730s, is the most sustained example of the motif. What Pope gives us in these poems is a series of compressed allusions to such an ideal. He nowhere presents such a self-portrait in its entirety, but the overall impression in reading these poems is to feel the cumulative effect of the references to the life of the 'happy man'. The ideal of the *beatus vir* emerges as a mosaic portrait that gives positive substance to the charges made against a corrupt and vicious world.

Horace's *Second Epode* was by no means the only place in which he developed the retirement theme. Equally important, and perhaps even more influential in seventeenth- and eighteenth-century England, was his *Satire II, vi*, containing the celebrated fable of the town and country mouse. Horace's poem includes a wonderful evocation of the retired life – based on the best authors, good food and wine, cheerful company and serious conversation – that he led at his Sabine farm outside Rome. Horace emerges from the poem as a sophisticated person taking comfort in sophisticated moderation. Pope's imitation of the second half of Horace's poem begins by serenely re-enacting the poise and tranquillity of Horace's retirement:

> O charming Noons! and Nights divine!
> Or when I Sup, or when I dine,
> My Friends above, my Folks below,
> Chatting and laughing all-a-row,
> The Beans and Bacon set before 'em,
> The Grace-cup serv'd with all decorum:
> Each willing to be pleas'd, and please,
> And even the very Dogs at ease! (133–40)

Pope then goes on to retell the fable of the town and country mouse. In doing so he captures, with urbanity and wit, the essence of Horace's fable defending the life of moderation free from anxieties. The closing speech of the country mouse, as he does his best to remain polite while the cat interrupts his courtly banquet, will have to suffice here to indicate Pope's control of ironic understatement and compression as he moves to a final emphasis on the retirement ideals of frugality and freedom:

> 'An't please your Honour,' quoth the Peasant,
> 'This same Dessert is not so pleasant:
> Give me again my hollow Tree!
> A Crust of Bread, and Liberty.' (220–3)

Allusions to the classical tradition of retirement are merged in Pope's later poetry with allusions to another literary tradition. This second tradition concerns the praise of certain seventeenth-century English poets for the country house.[20] Ben Jonson's *To Penshurst* and Marvell's *Upon Appleton House* are the outstanding achievements of this tradition. Both poets praise their respective houses because they are designed for dwelling in and not for display, and their estates because they yield a generous plenty but not a surfeit. The country house and its estate become symbolic in these poems of a social organism in which man and nature lead an interdependent existence. Man orders and cultivates nature: he does not ransack or despoil it. Above all the country house represents an acceptance, on the part of the owner, of the moral responsibilities falling on him to act as a generous host to the rural community. Such a way of life essentially belonged to the feudal past even in the seventeenth century, and it certainly did by the time Pope came to write about it. This, of course, makes it none the less real for Pope, but it is another reminder that he was, philosophically speaking, a conservative intent on preserving what he considered to be the best of the past.

What Pope did with his small villa and garden of five acres at Twickenham was to act out in miniature a fusion of these two literary traditions. The moderation of the happy man and the hospitality of the country house are merged in both the actual and the fictional life of Pope the husbandman-cum-host:

> Content with little, I can piddle here
> On Broccoli and mutton, round the year;
> But ancient friends, (tho' poor, or out of play)
> That touch my Bell, I cannot turn away.
> 'Tis true, no Turbots dignify my boards,
> But gudgeons, flounders, what my Thames affords.
> To Hounslow-heath I point, and Bansted-down,
> Thence comes your mutton, and these chicks my own:
> From yon old wallnut-tree a show'r shall fall;
> And grapes, long-lingring on my only wall,
> And figs, from standard and Espalier join:
> The dev'l is in you if you cannot dine.
> Then chearful healths (your Mistress shall have place)
> And, what's more rare, a Poet shall say *Grace*.
> (*Imitation of Horace, Satire II, ii*, 137–50)

A detailed discussion of Pope's views on landscape gardening, and of his cultivation of his own and his friends' gardens, will be found in the next chapter, but one aspect of his garden calls for comment here. This is the famous grotto, which connected his house and garden by providing a passageway underneath the main London to Hampton Court road that separated them. If the need for a grotto can be explained in utilitarian terms, its decoration with shells, stones, pieces of tile, glass and rock soon outstripped bare necessity. 'He extracted an ornament from an inconvenience', says Dr Johnson in his *Life of Pope*, 'and vanity produced a grotto where necessity enforced a passage'.[21] Pope's grotto came to sum up, more than any other part of his estate, the deep significance, both for him and his poetry, of the retirement theme. As a series of decorated caverns or underground rooms opening up on one another, it suggested associations with worship (the temple of Zeus), with inspired pronouncement (the oracle at Delphi), with contemplation (the retreat of hermits and saints) and with refuge (David's Cave at En-gedi when pursued by Saul, in I Samuel, 24):

> Know, all the distant Din that World can keep
> Rolls o'er my *Grotto*, and but sooths my Sleep.
> There, my Retreat the best Companions grace,
> Chiefs, out of War, and Statesmen, out of Place,
> There *St John* mingles with my friendly Bowl,
> The Feast of Reason and the Flow of Soul:
>
> (*Imitation of Horace, Satire II, i*, 123–8)

I have suggested in the foregoing paragraphs some of the connotations and allusions that the country held for Pope, especially in his later poetry. One last account of the retirement ideal, found in his *Imitation of Horace, Epistle I, vii*, written in the octosyllabic manner of Dr Swift, will bring this chapter to an appropriate close since it relates the ideal to the poet's own life at Twickenham:

> Give me, I cry'd (enough for me)
> My Bread, and Independency!
> So bought an Annual Rent or two.
> And liv'd – just as you see I do;
> Near fifty, and without a Wife,
> I trust that sinking Fund, my Life.
> Can I retrench? Yes, mighty well,
> Shrink back to my Paternal Cell,
> A little House, with Trees a-row,
> And like its Master, very low,
> There dy'd my Father, no man's Debtor,
> And there I'll die nor worse nor better.   (69–80)

We have here the familiar stress on self-sufficiency ('My Bread'), and self-reliance ('Independency'), coupled with an acceptance that further retrenchment is possible if necessary. The poet rejects the hectic life of the town (see lines 7–14) in favour of the tranquil life of the country. The ideal of the 'little House with Trees a-row', which takes over from the 'dust' (11), 'fevers' (13) and 'pox' (14) of the town, is saved from becoming sentimental by the poet's ironic treatment of himself – the joking comparison of his old age to Walpole's Sinking Fund, which likewise had done nothing to hinder inexorable accumulation, and the pun on his own stature, 'And like its Master very low'.

Pope's affirmation of the life of rural retirement is not to be confused with a life of rural solitude, or with a life of rural ease. His retirement is not a hermit-like retreat undertaken for the sake of meditation, as in the poetry of Vaughan, where the poet uses his natural surroundings in order to achieve a mystical union with God, nor is it an indolent withdrawal to pleasure and plenty, such as we find in Pomfret's extraordinarily popular poem, *The Choice*, first published in 1700. Pope's retirement is an alternative to the ambitious bustle of the city. His commitment is to society, and his retirement is offered as a better model for society to form itself on, not as personal seclusion or comfortable escape.

Notes

1. James Boswell, *Life of Johnson* (Oxford University Press, Oxford, 1965) p. 859. Saturday, 20 September 1777.
2. Sir John Fielding, *A Brief Description of the cities of London and Westminster* (London, 1776). p. v.
3. Pat Rogers, *Hacks and Dunces: Pope, Swift and Grub Street* (Methuen, London, 1980), p. 3.
4. John Stow, *A Survey of the Cities of London and Westminster* (1598; Corrected, Improved and very much enlarged by John Strype, in Six Books, London, 1720), Book 1, p. 9.
5. Isaac Kramnick, *Bolingbroke and His Circle* (Harvard University Press, Cambridge, Mass., 1968), pp. 66–7.
6. Max Weber, *The Protestant Ethic and the Spirit of Capitalism*, translated by T. Parsons (George Allen and Unwin, London, 1930).
7. John Noorthouck, *A New History of London, including Westminster and Southwark* (London, 1773), p. 695.
8. Ibid., p. 718.
9. Derek Jarrett, *Britain 1688–1815* (Longman, London, 1965), p. 28.
10. Pope's own footnote to the poem.
11. J. V. Guerinot, *Pamphlet Attacks on Alexander Pope, 1711–44* (Methuen London, 1969).
12. Ibid., p. 3.
13. Ibid., p. 44.
14. Jonathan Swift, 'The Battle of the Books' (1697), *Swift: Prose Works*, ed. Herbert Davis (Blackwell, Oxford, 1965), Vol. I, p. 149.
15. J. V. Guerinot, op. cit., p. 155.
16. Ibid., pp. 178–9.
17. Ibid., pp. 293–4.
18. Ibid., p. 1.
19. Sir Walter Besant, *London in the Eighteenth Century* (Adam and Charles Black, London, 1902), p. 78.
20. See G. R. Hibbard, 'The Country House Poem of the Seventeenth

Century', *Journal of the Warburg and Courtauld Institute*, XIX, 1956, pp. 159–74. This article is reprinted in *Essential Articles for the Study of Alexander Pope*, ed. Maynard Mack (Archon Books, Hamden, Conn., 1964).

21. Johnson, 'Pope' in *Lives of the English Poets* (1779–81); ed. G. B. Hill, 3 vols (Clarendon Press, Oxford, 1905), Vol. III, p. 135.

3 The kindred arts

> First follow NATURE, and your Judgment frame
> By her just Standard, which is still the same:
> *Unerring Nature*, still divinely bright
> One *clear, unchang'd,* and *Universal* Light,
> Life, Force, and Beauty, must to all impart,
> At once the *Source,* and *End,* and *Test of Art.*
>
> > (*Essay on Criticism*, 68–73)

> How oft' our slowly-growing works impart,
> While images reflect from art to art?
>
> > (*Epistle to Mr Jervas*, 19–20)

Different kinds of artists express the consciousness of their age through different media and in different ways. But to the extent that any creative artifact is the product of the civilization in which it is born, so the different art forms of any period are bound to bear a certain analogous relationship to one another. Pope's poetry, however, bears very much more than this inevitable relationship to the other art forms of his time. Pope was himself an enthusiastic amateur painter and an ardent landscape gardener. In addition he was knowledgeable about architecture, interested in sculpture and appreciative of music. As a result we find in his work not just a general relationship between poetry and the other arts, but a detailed set of correspondences in which the technical terms of other art forms are frequently used as images and allusions in his own.

Without falling into the trap of drawing simplistic parallels between different art forms, Pope managed to use his awareness of the different potential of contrasting media to extend the expressiveness and complexity of his poetry. As he says in his *Epistle to Mr Jervas*, 1716, while talking about the relationship between poetry and painting:

> How oft' our slowly-growing works impart,
> While images reflect from art to art?   (19–20)

The idea of images reflecting, rather than repeating, from art to art is crucial, for it enables the viewer or reader to see or imagine the same object recreated in a varying light, and in different degrees of distortion from reality, depending on the reflecting surface. Pope is fully aware of the autonomous nature of each of the kindred arts, but he is also aware of the rich response available to the person who is sensitive to a variety of art forms. In his poetry we find a mutual commerce, rather than a strict barter, between the arts. In this chapter I discuss Pope's knowledge of, and delight in, the other fine arts of his time, and show how an understanding of these relation-ships can enrich our appreciation of his poetry.[1]

Architecture

Pope's interest in architecture is closely related to his friendship with Lord Burlington. Richard Boyle, the Third Earl of Burlington, was a young man of twenty when Pope, six years his senior, first met him in 1715. The two men seem to have taken an immediate liking to one another, and, as Pope's correspondence bears witness, struck up an affectionate friendship that lasted throughout Pope's life. Lord Burlington was immensely wealthy, owning extensive properties in Yorkshire and Ireland. He used his wealth to support most of the fine arts, but especially that of architecture. He became patron to a group of persons, including William Kent and Colen Campbell, who were instrumental in changing the direction of English architec-ture away from the baroque style that had been made so popular by Wren, towards the Palladian style that was to become the leading fashion in the eighteenth century.

Burlington and his circle popularized the simple and classical lines of the Italian architect, Andrea Palladio (1508–80), and his English successor, Inigo Jones (1573–1652). They were especially influential in establishing Palladianism with respect to the gentle-man's country house, which they saw as a villa that was a dwelling place related to its rural surroundings rather than a palace full of magnificence, such as Vanbrugh had designed for Marlborough at Blenheim. The Palladian villa should be formal enough to be elevated and elegant, but it must avoid becoming massive and extravagant. The most notable Palladian villa in the eighteenth century was Burlington's own temple of the arts at Chiswick (see facing page), built between 1725 and 1729, and modelled on Palladio's Rotonda on the outskirts of Vicenza. Pope's own house at Twickenham, only five miles upstream from Chiswick House, also worked on by Kent,[2] was another example of the Palladian villa, but this time on a more modest scale. It is revealing that Pope kept busts of both Palladio and Inigo Jones in his library, as did Burlington at the entrance to his villa.

The essential principle of Palladio's architecture was that it should imitate nature. 'Since architecture, like all the other arts, imitates nature, nothing in it can satisfy that is foreign from what is found in nature', he wrote in his architectural treatise, *I Quattro Libri dell' Architettura*, first published in Venice in 1570 but not translated into

Palladio's Rotonda at Vicenza

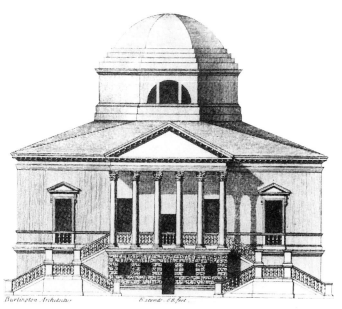

Burlington's Villa at Chiswick. Design by Earl of Burlington

English until 1715.³ Such a definition depends, of course, on what one understands by nature. Palladio did not mean that architecture had to copy visible reality, but that it should base itself on the principles of hierarchy, proportion and harmony that he considered to permeate God's creation at large. For Palladio and his admirers, the best architecture must have a direct, albeit stylized, relationship to nature. This involved accepting certain rules inherent in nature – especially those of mathematical proportion – and working as harmoniously as possible within them. It is not difficult to see a similar principle of artistic creation underlying Pope's handling of his couplet art.

Pope's views on Palladian architecture are most clearly set out in his *Epistle to Burlington*, first published in 1731. In this poem he insists that Taste is not something that can be bought. Lord Burlington shows us, he says, that Rome was 'glorious not profuse', and that in the best architecture design is directly related to use. In architecture, as in poetry, mere outward show does not fool the connoisseur:

> Oft have you hinted to your brother Peer,
> A certain truth, which many buy too dear:
> Something there is more needful than Expence,
> And something previous ev'n to Taste – 'tis Sense:
> Good Sense, which only is the gift of Heav'n,
> And tho' no science, fairly worth the sev'n:
> A Light, which in yourself you must perceive;
> Jones and Le Nôtre have it not to give.   (39–46)

True taste is shaped by 'Sense'. The word suggests various levels of meaning. It involves a proper use of judgment, a kind of commonsense; it involves an ability to respond with feeling, a use of the physical senses; and it involves a certain intuitive grasp, or sixth sense. Finally, it is a quality that one can only discover for oneself; it cannot be copied or acquired secondhand. Thus those who build according to Burlington's rules without understanding them, like those who try to write couplets by rote, merely make blunders out of beauty and fill half the land with imitating fools.

Pope's second great architectural principle in this poem involves a restatement of that emphasis on imitating nature seen in the quotation from Palladio:

> To build, to plant, whatever you intend,
> To rear the Column, or the Arch to bend,
> To swell the Terras, or to sink the Grot;
> In all, let Nature never be forgot.   (47–50)

Again a similar principle underlies Pope's conception of poetry as underlies his conception of architecture. These lines binding the two arts of architecture and landscape gardening together – 'To build, to plant, *whatever* you intend' – express a similar insistence on the primacy of nature for the architect and landscape gardener as the famous lines in *An Essay on Criticism* do for the poet:

> First follow NATURE, and your Judgment frame
> By her just Standard, which is still the same:
> *Unerring Nature*, still divinely bright,
> One *clear, unchang'd*, and *Universal* Light,
> Life, Force, and Beauty, must to all impart,
> At once the *Source*, and *End*, and *Test* of *Art*.   (68–73)

The appeal to 'Nature' in these lines, and many others, is notoriously difficult to define, but it is important to pause over it, for the appeal lies at the base of Pope's aesthetic position.[4]

It would be a mistake to look for any one fixed meaning or set of meanings for the term, for the repeated appeals to 'Nature' in *An Essay on Criticism*, and throughout Pope's poetry, are part of a complex web of significances connected with the word, partly defined, in each instance, by the context of the passage in which it appears. Partly the appeal to nature in Pope is an appeal to an empirical and observed reality. This is the concept of nature that Davenant seems to have had in mind, in his Preface to *Gondibert*, when he said, 'Nature is the only visible power and operation of God'.[5] But partly, too, the appeal to nature in Pope is an appeal to what one might call invisible reality, to the essence of things, or to a Platonic idea of something imperfectly realized in empirical reality. This is closer to what Palladio seems to have in mind in the quote from *I Quattro Libri dell' Architettura* given above. These two contrasting meanings of nature play against each other in Pope's poetry so that nature becomes a way to refer to that which is universal and immutable in thought and feeling because it is both present and absent from reality, both all around us on earth and an idea in the artist's mind of God's ideal order in the created cosmos. Pope is having things both ways at once. The appeal to nature in his poetry is both an appeal to that which can be tested in observable reality and an appeal to the artist's perception of the ideal order and harmony revealed in God's creation.

Although in the main Pope clearly saw Palladianism as the highest contemporary architectural expression of that ideal, it is interesting to note that the catholicity of his taste also enabled him to embrace a very different architectural style. Pope can be seen not only as a keen supporter of Palladianism, but as an early enthusiast for the Gothic revival that became so popular in literature and art later in the century. The most obvious examples of his enjoyment of the Gothic are the construction of the fanciful Shell Temple (see illustration on p. 74) and the elaborately embellished grotto in his own garden at Twickenham. Both structures shared the roughness, shagginess and irregularity associated with the Gothic. Yet another garden structure in this style that he had a hand in was the mock Gothic ruin, known as Alfred's Hall, erected by Lord Bathurst during the 1730s in his park at Cirencester. Pope seems to have been largely responsible for designing this for Bathurst and has been described by Brownell as 'in all probability the designer of the earliest sham ruin in an English landscape garden'.[6]

Pope's interest in the Gothic can be found influencing his poetry in various places, but nowhere, perhaps, so strongly as in *Eloisa to Abelard*, where he uses it to accentuate the romantic mood that suffuses the whole poem. The poem opens in the solemn and sombre setting of the Paraclete:

> In these deep solitudes and awful cells,
> Where heav'nly-pensive, contemplation dwells,   (1–2)

A few lines further on Eloisa addresses the walls of her cell as follows:

> Ye rugged rocks! which holy knees have worn;
> Ye grots and caverns shagg'd with horrid thorn!   (19–20)

The gloomy scene undoubtedly draws something from Milton's *Il Pensoroso*, as the Twickenham editors point out, but it also owes much to the bristling irregularity and desolation of the Gothic. This mood of loneliness, dankness and darkness is developed further at later points in the poem:

> In these lone walls (their day's eternal bound)
> These moss grown domes with spiry turrets crown'd,
> Where awful arches make a noon-day night
> And the dim windows shed a solemn light;   (141–4)

> But o'er the twilight groves, and dusky caves,
> Long-sounding isles, and intermingled graves,
> Black Melancholy sits, and round her throws
> A death-like silence, and a dread repose:
> Her gloomy presence saddens all the scene,
> Shades every flow'r, and darkens ev'ry green,
> Deepens the murmur of the falling floods,
> And breathes a browner horror on the woods.   (163–70)

Pope has carefully built up Gothic settings in these passages to establish a mood of awed solemnity with regard to the whole poem and to heighten the pathos of Eloisa's particular situation.

The significance of Pope's ability to gain pleasure and enjoyment from two architectural traditions as seemingly opposed to each other as the regularity of Palladianism and the irregularity of the Gothic, is that it demonstrates the inclusiveness of his taste and imagination. Pope believed that a perfect judge should show generosity and judge a work of art in the spirit in which it was created. He was open-minded in his willingness to appreciate and value whatever style was most appropriate for the expressive purposes in hand:

> For diff'rent *Styles* with diff'ent *Subjects* sort,
> As several Garbs with Country, Town and Court.
>
> (*Essay on Criticism*, 322–3)

Not for Pope the narrow exclusivity of critics who simply judged by a preconceived set of rules:

> So modern Pothecaries, taught the Art
> By Doctor's Bills to play the Doctor's part,
> Bold in the practice of mistaken Rules,
> Prescribe, Apply, and call their Masters Fools.
>
> (*Essay on Criticism*, 108–11)

The architectural critic cannot write a set of rules on how buildings are to be designed any more than the literary critic can 'write dull Receits how poems may be made'. Above all the critic, whether architectural or literary, should consider the whole effect of a work of art and not pay too much attention to its individual parts;

> 'Tis not a Lip, or Eye, we Beauty call,
> But the joint Force and full Result of all.
>
> (*Essay on Criticism*, 245–6)

Landscape gardening

After the Restoration of the English monarchy and the return of Charles's II's Court from Paris, the prevailing taste in English gardening became clearly based on the formal gardens of Holland and France. The most influential gardener in Europe was the Frenchman, André Le Nôtre (1613–1700) who was responsible for Louis's XIV's elaborate display at Versailles, where the gardens covered more than 15,000 acres. In gardens of this style everything was laid out according to a strict geometric pattern, divided into symmetrical units composed of parterres embroidered in floral scrollwork, terraces, rectangular pools and fountains, and intersecting avenues of trees. Each section of the garden would be marked off with straight boundaries of clipped hedges, canals or walls so that the total effect was that of a vast ornamental quilt.

At the beginning of the eighteenth century a few English professional gardeners, notably Charles Bridgeman (d. 1738) who created the famous gardens at Stowe; Stephen Switzer (*c.* 1682–1745) the royal gardener; and William Kent (1684–1748) Lord Burlington's protégé, began to break away from such artificial and restricted designs. While not departing completely from the formal garden, they strove for something less regular and more natural. Switzer says in his *Ichnographia Rustica*, 1718, that a little regularity may be permitted near the house, but beyond that the designer should pursue nature.[7] Bridgeman is perhaps best-known for his introduction of the sunken fence, or *ha-ha*, which was borrowed from the art of fortication and enabled the gardener to open up vistas, previously shut off by fences and walls, by concealing the bounds. In this way the gentleman's park could be 'called in' to the view of his garden. Kent, according to Horace Walpole, 'leaped the fence and saw that all nature was a garden'.[8]

Later in the century the movement against regularity and symmetry became more pronounced until, by the time of Lancelot ('Capability') Brown (1716–83), gardens were created that were meant to look as much like nature as possible, although the prospect was, of course, very carefully shaped by man. All boundaries and sharp edges were softened; trees were placed in belts or clumps rather than avenues or quincunxes; rivers and lakes were used wherever possible to give gentle serenity to the middle distance; and everything was done to bring out undulating contours that would provide a natural equivalent to Hogarth's serpentine line of grace, and 'lead the eye a wanton kind of chase'.[9]

Pope's place within this tradition is contemporaneous with that of Bridgeman, Switzer and Kent.[10] According to Brownell, Pope was the most dominant influence in this group and the single most important innovator in English landscape gardening. Brownell also argues that Pope was the originator of the picturesque sensibility in England as a significant aesthetic, and calls him 'as much the poet of picturesque landscape as Thomson is of the sublime' (97). He points out that Pope was one of the first English writers to use the word 'picturesque', introduced from the French, to describe graphic vividness, or a scene suitable for painting. Brownell focuses in particular on Pope's animated account in a letter to Patty Blount of an excursion he made to Nettley Abbey in 1734 with the Earl of Peterborough and says Pope 'can properly be called the first picturesque tourist of the eighteenth century' (89). Brownell describes Pope's garden at Twickenham as the 'paradigm of the picturesque garden', and Pope as 'the founder of the English landscape garden' (147).[11]

Pope belongs then in the forefront of those who were striving to create gardens of greater irregularity and contrast. As early as 1713 we find him attacking the artificiality of formal gardens, and especially the modern practice of topiary, in *Guardian*, no. 173. The main principle on which his views of gardening in this essay are founded is similar to that underlying his views on architecture and poetry: 'There is certainly something in the amiable Simplicity of unadorned Nature that spreads over the Mind a more noble sort of Tranquillity, and a loftier Sensation of Pleasure than can be raised from the nicer Scenes of Art'.[12] His preference for nature over art in gardening leads on to his view, expressed later in the essay, that 'all Art consists in the Imitation and Study of Nature'.

Pope's own practice as a gardener dates from 1719, when he rented his villa at Twickenham, together with five acres of ground on the other side of the London to Hampton Court road. During the remaining twenty-five years of his life this garden and the grotto that he excavated to join it to his house became the cherished pastime of his recreation. In October 1725, he wrote to the Earl of Strafford describing his work on it:

> I am as busy in three inches of Gardening, as any man can be in threescore acres. I fancy myself like the fellow that spent his life in cutting the twelve apostles in one cherry-stone. I have a Theatre, an Arcade, a Bowling green, a Grove, and what not? in a bit of ground that would have been but a plate of Sallet to Nebuchadnezzar, the first day he was turn'd to graze. My chief comfort is, that it's too little to afford Tytle to the aforesaid Parson. (II, 328)

We know quite a lot about Pope's garden, not least because of the plan made by his gardener and trusted servant, John Serle, in 1745 (see p. 76). Fifteen years after this, Horace Walpole described it in a letter to Horace Mann, written on 20 June 1760:

> In short, it was a little bit of ground of five acres, enclosed with three lanes, and seeing nothing. Pope had twisted and twirled and rhymed and harmonised this, till it appeared two or three sweet little lawns opening and opening beyond one another, and the whole surrounded with thick inpenetrable woods.[13]

The guiding principle in its layout seems to have been to surprise the viewer pleasantly with contrasting perspectives and moving patterns of light and shade. Around the boundary of the garden there was the darkness of the woods, or 'wilderness', and the shade of the serpentine paths that meandered through them. At the centre lay a light and open lawn used as a bowling green. From this point one had views of the garden's two main features which lay at

William Kent's drawing of the Shell Temple in Pope's garden

opposite ends of a central axis. At the western end stood an obelisk in memory of his mother, and at the eastern end the Shell Temple that marked the entrance to the grotto. 'From the River Thames', wrote Pope in a letter to Patty Blount's father in June 1725,

> you see thro' my arch up a walk of the wilderness to a kind of open temple, wholly composed of shells in the rustic manner; and from that distance under the temple you look down thro' a sloping arcade of trees, and see the sails on the river passing suddenly and vanishing, as thro' a perspective glass.   (II, 296)

Such surprising images and disappearing glimpses were an indispensable part of the overall effect of ever-changing delight that Pope tried to create in his garden.

It was, of course, a garden designed on a miniature scale compared with the great landscape estates of Pope's wealthy and noble friends – such as Lord Bathurst's at Cirencester, or Viscount Cobham's at Stowe, or Lord Burlington's at Chiswick, or Ralph Allen's at Prior Park – but this does not mean that it was either trivial or inconsequential, as anyone who has ever tried to cultivate a garden of even half an acre will know. Pope's friends took his gardening as seriously as he did and frequently sent him presents of plants or statues for the garden and a wide variety of stones, fossils, bits of marble, flints, pebbles, fragments of crystal, shells and pieces of rock for his grotto. Pope's garden was as carefully and minutely wrought as his poetry. Like his poetry it was full of allusions to the past, such as the busts of classical figures and the memorial to his mother, and like the poetry it was imbued with a basic moral significance that enabled it to stand as a natural expression of the peaceful life of rural retirement he so valued.

His views on gardening are developed most fully in the same poem as are his views on architecture, the *Epistle to Burlington*. The two arts have much in common. Whether one intends to build or plant, nature must 'never be forgot'. This is the great principle that Burlington exemplifies at Chiswick and that Bridgeman had demonstrated so triumphantly for Cobham at Stowe:

> Nature shall join you, Time shall make it grow
> A Work to wonder at – perhaps a Stow. (69–70)

Conversely, this is what Timon singularly fails to do in the rigid formal gardens that surround his villa:

> The suff'ring eye inverted Nature sees,
> Trees cut to Statues, Statues thick as trees, (119–20)

Nature then is the most important guiding principle, but in treating nature the artist, whether architect or gardener, must use an urbane tact. He must neither over- nor under-dress her. The key thing is to suggest as well as to show:

> Let not each beauty ev'ry where be spy'd,
> Where half the skill is decently to hide.
> He gains all points, who pleasingly confounds,
> Surprizes, varies, and conceals the Bounds. (53–6)

The last couplet here is as apposite to Pope's own poetry as it is to gardening. He 'pleasingly confounds' the reader by surprising, varying and concealing, through a great variety of ways fully discussed in Part Two, the regular bounds of the closed couplet form. The pleasure comes in not knowing what is going to come next, unlike in Timon's garden where:

> No pleasing Intricacies intervene,
> No artful wildness to perplex the scene;
> Grove nods at grove, each Alley has a brother,
> And half the platform just reflects the other. (115–18)

Pope next goes on to argue that the gardener must 'consult the genius of the place'; that is, he must consider the inherent quality or prevailing character, of the place and bring it out in its best colours rather than force a preconceived pattern on the area:

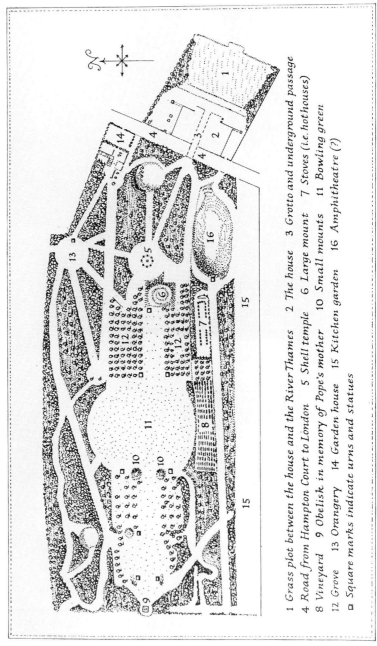

1 *Grass plot between the house and the River Thames*   2 *The house*   3 *Grotto and underground passage*
4 *Road from Hampton Court to London*   5 *Shell temple*   6 *Large mount*   7 *Stoves (i.e. hothouses)*
8 *Vineyard*   9 *Obelisk in memory of Pope's mother*   10 *Small mounts*   11 *Bowling green*
12 *Grove*   13 *Orangery*   14 *Garden house*   15 *Kitchen garden*   16 *Amphitheatre (?)*
□ *Square marks indicate urns and statues*

Plan of Pope's garden, re-drawn from Serle's plan, 1745

76

Consult the Genius of the Place in all;
That tells the Waters or to rise, or fall,
Or helps th' ambitious Hill the heav'n to scale,
Or scoops in circling theatres the Vale,
Calls in the Country, catches opening glades,
Joins willing woods, and varies shades from shades,
Now breaks or now directs, th' intending Lines;
Paints as you plant, and, as you work, designs. (57–64)

Pope describes the gardener's method here in terms of a landscape painter's. Indeed the landscape paintings of Claude Lorrain and the Poussins were an important influence on the development of gardening in eighteenth-century England. Spence records Pope as saying, in 1734, that 'all gardening is landscape painting. Just like a landscape hung up' (606). In the lines from the *Epistle to Burlington* just quoted, the gardener, by consulting the genius of the place, 'catches' opening glades as a landscape painter catches a special mood, or he 'varies shades from shades' as a landscape painter plays with colouring effects through the disposition of lights and shades (612) on his canvas. In the last line of the paragraph the analogy becomes explicit, 'paints as you plant', and then moves on to incorporate an image from architecture as well, 'and, as you work, designs'. This is a good example of the reflection of images from art to art that we find in Pope's poetry. Technical terms from landscape painting and architecture are used to describe the guiding principles of landscape gardening, and the better one understands the background of the terms the more one appreciates the allusiveness of Pope's poetry.

Landscape gardening clearly became for Pope a pastime through which he could express his visionary hopes without being constantly plagued by his enemies as he was in his poetry. Whereas anyone could read his published poetry, since the very act of publication put it in the public domain, only those could 'read' his garden whom he invited to do so. He spent the summers of the last twenty-five years of his life 'rambling' round the great landscape gardens of southern England that were being developed by his mainly noble friends – Lord Bathurst's at Cirencester Park and Riskins; Lord Burlington's at Chiswick; Viscount Cobham's at Stowe; Lord Peterborough's at Bevis Mount; Lord Bolingbroke's at Dawley Farm; and Ralph Allen's at Prior Park. From these visits he assimilated ideas and scenes of visual reflection that shaped and expanded his own 'visionary scene' at Twickenham. Pope's garden became an emblem of his belief in the value of myth, friendship and renewal and a symbolic expression of his hope for a better ordered world. If nature could be cultivated to show her finest and most serene face, was there not some possibility, however remote, that mankind too might put on a better countenance? There is really nothing contradictory or paradoxical about a poet who increasingly saw the public world as one of encroaching decay and darkness deliberately devoting so many hours of his life to creating a personal world constructed as an image of composure, reflection and light.

Painting

Poetry and painting have traditionally had close links with one another. Of all the visual arts these two have been referred to most frequently as the 'sister arts', while the correspondences between them have been commented on by literary critics, art historians and aestheticians alike. One of the earliest of such comments is Horace's celebrated phrase *ut pictura poesis*, 'as a painting, so a poem'.[14] Unfortunately Horace's phrase has too frequently been taken out of context to assert a parallel relationship between the two arts rather than to suggest, as Horace does, a comparison between them. What Horace actually says is that some poems please only once whereas others bear continual rereading, just as some paintings only please when placed in a dark corner of a gallery while others continue to please after constant viewing in full light. He is not saying that poetry must always be like painting, although many later critics have tended to take his phrase this way.

The Frenchman, Charles Alphonse Du Fresnoy, in his influential Latin poem *De Arte Graphica*, originally published in 1667 but first translated into English as *The Art of Painting*, by John Dryden in 1695, takes up such a position.[15] He quotes Horace's phrase, *ut pictura poesis*, in the opening lines of the poem and then goes on to argue that not only should poetry be like painting, but painting should be like poetry. Du Fresnoy's poem is expanded by a set of remarks, written by Roger de Piles and also translated by Dryden, who argues that poetry and painting are so nearly related that whoever thoroughly examines them will find them so much resembling one another that he cannot take them for less than sisters:

> They both of them aim at the same end, which is Imitation. Both of them excite our passions, and we suffer ourselves willingly to be deceiv'd, both by the one, and by the other; our eyes and souls are so fixt to them, that we are ready to persuade ourselves that the painted bodies breath and that the fictions are truth.[16]

Dryden, in his preface to the translation, entitled 'Preface of the Translator, With a Parallel of Poetry and Painting', lists three main ways in which the two arts are parallel – the Invention, the Design, and the Colouring – and then goes on to elaborate on these general areas of parallelism in considerable detail.

We know that Pope was familiar with Du Fresnoy's treatise and Dryden's translation because he wrote his *Epistle to Mr Jervas* to accompany a revised version of it. In this poem, written about 1715, Pope expresses the hope that his poetry and Jervas's paintings may share a similarly successful partnership:

> Read these instructive leaves, in which conspire
> *Fresnoy's* close art, and *Dryden's* native fire:
> And reading wish, like theirs, our fate and fame,
> So mix'd our studies, and so join'd our name,
> Like them to shine thro' long succeeding age,
> So just thy skill, so regular my rage. (7–12)

It is noticeable that Pope does not say in these lines, as Dryden does in his Preface, that painting and poetry should have a 'parallel' relationship, but that they should share a partnership. The painter and the poet should mix, not repeat or copy, their studies. They should draw inspiration from each other, but remain autonomous. Pope continues:

> Smit with the love of Sister-arts we came,
> And met congenial, mingling flame with flame;
> Like friendly colours found them both unite,
> And each from each contract new strength and light. (13–16)

The image Pope presents is that of two artists sharing ideas for the sake of mutual, but independent, re-creation.

Pope was interested in painting throughout his life. 'Which, Sir, gives you the most pleasure, poetry or painting?' asked Spence in May 1730. 'I really can't well say,' Pope replied, 'both of them are so extremely pleasing' (110). This interest in painting reached its greatest intensity in 1713 when he took a course of lessons with Charles Jervas, a well-established portrait painter. Pope wrote to Caryll on 30 April 1713 saying: 'I've been almost everyday employed in following your advice in learning to paint in which I am most particularly obliged to Mr Jervas, who gives me daily instructions and examples' (I,174). Four months later we find him writing to Gay giving a long and witty account of his progress:

I have been near a week in London, where I am like to remain, till I become by Mr. Jervas's help, *Elegans Formarum Spectator.*[17] I begin to discover beauties that were till now imperceptible to me. Every corner of an eye, or turn of a nose or ear, the smallest degree of light or shade on a cheek, or in a dimple, have charms to distract me. . . . I have thrown away three Dr. Swift's, each of which was once my vanity, two Lady Bridgewaters, a Duchess of Montague, besides half a dozen Earls, and one Knight of the Garter. I have crucify'd Christ over again in effigie, and made a Madonna as old as her mother St. Anne. Nay, what is yet more miraculous, I have rival'd St. Luke himself in painting, and as 'tis said an Angel came and finished his Piece, so you would swear a Devil put the last hand to mine, 'tis so begrimed and smutted. However I comfort myself with a Christian reflection, that, I have not broken the Commandment, for my pictures are not the likeness of anything in heaven above or in earth below, or in the waters under the earth. Neither will anybody adore or worship them, except the Indians should have a sight of 'em, who they tell us, worship certain Pagods or Idols purely for their ugliness.   (I, 187–8)

This period of total immersion in the sister art of painting seems to have come to an end about the spring of 1714 when he turned back to the serious business of translating the *Iliad*. 'I shall now be very much taken up in this work', he says in a letter to Caryll on 25 February 1714, 'which will keep me a poet (in spite of something I lately thought a resolution to the contrary) for some years longer' (I, 210). Pope's friendship with Jervas did not end at this point; indeed he continued to use Jervas's house in Cleveland Court as his regular residence when he was in London, but the temptation to give up poetry for painting did.

We get some idea of the extent of Pope's love of painting from the 'Inventory of Pope's Goods Taken After His Death', probably for valuation purposes.[18] The Inventory shows that he owned fifty-six or more portraits; twelve landscapes, including one by Peter Tillemans (1684–1734) and another by John Wootton (1682–1765) about whom Pope told Spence that 'they were the two best landscape painters in England'; four still lifes and numerous drawings and prints. One of the things this list brings out is that painting, like poetry, was divided up into different kinds which, ideally, fell into an ordered hierarchy in which each kind had its fit place. As with the literary kinds, however, the exact ordering of the different kinds tended to vary. The indisputably pre-eminent kind of painting in the early eighteenth century was history painting. The cost and scale of such paintings prevented Pope from owning more than the three grisaille panels of Hercules, Venus and Apollo, on his staircase, which Sir Godfrey Kneller had executed for him. The next most valued kind however was landscape painting, and as we have seen Pope owned twelve landscapes. In defending *Windsor-Forest* as a form of composition, in his *Essay on the Genius and Writings of Pope*, 1756, Joseph Warton says he wishes to remind despisers, or what he calls 'contemners' of it:

that, in a sister-art, landscape-painting claims the very next rank to history-painting, being ever preferred to single portraits, to pieces of still-life, to droll figures, to fruit and flower pieces; that Titian thought it no diminution of his genius to spend much of his time in works of the former species.[19]

The opening lines of *Windsor-Forest*, (7–42), after the invocation to Granville, are organized and shaped like an idealized landscape painting. The groves of Windsor Forest are compared to the groves of Eden:

> The Groves of *Eden*, vanish'd now so long,
> Live in Description, and look green in Song:
> *These*, were my Breast inspir'd with equal Flame,
> Like them in Beauty, should be like in Fame.   (7–10)

The whole scene, like so many of the landscapes of Claude Lorrain, (1600–82), looks back to an earlier Golden Age. As in a Claude landscape contrasts are immediately brought to the reader's attention:

> Here Hills and Vales, the Woodland and the Plain,
> Here Earth and Water seem to strive again,   (11–12)

but these contrasts only serve to confirm, rather than dispel, the overriding harmony of the scene:

> Not *Chaos*-like together crush'd and bruis'd,
> But as the World harmoniously confus'd.   (13–14)

The poet then points out, through a visually directive syntax, the different planes of the view, corresponding to the immediately present foreground, 'Here'; the more distant middleground, 'There'; and the far distant horizon, also indicated by the demonstrative adverb, 'There', of a landscape painting:

> Here waving Groves a chequer'd Scene display,
> And part admit and part exclude the Day,   (17–18)
> . . . .
> There, interspers'd in Lawns and opening Glades,
> Thin Trees arise that shun each others Shades.   (21–2)

The flickering chiaroscuro of the 'chequer'd Scene' and the play of light and shade between the 'opening Glades' and 'Thin Trees' contrast with the 'full light' of the heather-covered tracts of land:

> Here in full light the russet plains extend;   (23)

The haziness of the far distance makes the colour of the horizon a little uncertain, which Henry Peacham in *The Art of Drawing*, 1606, said, in his rules for drawing a 'landskip', it would:

The colours too must be changed in painting things a long way off. Begin with dark green but move gradually to blue which the density of the air between the near ground and the high ground effects.[20]

The poet therefore has to approximate his description, to move 'gradually to blue':

> There wrapt in Clouds the bluish Hills ascend   (24)

The eye, having been swiftly led through this framed picture to the horizon, is then brought back to linger on the more dominant features that intervene: the wild heath with her 'Purple dies' (25), and the fruitful fields which adorn 'the sable Waste' of the desert like 'verdant Isles' (28). The landscape view is an extensive, even panoramic, one, and of course Pope can do things in poetry, such as comparing the prospect to other landscapes at other places and in other times, like those of India (29–30) or Mount Olympus (33–4), which a landscape painter could not do without executing a separate painting. Nevertheless the underlying influence of landscape painting on the design and structure of the passage is clear and irrefutable. The closing vision, as in so many of Claude's landscapes, and those of his English imitators, such as John Wootton, imagines a time of classical tranquillity and peace. Pan, Pomona, Flora and Ceres each make their appearance in a scene of serenity and fruitfulness carrying explicit allegorical and political significances:

> Rich Industry sits smiling on the Plains,
> And Peace and Plenty tell, a STUART reigns.   (41–2)

The model of landscape painting has begun here to merge with that of history painting.

There are other passages in *Windsor-Forest* of a similarly pictorial quality that draw on different kinds of painting. The 'exquisite picture' of the dying pheasant (111–18), as Joseph Warton calls it,[21] that depicts the distress of an expiring bird, draws on the convention of still life painting. The passage opens with Pope focusing on the abundant life of the pheasant. We hear, as well as see, the bird as it flaps its wings and bursts into flight:

> See! from the Brake the whirring pheasant springs,
> And mounts exulting on triumphant Wings;
> Short is his Joy! he feels the fiery Wound,
> Flutters in Blood, and panting beats the Ground.   (111–14)

Its momentary and ironic thrill at life is captured in the verse both by the trochaic opening to line 113 and by the monosyllabic first half of the line. Injury and death immediately ensue however, and their process is described with telling compactness and effect as the pheasant first feels the shot, then struggles to survive and finally goes through anguished death throes on the ground.

Only after the bird's death does Pope focus on its brilliant colours, partly to heighten the pathos of its death but partly too as a pictorial metaphor for the transience of all life. The riot of painted colours, purple, scarlet, green and gold, and their dazzling hues as they shine out and flame forth, are an evanescent and deceiving splendour:

> Ah! what avail his glossie, varying Dyes,
> His purple Crest, and Scarlet-circled Eyes,
> The vivid Green his shining Plumes unfold;
> His painted Wings, and Breast that flames with Gold?
>
> (115–18)

Life and death come together in the description, and the fragility of life is paradoxically established through the temporarily dazzling colours noted in the dead bird. In this way Pope's pictorial sensitivity and awareness intensifies and enhances the moral significance of the passage.

We find a similar pictorial stylization of nature when we come to the description of the fishes the angler hopes to catch a little later in the poem:

> Our plenteous Streams a various Race supply;
> The bright-eyed Perch with Fins of *Tyrian* Dye,
> The silver Eel, in shining Volumes roll'd,
> The yellow Carp, in Scales bedrop'd with Gold,
> Swift Trouts, diversify'd with Crimson Stains,
> And Pykes, the Tyrants of the watry Plains.   (141–6)

The rich variousness of the colours here pays tribute to the plenitude of God's creation. There is no motion to the scene: the fish are caught in stasis, so that their scintillating colours become the focus of attention. Visually the scene is highly stylized, for although one might be able physically to see the colours attributed to each fish if one examined it out of water, one would never be able to see the colours of individual fishes, let alone those of the whole school presented, by looking at the river. Pope describes the colours he knows to be there rather than those one might actually see. Through his pictorially poetic imagination he enables us to see the fish much more brilliantly in our imaginations than we ever could do in the real world.

Pope's painterly interest in colour is just as strong when he is dealing with personified concepts or realms of imaginary being as when he is responding to actual Nature. His descriptions of 'Black Melancholy' in *Eloisa to Abelard* (163–70), or of 'the gloomy Cave of Spleen' in *The Rape of the Lock* (Canto IV, 17–54) are presented with a painter's sensitivity for delicate contrasts of light and shade. A further example of the pictorial quality of Pope's poetry occurs in *The Dunciad* (Book IV, 21–30). In these lines Pope uses neither colour nor light and shade. Nevertheless the reader is made to visualize the scene through a series of descriptive details that make the Queen of Dulness's abstract captives vividly real:

> Beneath her foot-stool, *Science* groans in Chains,
> And *Wit* dreads Exile, Penalties and Pains.
> There foam'd rebellious *Logic*, gagg'd and bound,
> There, stript, fair *Rhet'ric* languish'd on the ground;
> His blunted Arms by *Sophistry* are born,
> And shameless *Billingsgate* her Robes adorn.
> *Morality*, by her false Guardians drawn,
> *Chicane* in Furs, and *Casuistry* in Lawn,
> Gasps, as they straiten at each end the cord,
> And dies, when Dulness gives her Page the word.

The descriptions of the forms of imprisonment and torture and the details of dress are highly pictorial. The scene is based on a satirical inversion of one of those grand allegorical history tableaux, such as Sir James's Thornhill's painting of William III trampling over Tyranny on the ceiling of the Great Hall at Greenwich, or Rubens's painting of the apotheosis of James I on the ceiling of the Banqueting Hall at Whitehall, that were so popular during the seventeenth and eighteenth centuries.

Another way in which Pope's interest in art seems to have influenced his poetry can be traced in his satirical character sketches. Although these partly derive from the literary tradition of the *character* going back to Theophrastus, they also derive from the pictorial tradition of the caricature originating with Annibale Carracci (1560–1609). The literary tradition of the *character* tended to describe types rather than individuals and to do so in a fairly realistic way, while the pictorial tradition of the caricature attacked recognizable persons by exaggerating certain defects at the expense of any attractive qualities. To this extent Pope's lines on Atticus, Bufo and Sporus in *An Epistle to Dr Arbuthnot* owe as much, if not more, to the caricature as to the *character*. The similarities between the artistic re-creation and the actual person are sufficient to cause recognition, while the distortions are strong enough to cause laughter or disgust.

One of the best examples of Pope the caricaturist at work is the *Epistle to a Lady*. Here the reader eavesdrops as the painter-poet and his companion, Patty Blount, stroll round an art gallery:

> How many pictures of one Nymph we view,
> All how unlike each other, all how true!   (5–6)

The poet shows us outline portraits of twelve 'ladies' in all, and each one is presented as being consistent only in being inconsistent. Pope establishes their inconsistency in a series of taut and witty couplets, much as a caricaturist would with a few quick strokes of the brush:

> Pictures like these, dear Madam, to design,
> Asks no firm hand, and no unerring line;
> Some wand'ring touch, or some reflected light,
> Some flying stroke alone can hit 'em right:
> For how should equal Colours do the knack?
> Chameleons who can paint in white and black? (151–6)

The glittering surface attraction of each portrait rapidly gives way to the inconsistency beneath. The unreliable, even 'treacherous', colours of the artist's palette are necessary, as Pope ironically claims in the last couplet above, to capture such superficial and changeable personalities.

A further influence of painting on Pope's poetry is suggested by comparing the narrative technique of his tale of Sir Balaam at the end of the *Epistle to Bathurst* with that of Hogarth in his comic history cycles. Pope's lines describe Balaam rising, by various stages, to a position of great social success, only to conclude with a crashing fall as Balaam 'curses God and dies'. The narrative structure of rise and fall and the strong moral disapproval of affectation are similar to those of Hogarth, but at the same time it needs to be made clear that Pope draws a somewhat different moral from that which Hogarth draws. Pope sees Sir Balaam's financial success as a merchant as the inevitable beginning of his downfall, whereas Hogarth would be more likely to have seen it as a just reward for his industry.

Finally it is worth noting that Pope also uses his knowledge of the technical terms of painting in the traditional Horatian way, that is, as a form of imagery for writing about poetry. Thus in *An Essay on Criticism* he uses the analogy with painting to illustrate his belief that literary reputations will fade away as language changes:

> So when the faithful *Pencil* has design'd
> Some *bright Idea* of the Master's Mind,
> Where a *new World* leaps out at his command,
> And ready Nature waits upon his Hand;
> When the ripe Colours *soften* and *unite*,
> And sweetly *melt* into just Shade and Light,
> When mellowing Years their full Perfection give,
> And each Bold Figure just begins to *Live*;
> The *treach'rous Colours* the fair Art betray,
> And all the bright Creation fades away! (484–93)

Pope was fortunately wrong about true literary merit, which has always endured despite changes in the language, but the analogy remains a good one with which to close this section, for the traditional comparison between poetry and painting could hardly be more fully developed than in this passage. The three main ways in which Dryden claimed in his Preface to Du Fresnoy that the two arts are parallel – through the Design, the Invention and the Colouring – are each elaborated by Pope before he moves to the final comparison between the fading colours of a painting and the fading language of a poem. Pope loved colour but so far as he is concerned the colours of a painting are its least reliable element. They are potentially 'treach'rous'; the painter who indulges in them for themselves alone is like the poet who has mere verbal ornamentation to offer and no powers of overall design. This is the reason why Pope describes the human and the supernatural beings in *The Rape of the Lock* in such glittering colours. It is his metaphor for establishing their momentary attraction and their long term transience at one and the same time.

Sculpture

Sculpture had been considered one of the sister arts in England since the time of the Restoration when, as Pope says in the *Imitation of Horace, Epistle II, i,* 'Marble soften'd into life grew warm' (147). In the last forty years of the seventeenth century the analogy between sculpture and poetry became almost as common with literary critics as that between painting and poetry. Indeed one might well talk of an *ut sculptura poesis* tradition existing alongside *ut pictura poesis*. Pope more or less does this when, in writing about the art of classical times in his poem *To Mr Addison, Occasioned by his Dialogue on Medals,* 1720, he says:

> The verse and sculpture bore an equal part,
> And Art reflected images to Art. (51–2)

As in his lines on the relationship of painting and poetry in the *Epistle to Mr Jervas*, the key word in establishing the relationship between sculpture and poetry is 'reflect'. The two arts mutually reinforce one another. At the same time as one remarks on this relationship, however, one should beware of making too much of it. Pope never became as deeply immersed in sculpture as he did in painting, and his verse never took on marked sculptural qualities in the same way that it clearly took on marked pictorial ones.

   The growth of interest in sculpture that occurred in England after the Restoration was a revival of earlier sculpture, especially that of Rome, rather than a growth in creative output. As Margaret

Whinney says in her definitive study, *Sculpture in Britain, 1530–1830*, 'it is a regrettable fact that the general level of English sculpture of the second half of the seventeenth century is far below the Continental average'.[22] The best sculptor of the time was Caius Gabriel Cibber, a native of Holstein who settled in England at the time of the Commonwealth, and who was the father of Pope's great enemy, Colley Cibber. By far the most successful of Cibber's sculptures were the two highly realistic figures of Raving and Melancholy Madness made for the entrance to Bedlam Hospital. These are the statues which Pope refers to at the beginning of the revised *Dunciad* of 1743 as 'Great Cibber's brazen, brainless brothers' (I, 32).

English sculpture of the first half of the eighteenth century was very much more distinguished than that of the preceding period. It was, however, almost entirely dominated by foreign sculptors, especially the Fleming, Michael Rysbrack (1694–1770), who was the leading sculptor of the 1720s and 1730s; and the Frenchman, Louis François Roubiliac (1702/05–62), who succeeded him in eminence from about 1740. These sculptors introduced a strong classical influence, the popularity of which was increased by the fashion for the English gentleman to finish his education by going on the Grand Tour. As a result most sculptors showed their subjects in Roman drapes and in heroic attitudes. The portrait bust grew greatly in popularity and, from the death of Kneller in 1723 to the return of Reynolds from Italy in 1753, it seemed to take over from portrait painting as the most fashionable way of preserving one's image for posterity. According to Margaret Whinney, a gallery of busts became 'the normal decoration of a gentleman's library'.[23] The *Inventory of Pope's Goods Taken after his Death* lists no pictures in his library, which is the more striking when we consider that the inventory lists over fifty portraits on display at other points in the house. In the library the *Inventory* lists marble busts of Homer, Newton, Spenser, Shakespeare, Milton and Dryden, and plaster of paris busts of Shakespeare, Palladio and Inigo Jones. Thus Pope's library, like his garden and his poetry, was packed with literary and classical allusions.

Pope himself sat for both Rysbrack and Roubiliac. Rysbrack's marble bust of him, made about 1725–30, was done in the prevailing Roman style. It shows Pope in a heroic and lofty pose, and as an idealization of him it has great strength. But it apparently bore little likeness to Pope, who wrote to the Earl of Oxford saying that all he could say for it was that 'he neither made the Busto, nor himself' (III, 100). Roubiliac carved four marble busts of Pope between 1738 and 1741, and these seem to have earned far greater approval from Pope. They are all similar in size and attitude and suggest, with polished simplicity, both the power of the poet's intellectual penetration and the physical suffering he endured (see frontispiece).

The poem that most clearly demonstrates Pope's interest in sculpture is *The Temple of Fame*, an allegorical dream vision based on Chaucer's *House of Fame*, first published in 1715. It is a highly pictorial poem, full of visual effects linked to Pope's interest in architecture and painting as well as sculpture. The opening landscape, as the dreamer-poet looks down on the earth, has a Claude-like quality, while the temple of fame itself is a 'glorious pile' designed to excel the architectural beauty of anything in Rome, Greece or Babylon. Statues of heroes in 'animated marble' and legislators who 'seem to think in stone' grace the walls of the temple, which has four fronts, each one standing for a different civilization. Rising from the architrave on the Western Front, which represents Greek civilization, there are statues of Theseus, Perseus, Alcides (i.e., Hercules), Orpheus, Amphion and Cytheraea. Pope's own footnote tells us that the description of Hercules is 'drawn with an eye to the position [posture] of the famous statue of Farnese'.

In the middle of the temple are six columns on which are placed the statues of the greatest men of learning of all time. The select six are Homer, Virgil, Pindar, Horace, Aristotle and Cicero, and each column is adorned, as Pope's note tells us 'with Sculptures taken from the most striking subjects of their works; which Sculpture bears a Resemblance in its Manner and Character, to the Manner and Character of their Writings'. *Ut sculptura poesis* has become *ut poesis sculptura*. The relationship is a two-way one: images reflect from art to art. The distinguishing quality of the carving that ornaments the column reflects that of the writer's work who stands above it. Thus the carvings around Homer's column suggest the greatly admired 'fire' of his invention:

> The Wars of *Troy* were round the Pillar seen:
> Here fierce *Tydides* wounds the *Cyprian* Queen;
> Here *Hector* glorious from *Patroclus* Fall,
> Here dragg'd in Triumph round the *Trojan* Wall.
> Motion and Life did ev'ry Part inspire,
> Bold was the Work, and prov'd the Master's Fire;
> A strong Expression most he seem'd t'affect,
> And here and there disclos'd a brave Neglect.   (188–95)

By contrast, Virgil's column suggests the perfection of his craftmanship:

> A Golden Column next in Rank appear'd,
> On which a Shrine of purest Gold was rear'd;
> Finish'd the whole, and labour'd ev'ry Part,
> With patient Touches of unweary'd Art:

The *Mantuan* there in sober Triumph sate,
Compos'd his Posture, and his Look sedate;
On *Homer* still he fix'd a reverend Eye,
Great without Pride, in modest Majesty.   (196–203)

Pope refers to sculpture in other poems, but nowhere as extensively as in *The Temple of Fame*. Nevertheless it is quite clear that he sees sculpture as an essential member of the sisterhood of the arts in a cultured civilization. He makes this specific point in heralding the arrival of the Renaissance in *An Essay on Criticism*:

Then *Sculpture* and her *Sister-Arts* revive;
Stones leap'd to *Form*, and *Rocks* began to *live*;
With *sweeter Notes* each *rising Temple* rung;
A *Raphael* painted and a *Vida* sung!   (701–4)

One of Pope's most significant allusions to the art of sculpture is found in *The Dunciad*, Book III. At this point in the action Cibber has been transported to the Underworld and is experiencing a vision of what has happened, and what will happen, in the Empire of Dulness. The view of Rome is particularly distressing:

See, the Cirque falls, th' unpillar'd Temple nods,
Streets pav'd with Heroes, Tyber choak'd with Gods:
'Till Peter's keys some christ'ned Jove adorn,
And Pan to Moses lends his pagan horn;
See graceless Venus to a Virgin turn'd,
Or Phidias broken, and Apelles burn'd.   (107–12)

For Pope the great works of sculpture are as important a part of the creative achievements of mankind as the great works of literature, and this vision of their destruction is a significant pointer to the great Anarch's final triumph at the end of the poem.

Music

Of all the arts Music has the most right to be called the sister of poetry. A primitive harmony, symbolized in the mythical figure of Orpheus, had linked the two arts since classical times, although they had separated somewhat with the development of instrumental music in the sixteenth century. There was, however, a renewed impetus in the second half of the seventeenth century towards unifying them again. As Dryden says in his Dedication to *The Vocal and Instrumental Music of the Prophetess*, 1691:

Music and poetry have ever been acknowledged Sisters, which walking hand in hand, support each other: As poetry is the harmony of words, so music is that of notes: and as poetry is a rise above prose and oratory, so is Music the exaltation of poetry. Both of them may excel apart, but sure they are most excellent when they are joined, because nothing is then wanting to either of their perfections: for thus they appear, like wit and beauty in the same person.[24]

Dryden himself had considerable success in joining the two arts in his two lyrics, *A Song for St Cecilia's Day*, 1687 and *Alexander's Feast; Or the Power of Music, An Ode in Honour of St Cecilia's Day*, 1697, in which he suggests musical effects through a careful manipulation of words and metre. These two poems, and especially *Alexander's Feast*, were greatly admired in the eighteenth century, and we may perhaps take Dr Johnson's comment on this poem as a reasonably typical expression of eighteenth-century acclaim for it: 'The *Ode for St Cecilia's Day* . . . has always been considered as exhibiting the highest flight of fancy, and the exactest nicety of art. This is allowed to stand without a rival'.[25]

Pope too tried his hand at this 'kind' of poem in his *Ode for Music, On St Cecilia's Day*, written about 1708. The poem is one of the young poet's experiments rather than something he felt deeply committed to, and it never reaches the heights of Dryden's two poems in this genre. Pope's account of Orpheus's journey to the Underworld, for example, becomes jangling rather than tragic, and the weight of rhythmical contrivance is far too heavily felt.

On his own admission Pope had no formal training in music. 'Did you ever learn anything of music?' asked Spence in 1744. 'Never,' Pope replied, 'but I had naturally a very good ear, and have often judged right of the best compositions in music by the force of that' (398). Despite Pope's lack of knowledge concerning the technical aspects of music he seems to have enjoyed it, and especially that of Handel whom he praised handsomely in *The Dunciad*, Book IV:

> Strong in new Arms, lo! Giant Handel stands,
> Like bold Briareus, with a hundred hands;
> To stir, to rouze, to shake the Soul he comes,
> And Jove's own Thunders follow Mars's Drums.   (65–8)

Pope knew Handel through their common friendship with Lord Burlington and is reputed to have written some of the libretto for Handel's masque, *Esther*, first performed in 1720. On the other hand there is no evidence of collaboration between the two men for Handel's famous setting of the aria, 'Where e'er you walk', in his opera, *Semele*, 1744. The words were taken, verbatim, from Pope's second pastoral, *Summer* (73 ff.), written forty years earlier, but the librettist seems to have borrowed them without Pope's knowledge.

Pope's views on the relationship of poetry and music are most clearly set out in *An Essay on Criticism* where he scorns the great number of critics who judge poetry solely by its musical effect:

> But most by *Numbers* judge a Poet's Song,
> And *smooth* or *rough*, with them is *right* or *wrong*;
> In the bright *Muse* tho' thousand *Charms* conspire,
> Her *Voice* is all these tuneful Fools admire,
> Who haunt *Parnassus* but to please their Ear,
> Not mend their Minds; as some to *Church* repair,
> Not for the *Doctrine*, but the *Musick* there.   (337–43)

This scorn for critics who overemphasize an attention to 'numbers' does not mean that he scorns a proper concern for 'numbers'. A concern for the sound of the poetry is an important part of the poet's craft, so long as it is fused with a concern for meaning and is not indulged in for itself. For Pope,

> 'Tis not enough no Harshness gives Offence,
> The *Sound* must seem an *Eccho* to the *Sense*.   (364–5)

Dryden's *Alexander's Feast* is specifically picked out for praise on this account:

> The *Pow'rs of Musick* all our Hearts allow;
> And what *Timotheus* was, is *Dryden* now.   (382–3)

Italian opera, on the other hand, is attacked in *The Dunciad*, Book IV, as 'a Harlot form soft sliding by, / With mincing step, small voice, and languid eye' (IV, 45–6), precisely because Pope felt it offered sound without sense. He sees it as an actual example of Dulness's success in triumphing over the arts of a civilized country. Pope was not alone in attacking Italian opera. It was one of the favourite targets of the Scriblerus Club, and of course John Gay's famous *Beggar's Opera*, 1728, was partly written as a reaction against it. The highly moral and chauvinistic attitude of the Tory satirists towards Italian opera is nowhere more clearly expressed than in the following words of Lord Bolingbroke, writing in *The Craftsman*, 17 March 1727:

> A very little Reflection on History will suggest this Observation; that every Nation has made either a great or inconsiderable Figure in the World, as it has fallen into Luxury or resisted its Temptations. . . . Operas and Masquerades, with all the politer Elegancies of a wanton Age, are much less to be regarded for their Expence (great as it is) than for the Tendency, which they have to deprave our Manners. MUSIC has something so peculiar in it,

that it exerts a willing Tyranny, over the Mind, and forms the ductile Soul into whatever shape the Melody directs. Wise Nations have observed its Influence, and have therefore kept it under proper Regulations. . . . A well wrought story, attended with its prevailing Charms, will transport the Soul out of itself; fire it with glorious Emulation; and lift the Man into an Hero; but the soft *Italian* Music relaxes and unnerves the Soul, and sinks it into Weakness; so that while we receive their Music, we at the same time are adopting their Manners.[26]

It is interesting to note that both Pope and Bolingbroke use the same adjective, 'soft', to describe Italian opera. One senses that the Tory satirists objected more to its social and political associations than to its musical quality.

It would be wrong to give the impression that Pope's poetry was deeply influenced by an interest in music, for this was clearly not the case. Of all the sister arts it probably influenced his poetry least. But it would be equally wrong not to challenge the charge, made by Dr Johnson of all people, that Pope was not only ignorant of the principles of music but was also 'insensible of its effects'.[27]

I have tried to show in this chapter that Pope was interested in, and familiar with, the different art forms in the eighteenth century, and how his understanding and appreciation of them affected his poetry. This is not to say that the boundaries between the art forms were blurred in his mind. He was aware of their respective autonomy, but he was also aware of their sisterhood. It does not follow that six sisters have no individuality because they have one mother. Pope accepted the *ut pictura poesis* tradition because he wanted to draw attention to certain similarities between the arts that he believed enriched the artistic experience; Lessing rejected it later in the century because he wanted to draw attention to the differences between the arts that he believed to be more fully experienced in isolation.[28] A Romantic emphasis on the separateness and individuality of the different arts replaced an Augustan emphasis on the coherence and harmony that could exist when 'images reflect from art to art'.

Notes

1. There have been a number of most useful studies of this aspect of Pope's work in recent times. Among those I have made particular use of are the following: Robert J. Allen, 'Pope and the Sister Arts' in *Pope and his Contemporaries*, ed. J. L. Clifford and L. A. Landa (Oxford University Press, Oxford, 1949), pp. 78–88; Jean H. Hagstrum, *The Sister Arts*

(Chicago University Press, Chicago, 1958); James Sambrook, 'Pope and the Visual Arts' in *Writers and Their Background: Alexander Pope*, ed. Peter Dixon (G. Bell & Sons, London, 1972), pp. 143–71; and especially Morris R. Brownell, *Alexander Pope and the Arts of Georgian England* (Clarendon Press, Oxford, 1978), referred to hereafter as Brownell.

2. Kent designed a portico for Pope's house, which was added in 1732–33. See Pope's *Correspondence*, III, 323, 329, 356 and 359.

3. This translation was published by Giacomo Leoni, a Venetian architect who had settled in London. Lord Burlington was not happy with this edition, which took some liberties with the original, and commissioned Isaac Ware to produce a more accurate version, which was published in 1738.

4. For a fuller consideration of some of these meanings see A. O. Lovejoy, '"Nature" as Aesthetic Norm', *Essays in the History of Ideas* (Johns Hopkins University Press, Baltimore, 1948), pp. 69–77.

5. Sir William Davenant, 'The Authors Preface', *Gondibert: An Heroic Poem* (1651); ed. David F. Gladish (Clarendon Press, Oxford, 1971), p. 7.

6. Brownell, p. 275.

7. Stephen Switzer, *Ichnographia Rustica; The Nobleman, Gentleman, and Gardener's Recreation*, 3 vols (London, 1718).

8. Horace Walpole, 'The History of the Modern Taste in Gardening', *Anecdotes of Painting in England*, 4 vols (1771; 2nd Edition London, 1782), Vol. IV, p. 289.

9. William Hogarth, *The Analysis of Beauty* (London, 1753), p. 25.

10. There has been extended interest in Pope's role as a landscape gardener in recent years and the following studies have each contributed significantly to our better understanding of it: Christopher Hussey, *English Gardens and Landscapes, 1700–1750* (Country Life Ltd, London, 1967); Maynard Mack, *The Garden and the City: Retirement and Politics in the Later Poetry of Pope, 1731–1743* (University of Toronto Press, Toronto, 1969); James Sambrook, op. cit.; John Dixon Hunt, *The Figure in the Landscape: Poetry, Painting and Gardening during the Eighteenth Century* (Johns Hopkins University Press, Baltimore and London, 1976); Morris Brownell, op. cit.; Peter Martin, *Pursuing Innocent Pleasures: The Gardening World of Alexander Pope* (Archon Books, Hamden, Connecticut, 1984).

11. Brownell, pp. 71–246. Page references in my text are to this edition. In this closely argued section of his book Brownell is attempting to move the origins of the picturesque sensibility, as defined by Christopher Hussey, *The Picturesque, Studies in a Point of View* (London, 1927), and Walter Hipple, *The Beautiful, the Sublime and the Picturesque in Eighteenth-Century British Aesthetic Theory* (Carbondale, Illinois, 1957), back to an earlier point in the century, and specifically to the writings, observations and works of Alexander Pope. The point has however been disputed by Peter Martin, op. cit., pp. 8–10 and 241.

12. 'On Gardens', *The Prose Works of Alexander Pope*, Vol. 1 *The Earlier Works, 1711–1720*, ed. Norman Ault (Shakespeare Head Press, Oxford, 1936), p. 145.

13. *Horace Walpole's Correspondence*, ed. W. S. Lewis (Yale University Press, New Haven, 1937; Vol. XXI, 1960), p. 417.

14. Horace, *Ars Poetica*, 361.
15. Du Fresnoy, *De Arte Graphica* (1667), translated by John Dryden as *The Art of Painting* (1695), in *The Works of John Dryden* (University of California Press, Los Angeles, Vol. XX, 1989).
16. Ibid., pp. 110–11.
17. The Latin phrase means 'a discriminating judge of beauty'.
18. The 'Inventory' was first published in *Notes and Queries*, 6th Series, V (1882), pp. 363–5. It has been recently re-published in Maynard Mack, *The Garden and the City*, Appendix B, pp. 244–58.
19. Joseph Warton, *An Essay on the Genius and Writings of Pope* (1756; Second edition corrected, London, 1762), Vol. I, p. 50.
20. Henry Peacham, *The Art of Drawing* (London, 1606), p. 30.
21. Warton, op. cit., Vol. I, p. 33.
22. Margaret Whinney, *Sculpture in Britain, 1530–1830* (Pelican History of Art (Penguin Books, Harmondsworth, 1964), p. 41.
23. Ibid., p. 73.
24. John Dryden, 'Epistle Dedicatory for the Vocal and Instrumental Music of the Prophetess' (1691), in *The Works of John Dryden* (University of California Press, Los Angeles. Vol. XVII, 1971), p. 324.
25. Samuel Johnson, 'Dryden', in *Lives of the English Poets* (1779–81); ed. G. B. Hill, 3 vols (Clarendon Press, Oxford, 1905), Vol. I, p. 456.
26. Caleb D'Anvers, *The Craftsman*, 14 vols (London, 1731–37), Vol. 1, pp. 173–7.
27. Johnson, 'Pope', op. cit., Vol. III, p. 22.
28. G. E. Lessing, *Laocoon* (1766), translated by Sir Robert Phillimore (Macmillan, London, 1874).

4   Augustan literary tenets

> A perfect Judge will *read* each Work of Wit
> With the same Spirit that its Author *writ*,
> (*An Essay on Criticism*, 233–4)

Any age makes certain intellectual and cultural assumptions about itself which seem dated, and sometimes totally foreign, to succeeding ages, but which come almost unconsciously to the age itself. Twentieth-century writers, for example, assume that their audience is familiar with Freudian or Marxist ideas. They refer to the Oedipus complex or to the class struggle without having to explain, what is meant. Such ideas form an area of allusion from which twentieth-century writers freely draw, and about which they can be sure of their readers' familiarity. But in two hundred years' time such allusions may well need footnotes to explain them, just as eighteenth-century allusions to the concepts of *concordia discors* and the *scala naturae* need them today. The aim of this chapter is to explain some of the critical assumptions that underlay Augustan expectations about literature, and to show how an understanding of such assumptions helps one to see better what Pope was trying to do in his poetry, and to judge more fairly the degree to which he succeeded in doing it.

One of the most important and helpful documents for an understanding of Augustan literary principles is Pope's *An Essay on Criticism*. Although most of this poem was written when he was only twenty or twenty-one, it hardly deserves the scorn poured on it by De Quincey who called it 'the feeblest and least interesting of Pope's writings, being substantially a mere versification, like a metrical multiplication table, of commonplaces the most mouldy with which criticism has baited its rat-traps'.[1] It is true that there is nothing especially new in what Pope says, but that is also its merit. It is an extremely thorough and often memorable account of the Augustan critical position, and, preferring Dr Johnson's words to those of De Quincey, 'exhibits every mode of excellence that can embellish or dignify didactic composition – selection of matter, novelty of arrangement, justness of precepts, splendour of illustration, and propriety of digression'.[2] Part of our difficulty with the poem, if we find one, is due to our lack of familiarity with didactic poetry. In the twentieth century we tend to feel that this is not quite the right subject matter for poetry. But the eighteenth century laid down no such limitations on what was or was not the right subject for poetry. Indeed it is not until one tries to extract a prose meaning from the lines that one realizes how poetically charged they in fact are.

The kinds

When we first read a new poem today we tend to come to it with certain accepted ideas concerning what is and is not good poetry. We expect, for example, that a good poem will be fresh and striking in its imagery, will use everyday colloquial language, and will offer a full expression of the poet's own feelings. But these are peculiarly post-Romantic criteria, and although eighteenth-century readers also judged poetry according to certain preconceived criteria, they would not have approached a new poem with anything like so narrow a set of preconceptions. They would have a different set of criteria for different *kinds* of poems. They would have read a new poem much as sixteenth- and seventeenth-century readers had done before them, and when they read a new poem the first question they would have asked would have been 'What *kind* of a poem is this?'

So far as the Renaissance was concerned particular kinds of poetry demanded particular kinds of subject matter. The epic, for example, required an elevated subject of a grand scope, while the epistle required a familiar subject of a more parochial scope. There was a wide variety of possible kinds of poetry, just as there was a wide variety of possible kinds of subject matter, but each kind made its own special rules and demands on the poet. What was appropriate for one kind of poetry might be totally inappropriate for another. This is what is meant by the concept of decorum.

The different kinds of poetry had different degrees of importance. Just as the Renaissance world fell into an ordered hierarchy, the Great Chain of Being (see chapter 5) in which all existence from the human to the inanimate had its fit place, so the literary kinds, ideally, fell into an ordered hierarchy in which each kind had its fit place. In practice, however, the order was never as strict or as clearcut as this comparison suggests, and there was considerable difference of opinion about the correct ordering of the kinds. In the sixteenth century we find the kinds ordered, in such works as Julius Caesar Scaliger's *Poetics*, 1561,[3] or George Puttenham's *Art of English Poesie*, 1589,[4] so that hymns and paeans are the highest kind of poetry, because of their divine subject matter, while incantations, epigrams and ditties are the lowest. What matters for us of course is not Scaliger or Puttenham's ordering of the kinds, but that of the eighteenth century. I have begun by mentioning the sixteenth-century belief in the doctrine of the kinds because it shows us that Pope in his acceptance of the doctrine was, as in so many other things, shaped by and faithful to the past. Furthermore we know that he was familiar with Scaliger's work in particular, for he told Spence in 1739 that 'Scaliger's *Poetics* is an exceeding useful book of its kind, and extremely well collected' (554).

The main difference between the seventeenth- and eighteenth-century ordering of the kinds and that of the Renaissance concerns the much higher valuation that the seventeenth and eighteenth centuries gave to the epic. The epic was pre-eminently the major literary kind, and any poet aspiring to greatness should have written one. For this reason, if no other, Spenser and Milton were accepted as the great English poets, and although Dryden and Pope, who were accounted the next greatest,[5] failed to write their planned epics (Dryden's was to be on King Arthur, and Pope's on Brutus, the legendary founder of Britain) they did the next best thing by writing translations of the two greatest epics in any language. The more one reads of post-Restoration poetry the more one becomes aware of the very great degree to which the epic shaped and formed it. Without the idea of the epic in the background *MacFlecknoe*, *Absalom and Achitopel*, *The Rape of the Lock* and *The Dunciad* would have been impossible.[6] Each of these poems constantly alludes to, quotes from, imitates, parodies or mocks specific lines and incidents from the great epics of Homer, Virgil and Milton. One can only fully appreciate the satiric wit of the poems when one has a knowledge of the epics on which they are based.

This is no place to discuss the separate traditions lying behind all the different kinds of poetry that Pope attempted, for he tried his hand, not always with equal success, at a great number – the mock-epic, the georgic, the pastoral, the dream vision, the didactic, the heroic epistle, the elegy, the familiar epistle, the formal verse satire, the moral epistle, the prologue, the epilogue, the ode, the epigram and the epitaph. What matters is that the reader should be aware that each kind of poem Pope writes has a different tradition behind it, and therefore a different framework in which it needs to be viewed. This is important because Pope expects the reader to recognize the tradition in which he is writing and then to admire the way in which he gives it a new turn. Where nineteenth- or twentieth-century poets hope the reader will think their poems original and new, eighteenth-century poets considered they had failed if they ignored tradition by being too original. They felt the need to fuse tradition and originality, the ancient and the modern, the old and the new. Dr Johnson praised Pope's *The Rape of the Lock* for exhibiting 'in a very high degree, the two most engaging powers of an author. New things are made familiar and familiar things are made new.'

At the same time as the doctrine of the kinds created certain formal expectations it also allowed an inventive poet to create surprise by breaking those expectations in unusual ways. This, of course, is the basis of the mock-epic where the poet uses an elevated form for unsuitable subject matter. In *The Rape of the Lock* a trivial event is treated with a mock seriousness that is totally inappropriate to its importance. The same sort of deliberate unrelatedness between form and subject lies behind many Augustan satiric writings. Gay's 'Newgate Pastoral', *The Beggar's Opera*, and Swift's mock aubade, *A Description of the Morning*, are two cases in point. In both these works the success of the satire depends not only on readers recognizing the fact that form and subject are at odds with one another, but also in their implicitly knowing how the literary kinds of the pastoral and the aubade would be correctly handled. The readers' appreciation of the poem is increased through their self-esteem in recognizing the distortion that has taken place.

One other way in which an awareness of the doctrine of the kinds helps in an appreciation of Pope's poetry concerns readers being responsive to the possibility of a shift in kinds, even within a single poem. Pope never allows the kinds to become so mixed that the overall effect is one of confusion, but he does frequently move into a style that is appropriate to a kind other than that in which he is writing. For instance, in his *Imitation of Horace, II, vi*, which tells the famous story of the town and country mice, Pope writes in the familiar and colloquial language appropriate to the formal verse satire. Then, suddenly, in describing the home of the town mouse he shifts into a mock-epic language that is strictly inappropriate to the kind of poem he is writing:

> Behold the place, where if a Poet
> Shin'd in Description, he might show it,
> Tell how the Moon-beam trembling falls
> And tips with silver all the walls:
> Palladian walls, Venetian doors,
> Grotesco roofs, and Stucco floors:
> But let it (in a word) be said,
> The Moon was up, and Men a-bed,
> The Napkins white, the Carpet red:
> The Guests withdrawn had left the Treat,
> And down the Mice sate, *tête à tête*.   (189–99)

The transition from the elegant pictorial language of the trembling moonbeams that tip the walls with silver in the first six lines to the curt and clipped telegrammatic language, that so perfectly captures the style of Swift, in the last five lines, shows a wonderfully urbane turn of wit.

Decorum

The Augustan concept of *decorum* is directly connected with the doctrine of the *kinds* just discussed. In the same way as there is an appropriate kind of poetry for a certain subject matter, so there is an appropriate language for each kind of poetry. Decorum is another word for propriety, and the literary concept of decorum involves proper words in proper places. The language must be suited to the purpose, or as Ian Jack puts it in his book *Augustan Satire*, the idiom must be level with the intention.[7]

Pope expresses the doctrine clearly enough in *An Essay on Criticism*:

> Expression is the *Dress of Thought*, and still
> Appears more *decent* as more *suitable*;
> A vile Conceit in pompous Words exprest,
> Is like a Clown in regal Purple drest;
> For diff'rent *Styles* with diff'rent *Subjects* sort,
> As several Garbs with Country, Town, and Court.

(318–23)

The analogy between literary decorum and civilized behaviour is a crucial one. Just as there is an art in doing certain things well – dressing, eating, courting – so there is an art in expressing them well. One dresses according to the occasion. It would be ridiculous to wear one's best suit and new shoes to go gardening in, and it would be disrespecful to wear one's tattiest clothes and oldest boots to attend a wedding. In the same way, it is ridiculous to use an elevated style to describe a trivial event like the removal of a lock of hair from a young lady's head, just as it is disrespectful to use an earthy style to praise the King. As the above examples imply there are times when Pope deliberately breaks the concept of decorum for satiric effect, but in breaking it he is of course tacitly acknowledging its fundamental importance.

The epic demands a specially well-chosen style. It should be written in a language appropriate to its grand purpose. Indeed, one of Pope's rare criticisms of Dryden concerns the inappropriateness of part of his translation of the *Aeneid*:

> I agree with you [he writes to his friend Henry Cromwell on 28 October 1710] in your censure of the use of sea-terms in Mr Dryden's Virgil; not only because Helenus was no great Prophet in those matters, but because no Terms of Art, or Cant-Words, suit with the majesty and dignity of style which epic poetry requires. (I, 101)

An understanding of the literary concept of decorum helps us to appreciate two particular aspects of Pope's vocabulary that have given readers trouble and concern over the years: his use of poetic diction, and his use of scatologic words.

Poetic diction is a term used by Pope in his Preface to the *Iliad* to describe that quality in Homer's expression which is especially alive and glowing and more highly charged than ordinary speech. But the term was taken up by the Romantics and used in a much narrower and more pejorative sense to describe the artificial language that they felt to be the overriding fault of eighteenth-century poetry. The most famous and influential attack on poetic diction comes in Wordsworth's Preface to *Lyrical Ballads*, 1800:

> There will also be found in these volumes little of what is usually called poetic diction; I have taken as much pains to avoid it as others ordinarily take to produce it; this I have done for the reason already alleged, to bring my language near to the language of men.[8]

Later on Wordsworth refers to poetic diction as 'adulterated phraseology' and a 'motley masquerade of tricks, quaintness, hieroglyphics and enigmas'.

Wordsworth's attack on poetic diction is particularly a rejection of personification and periphrasis: phrases like the 'scaly breed', used by Pope to describe fish in *Windsor-Forest*, or the 'glitt'ring forfex', to describe a pair of scissors in *The Rape of the Lock*. These are words specially chosen to raise the respective scenes in which they occur, either seriously or ironically, above an ordinary scene. Furthermore, they add a dimension to the meaning that the more ordinary words could not possibly add. In calling the fish the 'scaly breed' in *Windsor-Forest*, for example, Pope shows through the adjective what the individual fish that he is about to describe in great detail have in common that distinguishes them from other creatures in the *scala naturae*; through the noun he points out that they are at the same time a generative part of that *scala naturae*, thus adding to the sense of creative plenitude found in the forest at large. The more ordinary word 'fish' could not have suggested these additional areas of meaning. Similarly detailed reasons can be given for the periphrastic description of the scissors in *The Rape of the Lock* (see under 'Periphrasis' in the Glossary of technical terms, p. 241).

Because Pope can be shown to be using poetic diction here for a deliberate purpose, however, it does not follow that there is not a great deal of substance in Wordsworth's attack on it. There certainly was a decaying poetic style among the minor poets of fifty years later, who frequently used the formulaic quality of poetic diction as a way of constructing stock effects, and Wordsworth's rejection of this habit was more than welcome. What needs to be pointed out here is that the best poets, such as Pope, Thomson and Gray, used poetic diction as an integral support to their poetic feeling, not as a substitute for it.

The difficulty with scatologic words is similar. Pope is gratuitously obscene in *The Dunciad*, Book II, critics will say, or his image of excrement being passed on from 'hog to hog in huts of Westphaly', in *Epilogue to the Satires: Dialogue II*, 171–80, is unpardonably filthy. But this is exactly what Pope wants us to say. To an audience that is not shocked by his attack on moral decay, only the analogy with physical decay remains. Again the concept of decorum is at work, for just as the epic requires a suitably elevated style, so satire requires a suitably vigorous and scabrous one. Pope did not hesitate to call a spade a spade if it was appropriate, and he did not shrink from calling it a shovel if it was necessary. When Boswell objected to a certain phrase in Pope as being low, Dr Johnson replied: 'Sir, it is intended to be low: it is satire. The expression is debased to debase the character'.[9]

The rules

Much of the foregoing discussion might suggest that Pope and the Augustans believed poetry should be written according to a set of pre-ordained rules. But there is a great difference between the person who believes that poetry should be written according to a narrow set of sharply defined rules and the person who believes that the poet's imagination works the more freely for operating within a broad set of shared expectations. The theoretical discussion concerning whether a poet is born or made is a simplification of the same issue. A poet, of course, is both born and made: has both genius and skill. The critical question is where the emphasis should lie, which is the more important? The question was indeed a lively and perennial one in the seventeenth and eighteenth centuries, but only the most stereotyped of neoclassical critics, like Thomas Rymer, believed in a strict and uncompromising adherence to the rules. The great creative writers, especially Dryden and Pope, were far too aware of the complex workings of the imagination to subscribe to limiting formulae without making serious reservations.

The rules received their greatest support and popularity in seventeenth-century France. Boileau's *Art Poétique*, 1674, Rapin's *Réflexions sur la Poétique*, 1674, and Le Bossu's *Traité du Poème Épique*, 1675, belong to a common school of criticism in that they each set out to abstract a set of guidelines for the writing of poetry from the works of the Ancients, and particularly from Aristotle and Horace. Perhaps the most notorious rules abstracted from the Ancients were those concerning drama. The demand that plays be written according to the three unities of time, place and action has long since been shown to be totally irrelevant to the stage, and nowhere more effectively than by Dr Johnson in his *Preface to Shakespeare*, 1765.[10] But for a short period during the last quarter of the seventeenth century this theoretical demand held great sway in both France and England. Thomas Rymer's vituperative attack on Shakespeare in *A Short View of Tragedy*, 1692, shows such a position taken to its logical and absurd conclusion. Rymer's 'commonsense' approach demonstrates an extraordinary aesthetic insensitivity and has earned him the reputation among most latterday students of being, in Macaulay's words, 'the worst critic that ever lived'.[11]

Dryden's attitude to the rules is, like that of Pope, mixed. Both men skilfully pick their way between the strict rigidity of the formalist critics and the boundless freedom of their opponents. Where Rymer sees the rules as ends in themselves, Dryden and Pope see them as means to an end:

> I never heard of any other foundation of Dramatic Poesy than the imitation of nature; neither was there ever pretended any other by the Ancients, or moderns, or me, who endeavour to follow them in that rule. This I have plainly said in my definition of a play; that it is a just and lively image of human nature . . . if nature be to be imitated, then there is a rule for imitating nature rightly; otherwise there may be an end, and no means conducing to it.[12]

Pope begins his discussion of the rules in *An Essay on Criticism* in much the same way:

> Those RULES of old *discover'd*, not *devis'd*,
> Are *Nature* still, but *Nature Methodiz'd*;
> *Nature*, like *Liberty*, is but restrain'd
> By the same Laws which first *herself* ordain'd. (88–91)

The modern reader may feel that Pope is trying to have his cake and eat it, but there is a great deal of validity in what he says. He neatly sidesteps involvement in the debate between the proponents of rules and the proponents of imitating nature by saying that the two are essentially the same. He makes the identical point later in the poem when he says:

> Learn hence for Ancient *Rules* a just Esteem;
> To copy *Nature* is to copy *Them*. (139–40)

Pope draws, in *An Essay on Criticism*, on many of the same persons who so influenced Rymer – Boileau, Rapin and Le Bossu – but never in so slavish a way. He struggles throughout to effect a reasonable reconciliation between the adherents and the opponents of the rules, a reconciliation that is summed up in the antithetical force of the second line in the following couplet:

> Hear how learn'd *Greece* her useful Rules indites,
> When to repress, and when indulge our Flights.   (92–3)

He defends 'just precepts' drawn from 'great examples', but the emphasis in both phrases is as much on the adjective as the noun. What really counts, however, is the 'Poet's Fire', that is, his imagination (cf. Pope's admiration for Homer's fire which 'burns everywhere clearly and everywhere irresistibly', *Preface to the Iliad*), and for as long as critics admired that 'coelestial fire' (195) criticism remained in a healthy state:

> Then Criticism the Muse's Handmaid prov'd,
> To dress her Charms, and make her more belov'd.   (102–3)

But later critics grew jealous of what they could not themselves achieve and, elevating criticism above the art it presumed to study, used 'mistaken rules' to attack the poets they were meant to serve:

> But following Wits from that Intention stray'd;
> Who could not win the Mistress, woo'd the Maid;
> Against the Poets *their own Arms* they turn'd,
> Sure to hate most the Men from whom they *learn'd*.   (104–7)

Critics who slavishly adhere to precept are seen as quack apothecaries (108–11), insects (112–13) and even as cooks, who 'write dull *Receits* [recipes] how Poems may be made' (115).

For Pope the only true way to sharpen one's critical discrimination is to soak oneself in the classics:

> Be *Homer*'s Works your *Study*, and *Delight*,
> Read them by Day, and meditate by Night,
> Thence form your Judgment, thence your Maxims bring,
> And trace the Muses *upward* to their *Spring*.   (124–7)

Pope's strategy in effecting a reconciliation in the debate concerning the rules is to redefine what is meant by them so that following them becomes the same thing as following nature. Yet even when he has thus carefully qualified his approval he still finds it necessary to insist on the escape clause:

> Some Beauties yet, no Precepts can declare,
> For there's a *Happiness* as well as *Care*.   (141–2)

He goes on to stress the mysterious quality that exists in the greatest poetry, the '*nameless Graces* which no methods teach', and which depend on a 'Lucky LICENCE' [Pope's capitals], or a '*brave Disorder*' that will part from '*vulgar Bounds*' and '*snatch* a *Grace* beyond the Reach of Art' (144–55).

What this account of Pope's discussion of the rules in *An Essay on Criticism* shows us is that, far from being the fervent disciple of the rules that he is sometimes described as being, Pope gives them, at most, a qualified vote of approval. He admits their usefulness when they lead us back to the great works of creative genius, but once they become dogmatic or limiting they must be put aside. On the whole he is a far fiercer defender of the 'Liberties of Wit' than he is of the 'vulgar Bounds' of 'Foreign Laws despis'd'.

Wit

Of all the literary terms current in the Augustan period 'wit' is the most difficult to define. The word is used in the late seventeenth and early eighteenth centuries to cover a variety of widely different meanings, each one of which forces us to see the other in a slightly different light. Pope was concerned with the word's complexity from a very early age. In 1704, for instance, we find him writing to William Wycherley offering the following definition: 'True Wit I believe, may be defin'd as a justness of Thought, and a Facility of Expression; or (in the Midwives phrase) a perfect Conception, with an easy Delivery'. The definition is itself an example of one kind of wit, but the sixteen-year-old Pope was fully aware of the elusive nature of the term, for he continued in the next sentence: 'However this is far from a compleat definition; pray help me to a better, as I doubt not you can' (I, 2).

In his *Dictionary, 1755*, Dr Johnson lists eight different meanings of the word, while the *OED*, published almost two hundred years later, lists fourteen main meanings and any number of subordinate and compound ones. William Empson has pointed out in *The Structure of Complex Words* that the word appears on an average every sixteen lines in *An Essay on Criticism* and in a somewhat different sense nearly every time, though he adds that 'there is not a single use of the word, in the whole poem in which the idea of a joke is quite out of sight'.[13] All this is of little comfort to the new reader, but it is a warning against expecting a clearcut definition of so complex a word.

The basic meaning of the word, from which all others derive, concerns the various powers of the mind. The term could refer either to all the mental faculties working together, or to individual mental faculties, such as the imagination, judgment and memory. It is because the word originally covered each of these very different faculties that its meaning became so complex when writers tried to limit its application to a particular faculty. We still use the term in its overall sense, albeit somewhat unconsciously, when we talk about being at our 'wit's end', but by and large the word has a very much narrower meaning in its most commonly accepted usage today, referring to a person's ability to say clever and 'witty' things.

There are four main ways in which Pope uses the expression in *An Essay on Criticism*. First, he occasionally uses it in its original sense to refer to all the mental faculties considered together:

> Nature to all things fix'd the Limits fit,
> And wisely curb'd proud Man's pretending Wit:
> As on the *Land* while *here* the *Ocean* gains,
> In *other Parts* it leaves wide sandy Plains;
> Thus in the *Soul* while *Memory* prevails,
> The solid Pow'r of *Understanding* fails;
> Where Beams of warm *Imagination* play,
> The *Memory*'s soft Figures melt away.
> One *Science* only will one *Genius* fit;
> So *vast* is Art, so *narrow* Human Wit. (52–61)

Wit, as it is used in the last line of this passage, refers to each of the cognitive faculties in turn whether one is considering the 'soft figures' of Memory, the 'solid power' of Understanding [i.e. Judgment], or the 'beams of warm' Imagination. No person can excel in all the faculties of the mind, 'so vast is Art [Learning], so narrow Human Wit', and individuals must therefore fit their genius to one particular branch of knowledge.

The second meaning of the word, and the one with which he begins the poem, is as a synonym for genius, or the indefinable gift of the poet:

> In *Poets* as true *Genius* is but rare,
> True *Taste* as seldom is the *Critick's* Share;
> Both must alike from Heav'n derive their Light,
> These *born* to Judge, as well as those to Write.
> Let such teach others who themselves excell,
> And *censure freely* who have *written well*.
> *Authors* are partial to their *Wit*, 'tis true,
> But are not *Criticks* to their *Judgment* too? (11–18)

In the first line here the distinguishing mark of the poet is 'true Genius' which must be derived from Heaven (cf. *poeta nascitur non fit*), but by line 17 the distinguishing mark of the poet is 'Wit'. The term 'wit' has become interchangeable with 'genius' and distinct from 'judgment'. We shall see when we come to Pope's fourth meaning that, in other places, he stresses the importance of its liaison with judgment. Such paradoxes are an essential part of the word's complexity.

A third way in which Pope uses wit is to refer to the quality of ingenuity in a writer. It was this quality of verbal and intellectual agility that the Restoration Wits strove after. At its best the pursuit of such a quality leads to piercing illumination, but at its worst it leads to a purely superficial glamour, to writing that is all frothy extravagance without any ethical basis, or what Pope so aptly calls, 'One glaring Chaos and wild Heap of Wit' (292). Pope is totally scornful of this kind of wit:

> Some have at first for *Wits*, then *Poets* past,
> Turn'd *Criticks* next, and prov'd plain *Fools* at last;
> Some neither can for *Wits* nor *Criticks* pass,
> As heavy Mules are neither *Horse* nor *Ass*.
> Those half-learn'd Witlings, num'rous in our Isle,
> As half-form'd Insects on the banks of *Nile*;
> Unfinish'd Things, one knows not what to call,
> Their Generation's so *equivocal*:
> To tell 'em, wou'd a *hundred Tongues* require,
> Or one vain Wit's, that might a hundred tire.   (36–45)

The comparison of the 'Witlings' to insects (cf. the opening lines of *An Epistle to Dr Arbuthnot*), the pun concerning their proliferation, 'their Generation's so equivocal', and the final epigrammatic dig at their endless loquacity show the brilliant effectiveness of Pope's own satiric wit being used to annihilate the glittering falsity of the poetasters and pretenders to wit. At its best, wit of such intellectual agility adds a sprightliness to poetry that both charms and surprises the reader. It involves a liveliness of mind that should not be underrated, though, as Pope would be the first to admit, it is only part of the great poet's equipment.

The fourth and by far the most important meaning that Pope attributes to 'wit' concerns the imagination. Towards the end of the poem he describes Horace as:

> He, who supream in Judgment, as in Wit,
> Might boldly censure, as he boldly writ,
> Yet *judg'd* with *Coolness* tho' he sung with *Fire*;
> His *Precepts* teach but what his *Works* inspire.   (657–60)

Here wit involves the 'fire' of the imagination, an image that picks up the earlier reference to the 'Beams of warm *Imagination*' (58). Wit, as it refers to the imagination, is, like the sun, the source of all light. Pope explicitly makes the comparison when he compares 'envy'd Wit' to '*Sol* Eclips'd' (468). When the Sun's beams are too strong they draw up vapours that at first obscure but finally reflect added glory. In the same way Wit's shining light at first attracts dull critics, but finally endures despite them.

Perhaps the most important point Pope makes about wit in this sense, however, is that imagination is not in itself sufficient for the poet:

> Some, to whom Heav'n in Wit has been profuse,
> Want as much more, to turn it to its use;
> For *Wit* and *Judgment* often are at strife,
> Tho' meant each other's Aid, like *Man* and *Wife*.   (80–3)

In the best writing the imagination must be at one with the judgment. The two qualities cannot be separated. As 'grave *Quintilian*', whom Pope praises for his clear method (669–74), says in his *Institutio Oratoria*: 'I do not believe that invention can exist apart from judgment, since we do not say that a speaker has invented inconsistent two-edged or foolish arguments, but merely that he has failed to avoid them'.[14] La Rochefoucauld, whose maxims were translated into English in 1706, just a few years before Pope wrote his poem, says much the same thing:

> The making a Difference between Wit and Judgment, is a Vulgar Error. Judgment is nothing else but the exceeding Brightness of Wit, which, like Light, pierces into the very Bottom of Things, observes all that ought to be observed there, and discovers what seemed to be past anybodies finding out: From when we must conclude, that the Energy and Extension of this Light of the Wit, is the very Thing that produces all those Effects, usually ascribed to the Judgment.[15]

It is this idea of wit as the marriage of imagination and judgment that lies behind the best-known couplets in the poem:

> *True Wit* is *Nature* to Advantage drest,
> What oft was *Thought*, but ne'er so well *Exprest*,
> *Something*, whose Truth convinc'd at Sight we find,
> That gives us back the Image of our Mind.   (297–300)

True wit involves both the imagination and the judgment, both nature and art. It involves subject matter and form welded together in the creative mind so that the truth that results convinces us at sight and 'gives us back the Image of our Mind'.

I have suggested four different ways in which wit is used by Pope in *An Essay on Criticism*, and the question that now arises is whether these differences in the meaning of one word are the result of confusion or deliberate strategy. In order to answer this we need to say something about the distrust of the imagination found in the writings of the most influential seventeenth-century philosophers and scientists. Contrary to popular opinion, this is not a distrust that is found among Augustan poets. On the other hand they could not help being aware of it and of the corresponding attempt to downgrade the importance of poetry as a medium for expressing truth about human nature.

Francis Bacon was the chief originator of this distrust of the imagination. For Bacon poetry was almost totally a means of escapism that allowed deception to triumph. In *The Advancement of Learning*, 1605, he admitted the power of poetry and the imagination but he distrusted it as a vehicle for truth because it transformed reality. For Bacon poetry was 'the play of the mind'.[16] This distrust was taken up by Bacon's disciples, the members of the Royal Society, and eloquently expressed by their official historian Thomas Sprat in his *History of the Royal Society*, 1667. Sprat described the wit and imagination of the poet as being inconsistent with a sincere enquiry into the works of Nature.[17]

A further example of the philosopher's distrust of the imagination occurs in Thomas Hobbes's *Leviathan*, 1651. For Hobbes imagination 'is nothing but *decaying sense* and is found in men, and many other living creatures, as well sleeping as waking'.[18] John Locke also considered the imagination a hindrance in arriving at the truth. The emphasis in his *Essay Concerning Human Understanding*, 1690, falls on the importance of judgment and the frailty of imagination. He defines wit as 'lying most in the assemblage of ideas, and putting those together with quickness and variety, wherein can be found any resemblance or congruity, thereby to make up pleasant pictures and agreeable visions in the fancy'. Judgment on the other hand 'lies quite on the other side in separating carefully ideas one from another, wherein can be found the least difference, thereby to avoid being misled by Similitude'.[19] In aligning wit with fancy and opposing it to judgment, Locke is managing further to discredit poetry as likely to mislead the mind. If a child has a poetic vein, he argues in *Some Thoughts Concerning Education*, 1693, the parents 'should labour to have it stifled and suppressed as much as may be'.[20]

It is against this background that we need to consider Pope's definition of 'wit' in *An Essay on Criticism*, in which he defends poetry against these attacks as subtly as he can. He does this by taking the word most frequently associated with poetry – namely wit – and working it over and over in a variety of different ways that stress the complexity of the creative process and, above all, the fusion of those faculties of judgment and imagination that Bacon, Hobbes and Locke had been trying to separate. In redefining 'wit', Pope is attempting to redefine and secure poetry itself. For Pope 'wit' is what E. N. Hooker calls 'the unique mode of the creative artist'.[21] It is the essence of poetry entailing the inspiration of genius, the mental agility of ingenuity, the fire of imagination and the control of judgment. It involves, in direct contrast to Eliot's notorious phrase, an association of sensibility.[22]

Imitation

One thing that should be clear from the foregoing discussion is that Augustan wit and Augustan poetry have nothing to do with originality in itself. The best poets should say things in a new way, but the idea that they can say things that have never been said before, that they can be totally original, is a post-Romantic one. For the Augustan poet there are only a few irrefutable human truths, and they were discovered long ago. The idea that anyone can come up with original truths is seen as an indication of human presumption and pride. All the living poet can do is reinterpret the validity of established truths as they apply to the modern world:

> *True Wit is Nature* to Advantage drest,
> What oft was *Thought*, but ne'er so well *Exprest.*   (297–8)

A person who claimed to be original was looked on with some suspicion. Indeed the noun, an 'original', was a term of abuse reserved for laughing at eccentric and singular persons like Captain Lismahago in Smollett's novel *Humphry Clinker*, 1771.

Instead of trying to be original Augustan poets assimilated their knowledge of the past into their awareness of the present. Dryden praises the young Anne Killigrew's poetry by saying that:

> Such noble vigour did her verse adorn
> That it seem'd borrow'd, where 'twas only born.
> (*To the Memory of . . . Mrs Anne Killigrew*, 75–6)

Although her poetry had the limitation of being original, it had such vigour that it seemed to have the excellence of imitating the Ancients.

Augustan poets, then, saw imitation as at least, if not more, important than originality. But this does not mean that they felt in duty bound simply to copy earlier writers. 'Those who say our thoughts are not our own because they resemble the Ancients', wrote Pope in the Preface to his *Works*, 1717, 'may as well say our faces are not our own, because they are like our fathers'. True imitation involves both borrowing and recasting. The youthful Pope, writing to his friend William Walsh in 1706, said:

> I wou'd beg your opinion too as to another point: it is how far the liberty of *Borrowing* may extend? I have defended it sometimes by

saying, that it seems not so much the Perfection of Sense to say things that have *never* been said before, as to express those *best* that have been said *oftenest*; and that Writers in the case of borrowing from others, are like Trees which of themselves wou'd produce only one sort of Fruit, but by being grafted upon others, may yield variety. A mutual commerce makes Poetry flourish; but then Poets like Merchants, should repay with something of their own what they take from others; not like Pyrates, make prize of all they meet. (I, 19–20)

Poets, like merchants, take from others and repay with something of their own. Like Swift's famous bee in *The Battle of the Books*, they visit 'all the flowers and blossoms of the field and garden', and 'by an universal range, with long search, much study, true judgment, and distinction of things, bring home honey and wax'.[23]

Pope visited the flowers and blossoms of the literary field widely, especially in his youth. He told Spence, shortly before he died, that in his great reading period (from about thirteen or fourteen to twenty-one), he went through 'all the best critics, almost all the English, French and Latin poets of any name, the minor poets, Homer and some of the greater Greek poets in the original, and Tasso and Ariosto in translations'(44). He not only read widely in classical and English literature, but he also wrote many imitations of earlier English poets including Chaucer, Spenser, Waller and Cowley, and many translations of earlier classical poets including Homer, Virgil, Ovid and Horace. This was an essential part of his apprenticeship as a poet for, as he put it to Spence, 'my first taking to imitating was not out of vanity, but humility. I saw how defective my own things were, and endeavoured to mend my manner by copying good strokes from others'.(46) Reuben Brower has revealed in his illuminating and subtle book, *Alexander Pope: The Poetry of Allusion*, just how present the classical poets were to Pope and his eighteenth-century readers. Brower shows how, for Dryden and Pope, allusion to the past 'especially in ironic contexts is a resource equivalent to symbolic metaphor and elaborate imagery in other poets'.[24] We find the same thing, in a more strained and self-conscious way, in the poetry of T. S. Eliot.

But imitation was more than just a frame of mind for the Augustan poet. It was also an accepted form, or literary 'kind', that grew out of the great interest and activity in verse translation that took place in the seventeenth century. During the first half of the seventeenth century most English verse translation tended toward a fairly close adherence to the original, for example Ben Jonson's translation of Horace's *Ars Poetica*, but during the second half of the century verse translators increasingly took more freedom with their models. It became more important for a translator to catch the spirit of a work than to give a word-for-word rendition.

The imitations written in post-Restoration England are a further extension of this concept of free translation. In the 'Advertisement' prefacing his version of Horace's *Ars Poetica* Oldham says that he thought of turning the work to an advantage which had not occurred to those who went before him in the translation (Ben Jonson and the Earl of Roscommon) by making Horace speak as if he were then living:

> I therefore resolved to alter the scene from Rome to London, and to make use of English names of men, places, and customs, where the parallel would decently permit, which I conceived would give a kind of new air to the poem, and render it more agreeable to the relish of the present age.[25]

Oldham was not the first to modernize classical poems in this way. Cowley, Sprat and Rochester had each done it before him and would each have agreed with his reasons for taking such liberties. As the imitation developed and became more popular, so it became completely independent of various levels of translation. It made different assumptions of its audience: where translation was primarily intended to help those readers who could not understand the original, imitation assumed that the reader would be sufficiently familiar with the original to appreciate the author's wit in adapting it. For this reason the Latin (and most imitations were of Roman poetry) was frequently printed on the facing page or at the foot of the poem, on the same page, while parallel passages were indicated by linking arabic numerals.

Imitation was a way for poets to give depth and authority to their writing. Poets did not simply rely on their own opinion, they called on acknowledged classical masters to support their case. They sought for a peculiarly appropriate classical equivalent to the modern subject they wanted to write about, or for a peculiarly appropriate modern equivalent to the classical poem they wanted to adapt, and then fitted their treatment to the overall organization of the classical poem. This relationship between the present and the past could be handled in a variety of ways. It could either be used to add emphasis to the condemnation of the present, as in Oldham's *Satire in Imitation of the Third of Juvenal*, where London was shown as not only bad but as bad as Juvenal's Rome, or it could be used ironically to undercut the present by creating a contrast with the past. The outstanding example of such a usage was Pope's *Imitation of Horace, Epistle II, i: To Augustus* where the compliments sincerely paid by Horace to the Emperor Augustus are ironically paid by Pope to King George Augustus Hanover, i.e. George II.

Satire

It seems appropriate to close this chapter by saying something about the chief mode of Augustan literature. When all is said and done, it is for the brilliance of its satire that the age in general, and Pope's poetry in particular, is most highly valued. But what did the Augustans understand by satire? What were its aims and intentions, and why was it so popular among Augustan writers? What kind of pressures impel someone to write satire in preference to other literary modes? These are some of the questions that a study of Augustan literature forces one to consider.

The word 'satire' as it is used today describes a mode of writing rather than a form. It describes a spirit of conception, or state of mind, that can operate through any number of different forms. Thus an epic poem, such as *The Dunciad*, or a prose account of imaginary travels, such as *Gulliver's Travels*, or an opera, such as *The Beggar's Opera*, are each referred to as satires because they share certain common qualities in terms of their overall conception.

At the most general level one can say that satire attacks human evil and stupidity by making fun of it from a standpoint that at least implies, if it does not state, a consistent moral position. There are three distinct elements of conception involved here – attack, laughter and morality – and a careful fusing of all three elements is necessary for successful satire. If the author concentrates on attack alone then the work of art tends towards mere invective; if the author concentrates on laughter alone, then the work moves into a region of the purely comic; and if the author concentrates on morality alone then the work moves towards the area of the homily. Clearly satire cannot be completely separated from other allied modes, especially comedy, and some of the greatest comic characters also have strong satiric dimensions. Falstaff's gluttony, cowardice and dishonesty, for example, are clearly satirized by Shakespeare, but since his superabundant jollity and massive zest for life so dwarf these vices we see him finally as a comic rather than satiric character.

I have suggested three main qualities that compose the satiric vision overall, but we can also point to certain particular structural elements that are common to most works of satire, whatever their form. Satire frequently involves, for instance, the imaginative creation of absurd, or even grotesque worlds, such as Swift's Yahoos in *Gulliver's Travels* or Pope's Cave of Spleen in *The Rape of the Lock*, that ridicule mankind by containing both exaggerations and real depictions of human pretensions and frailties. Satirists create at the same time as they destroy, and this paradox lies at the root of their power to excite our attention. There is a tendency among some readers to dwell on the destructiveness of satire and to see satire as a totally negative mode. It is, of course, a destructive mode, but the best satirists are never purely destructive. They protest against the viciousness and absurdity of the present world, both by creating grotesque transformations of it in a nightmare world and by suggesting alternative and better ways of proceeding. Their destructiveness goes along with equally important elements of creativity and constructiveness.

Satirists see through mankind's affectations, and set out to expose them to laughter and scorn. They do not do this out of meanness or envy but because they feel indignation at the wastage and corruption of human potential. They confront mankind with its own nakedness and with its own tenuous grasp on existence. They use their pens partly as swords with which to attack people and partly as scalpels with which to lay them open. Consider the defence put forward by Pope's irate satirist in his *Imitation of Horace, Satire II, i:*

> What? arm'd for *Virtue* when I point the Pen,
> Brand the bold Front of shameless, guilty Men,
> Dash the proud Gamester in his gilded Car,
> Bare the mean Heart that lurks beneath a Star;
> Can there be wanting to defend Her Cause,
> Lights of the Church, or Guardians of the Laws?
> Could pension'd Boileau lash in honest Strain
> Flatt'rers and Bigots ev'n in *Louis'* Reign?
> Could Laureate *Dryden* Pimp and Fry'r engage,
> Yet neither *Charles* nor *James* be in a Rage?
> And I not strip the Gilding off a Knave,
> Un-plac'd, un-pension'd, no Man's Heir, or Slave?

(105–16)

The satirist describes himself here in an aggressively militant way. He points, brands, dashes, bares, lashes and strips his enemy. The verbs draw comparisons between the satirist's profession and that of the public prosecutor: both see it as their duty to publish and punish, to strip bare and to whip.

Satirists force human beings to come face to face with the most brutal and least attractive parts of themselves. As a result we often find in satire scenes of crowded humanity portrayed at its most barbaric and uncivilized. The unthinking mob that surges through the stinking streets of London in *The Dunciad*, Book II, is related in this way to the wretched mass of humanity that accompanies Tom Idle on his way to execution at Tyburn in Hogarth's *Industry and Idleness*, Plate XI. The satirist forces us to watch not only a close clinical analysis of man's anatomy, but very often a dissection, or even a vivisection of it. 'Yesterday', says Swift's scientist persona in his most complex satire *A Tale of a Tub*,

113

I ordered the carcass of a beau to be stript in my presence; when we were all amazed to find so many unexpected faults under one suit of clothes. Then I laid open his brain, his heart, and his spleen, but I plainly perceived at every operation, that the further we proceeded we found the defects increase upon us in number and bulk.[26]

The satirist analyses man and his world with brutal and often horrifying frankness. At his most extreme he is not content with confronting man with his own nakedness, but lays open the flesh and exposes the festering innards.

Satirists protest against the state of the world as they find it, largely because they know there are other and better states. In looking for examples of better states satirists frequently look to the Golden Age of Mythology, or to the security of the past. Sometimes this becomes mere nostalgia for the good old days, but in Pope and Swift it is very much more than this. Both men share a deep-rooted belief in the stability of inherited order. Satirists nearly always find themselves in a minority position, for if their point was that of the majority they wouldn't feel the need to protest in the first place. Thus in the early part of the eighteenth century, when the Government was nearly always Whig, it is hardly surprising that most satire was written by opponents of the Whigs. Pope, Swift, Arbuthnot, Gay, Fielding and Thomson were each at various times and in various differing degrees of commitment, affiliated to either the Tory or Patriot opposition to Robert Walpole.

Satirists' traditional justification for their art is that they do it for the good of society. They hope to reform and correct corruption, and for this reason frequently take on roles as defenders of virtue or spokespersons for the public good. Whether or not they really believe in such a role is another question: it is sufficient for them that they have a conventional framework within which to carry out their attack. 'Ask you what Provocation I have had?' says Pope's satirist in the *Epilogue to the Satires, Dialogue II*:

> The strong Antipathy of Good to Bad.
> When Truth or Virtue an Affront endures,
> Th' Affront is mine, my Friend, and should be yours.

(198–200)

Above all else satirists need to be committed to the living world. They need to care about its decay, and if they do not, if they merely use their wit in a virtuoso way, then their satire is likely to be shortlived.

So far I have talked about satire as a mode in literature, but the word has not always been used in this all-embracing sense and it is helpful to consider briefly its origins as a particular form of poetry. The English word satire derives from the Latin word *satura* (meaning medley or mixture), which was the name Horace (65–8 B.C.) first gave to a genre of poetry he inherited from Ennius and Pacuvius. This genre, or form, was later taken up by Persius (A.D. 34–62) and Juvenal (A.D. 60–140) and imitated at the same time as it was further developed. Horace and Juvenal wrote poems in which they attacked particular vices and follies of their day. They were so effective that a word which was originally used to designate a particular literary form, with a definable rhetorical structure, has been extended to cover a whole mode of writing. That literary form does, however, have an independent and continuing tradition in English literature, usually referred to as formal verse satire. It is a form that reached its peak in England during the eighteenth century, particularly in the poetry of Pope, Swift and Dr Johnson.

Although Horace and Juvenal use the same form, *satura*, there are important differences in the way they use it. Where Horace's satirist sets out to persuade with witty and urbane ridicule, Juvenal's attempts to chastise with fierce and savage denunciation. Horace tries to laugh us into truth, while Juvenal sets out to provoke our indignation and horror. In the First Satire of his First Book Horace's satirist asks why one cannot tell the truth with laughter, as a teacher gives children sweets to persuade them to learn to read. Juvenal's in his first satire, tells us that it is indignation and anger that drives him to write satire. As a result of this difference of tone in the satires of Horace and Juvenal we have developed the habit of referring to milder, more gentle satire as Horatian, and of referring to harsh and savage satire as Juvenalian. The dominant influence on English verse satire from Skelton through Donne, Hall and Marston to the great satirists of the Restoration and Augustan periods has been that of Juvenal, and although it was Horace's poems that Pope chose to imitate so widely in the 1730s it makes a great deal of sense to say that in imitating Horace he has 'Juvenalized' him.

We can find useful hints about Pope's concept of satire and his reasons for writing it by consulting his *Correspondence*. He writes to Swift in March 1732 saying, 'I know nothing that moves strongly but Satire, and those who are ashamed of nothing else, are so of being ridiculous' (III, 276). He clearly feels that the satirist aims at an emotional as well as an intellectual response. Satire 'moves' the reader, and furthermore it moves him 'strongly'. Two years later, on 17 July 1734, Arbuthnot wrote to Pope urging him to 'continue that noble *Disdain* and *Abhorrence* of Vice which he seem'd naturally endued with', but begging him to show a certain regard for his own safety and to 'study more to reform than chastise' (III, 417). This distinction that Arbuthnot presses on Pope is similar to that we have already described between Horatian and Juvenalian satire.

Pope's reply to Arbuthnot's letter, written on 2 August 1734,

115

offers the clearest prose statement we have of his theory of satire. He thanks Arbuthnot for his comments about his disdain of vice and for the concern he expresses for his safety, but with regard to Arbuthnot's request that he study more to reform than chastise he argues that such a separation is impossible:

> But General Satire in Times of General Vice has no force, and is no Punishment: People have ceas'd to be ashamed of it when so many are joined with them; and tis only by hunting One or two from the Herd that any Examples can be made. If a man writ all his Life against the Collective Body of the Banditti, or against Lawyers, would it do the least Good, or lessen the Body? But if some are hung up, or pilloried, it may prevent others. And in my low Station, with no other Power than this, I hope to deter, if not to reform. (III, 423)

If the satirist merely tries to reform without using examples to enforce his reform, then his satire will have little effect. As Pope put it when he rewrote this letter for the publication of his *Correspondence* in 1737, 'to attack Vices in the abstract, without touching Persons, may be safe fighting indeed, but it is fighting with Shadows' (III, 419). Both the references to 'fighting', in this quotation, and to 'hunting', in the previous quotation, indicate that Pope sees the satirist's role in adversarial and militant terms.

It is this concept of the satirist's role that emerges most strongly from his poetry. Sometimes he appears as a hunter, as in the *Epilogue to the Satires: Dialogue II* where knaves are seen as 'game' (27) to be 'run down' (29) and where the satirist has to 'beat about' to find an honest man:

> To find an honest man, I beat about,
> And love him, court him, praise him, in or out. (102–3)

The broken movement of the second line here acts out the image of the hunter thrashing about in the undergrowth to raise the game. At other times the satirist is seen as a bird of prey hovering over the world ready to drop on its victim. Thus in the same poem the satirist 'sowzes' (15) and 'stoops' (110) on mankind. Both words are technical terms taken from falconry, where they describe the action of the bird swooping down on its prey. The image is also found in *An Epistle to Dr Arbuthnot* when the speaker tells us,

> That not in Fancy's Maze he wander'd long
> But stoop'd to Truth, and moraliz'd his song. (340–1)

The concept of the satirist that informs Pope's satirical poetry is one of a militant defender of the public good, determined to continue 'that noble *Disdain* and *Abhorrence* of Vice' that Arbuthnot urged on him. Contrary to what has frequently been said about the wounded and besieged poet who lashes out at his enemies in desperate retaliation, Pope usually directs his wrath from a position of personal detachment. The satirist's attack is not primarily the result of personal hurt or grievance, nor is it primarily a form of self-defence: it springs rather from a profound disgust at his '*Country's* Ruin' and from a correspondingly strong sense of public spiritedness concerning the '*Public* Weal'.

Notes

1. Thomas De Quincey, Review of 'Schlosser's Literary History of the Eighteenth Century', *Tait's Edinburgh Magazine* (Sep.–Oct. 1847), re-printed in *Essays, Sceptical and Anti-Sceptical* (James Hogg and Sons, Edinburgh, 1858), p. 64.
2. Samuel Johnson, 'Pope', in *Lives of the English Poets* (1779–81); ed. G. B. Hill, 3 vols (Clarendon Press, Oxford 1905), Vol. III, pp. 228–9.
3. Julius Caesar Scaliger, *Poetics* (1561), select translations by F. M. Padelford (New York, 1905). The *Poetics* of J. C. Scaliger (1484–1558) appeared posthumously in 1561 and, as James Osborn says, in his edition of Spence's *Anecdotes*, 'had a profound influence on the formation of neo-classical critical taste'. Pope refers to it in the *Narrative of Dr Norris* (1713) and in the Preface to the *Iliad* (1715).
4. George Puttenham, *The Arte of English Poesie* (1589), ed. G. D. Willcock and A. Walker (Cambridge University Press, Cambridge, 1936), p. 25.

   'As the matter of Poesie is diverse,' says Puttenham, 'so was the form of their [the Ancients] poems and manner of writing, for all of them wrote not in one sort, even as all of them wrote not upon one matter. Neither was every poet alike cunning in all as in some one *kind* of Poesie, nor uttered with like felicity. But wherein anyone most excelled, thereof he took a surname, as to be called a Poet *Heroic, Lyric, Elegiac, Epigramatic* or otherwise.'
5. See, for example, Joseph Warton, *An Essay on the Genius and Writings of Pope* (1756; Second edition corrected, London 1762) Vol. II, p. 480.

   'Where, then, according to the question proposed at the beginning of this essay, shall we with justice be authorized to place our admired Pope? Not, assuredly, in the same rank with Spenser, Shakespeare and Milton, however justly we may applaud the *Eloisa* and *Rape of the Lock*; but, considering the correctness, elegance and utility of his works, the weight of sentiment, and the knowledge of man they contain, we may venture to assign him a place next to Milton and just above Dryden.'
6. For further development of this idea see Ian Jack, *Augustan Satire* (Clarendon Press, Oxford, 1952).
7. Ibid. The subtitle of this book is 'Intention and Idiom in English Poetry, 1660–1750'.
8. William Wordsworth, Preface, *Lyrical Ballads*, 2 vols (Longman, London, 1800), pp. xviii–xix.

9. James Boswell, 'The Journal of a Tour to the Hebrides', 21 August 1773, in *Boswell's Life of Johnson*, ed. G. B. Hill, 6 vols (Clarendon Press, Oxford, 1934–50, Vol. V, p. 83.

10. Samuel Johnson, 'Preface to Shakespeare' (1765), *The Yale Edition of the Works of Samuel Johnson*, Vol. VII, *Johnson on Shakespeare*, ed. Arthur Sherbo (Yale University Press, New Haven, 1968), p. 76.
    'It is false, that any representation is taken for reality; that any dramatic fable in its materiality was ever credible, or, for a single moment, was ever credited.'

11. Thomas Babington, Lord Macaulay, Review of Croker's edition of 'Boswell's Life of Johnson' for *The Edinburgh Review*, Sep. 1831, reprinted in *The Complete Works* (Longmans Green & Co, London, 1898), Vol. VIII, p. 102.

12. John Dryden, 'A Defence of an Essay of Dramatique Poesie' (1667), *The Works of John Dryden* (University of California Press, Los Angeles, Vol. IX, 1966), pp. 13–14.

13. William Empson, *The Structure of Complex Words* (Chatto and Windus, London, 1951), p. 87.

14. Quintilian, *Institutio Oratoria* (Book III, iii, 5), translated by H. E. Butler, Loeb edition, 4 vols (Heinemann, London, 1921), Vol. I, p. 385.

15. La Rochefoucauld, *Moral Maxims and Reflections*, in 4 Parts (London, 1706), Moral Reflection 98, p. 22.

16. Francis Bacon, *The Advancement of Learning* (1605), ed. W. A. Armstrong (Athlone Press, London, 1975).

17. Thomas Sprat, *History of the Royal Society* (1667), ed. Jackson I. Cope and Harold Whitmore Jones (Washington University Studies, Saint Louis, Missouri, 1958).

18. Thomas Hobbes, *Leviathan* (1651), ed. Herbert W. Schneider (Bobbs-Merrill, New York, 1958), Part I, chapter 2, p. 27.

19. John Locke, 'Of Discerning, and other Operations of the Mind', *An Essay Concerning Human Understanding*, in 4 Books (London, 1690), Book II, chapter XI, p. 68.

20. John Locke, *Some Thoughts Concerning Education* (London, 1693), p. 207.

21. E. N. Hooker, 'Pope on Wit: The Essay on Criticism', *The Hudson Review*, Vol. 2 (1950), pp. 84–100. Reprinted in *Eighteenth-Century English Literature*, ed. J. L. Clifford (Oxford University Press, Oxford, 1959), pp. 42–61.

22. T. S. Eliot, 'The Metaphysical Poets' (1921), *Selected Prose*, ed. John Hayward (Penguin Books, Harmondsworth, 1953), p. 117.

23. Jonathan Swift, 'The Battle of the Books' (1704), *A Tale of a Tub, With Other Early Works*, ed. Herbert Davis (Basil Blackwell, Oxford, 1939), pp. 149–50.

24. Reuben Brower, *Alexander Pope: The Poetry of Allusion* (Clarendon Press, Oxford, 1959), p. viii.

25. John Oldham, *Poems and Translations* (London, 1684). The pages of the 'Advertisement' are not numbered.

26. Swift op. cit., pp. 109–10.

5   Pope's beliefs

Papist or Protestant, or both between,
Like good *Erasmus* in an honest Mean,
In Moderation placing all my Glory,
While Tories call me Whig, and Whigs a Tory.
(*Imitation of Horace, Satire II, i*, 65 8)

The separation of Pope's beliefs into the philosophical, religious and
political divisions propounded in this chapter is clearly an oversimpli-
cation of complex material. Philosophical ideas can never be set
apart from religious and political views for the fundamental reason
that any enquiry into the meaning of the universe must also be an
enquiry into the existence of God and the behaviour of mankind.
Pope's philosophical views are, therefore, both the result of and the
basis for his religious beliefs and political commitments. The divisions
used here for the sake of convenience are put forward in full
awareness of the false separation frequently involved.

   For most of his life Pope strove to avoid too contentious a position
with regard to any one of these areas of thought. In his religion he
was a practising member of the Catholic Church. At the same time
he was only too aware of the precariousness of his position as a
practising Catholic and took care not to make any too obvious
demonstration of his faith. In *An Essay on Man* we find him treading
a cautious path between respectable defence of established Christian
orthodoxy and open interest in new interpretations of it.

   In his politics he was by temperament and instinct a conservative,
but for most of his life took as much care not to commit himself
solely to the Tory party as he took not to draw special attention to
his Catholicism. As the lines from the *Imitation of Horace, Satire II, i*,
quoted at the head of this page, indicate, he cultivated the position
of being a moderate: 'In Moderation placing all my Glory'. Moderation is a useful screen to hide behind, especially in times of political
tension, and Pope's actual beliefs may have been rather stronger
than the word seems to imply. It was only during his later years,
when his social position was assured and his political disillusion
intense, that he openly espoused the joint efforts of the Tories and
the anti-Walpole Patriot Opposition.

   In his philosophical beliefs he was a clear and eclectic thinker, but
avoided extreme or original positions. As he says in the introductory
note to *An Essay on Man*, 'If I could flatter myself that this Essay has
any merit, it is in steering betwixt the extremes of doctrines seemingly

opposite. . . .' *An Essay on Man* is the clearest and most sustained expression Pope made of his philosophical and ethical beliefs. It is a concise and forceful introduction to ideas widely prevalent in early eighteenth-century England, and this chapter will be as particularly concerned with discussing this poem as the last chapter was with *An Essay on Criticism.*

Philosophy

Pope was not a professionally trained philosopher. He was widely read in philosophy, but he was not formally educated in the logical study of either science, ethics or metaphysics. He had an intellectual interest in the ordering of the universe and a profound concern for the behaviour of man and his pursuit of happiness,[1] but this interest and concern were those of the creative poet rather than the professional philosopher. Readers will be disappointed if they turn to *An Essay on Man* looking for a regular system of philosophical thought.

This is not to say that the poem is valueless as philosophy, but that its primary value is poetic rather than philosophical and that its philosophical content is subservient to its artistic purpose. *An Essay on Man* is a mélange of philosophical ideas, some traditional, some current, that show Pope's powers as an eclectic more than as a speculative thinker.[2] The only idea in the poem that might be called original is that of the *ruling passion*, and even that has distinct origins in the medieval belief concerning the shaping power of the bodily humours. Out of this mixture of ideas Pope precipitates a poetic realization of man and the universe he inhabits that is consistent in itself, powerfully felt and keenly visualized. It is a poem of changing moods in which the speaker steers 'from grave to gay' and 'from lively to severe' (IV, 380). Sometimes the tone is sombre and reasoning, at other times it is witty and satiric, but most of the time it is exhortatory and didactic. It is a poem that sets out to 'vindicate the ways of God to man' (I, 16), and though one would not want to call it a religious poem the voice of the Christian advocate is never very far away.

Pope believes in an ordered universe. 'ORDER is Heav'n's first law', he tells us in the fourth epistle (49). It is not an easy order to explain, however, for though the Universal Cause 'acts to one end', it 'acts by various laws' (III, 2). The result is that the scene of man is 'A mighty maze! but not without a plan' (I, 6). The universe has a 'frame', 'bearing' and 'ties' (I, 29) that give it a coherent structure similar to that of a building, but man is not able to see the structure of this building as clearly as he might like because of obstacles he himself has erected. Pope's poem is an attempt, an *essai*, to describe this structure and define the established order as he sees it.

120

Pope inherited the popular Medieval and Renaissance idea, familiar in their day to both Chaucer and Shakespeare, of the Great Chain of Being.[3] This was a metaphysical doctrine – based on *a priori* assumptions about God – that explained the existence, plenitude and unity of creation. It did this in accordance with deductive argument, concluding that the world was the best that God could have created, where nothing apart from him could be perfect. The important point for our purpose is that Pope adopted only certain parts of this belief. What he describes in *An Essay on Man* is the ladder of created nature, or *scala naturae*, which is one element in the Great Chain that can nevertheless be separated from it and argued on *a posteriori* grounds. The *scala naturae* describes the world of observable reality, 'Creation's ample range', from the 'green myriads in the peopled grass' to 'Man's imperial race' (I, 207–10). But it does not go any higher, as the Chain of Being does, and it is this limitation that Pope accepts when he says, near the beginning of the poem:

> Say first, of God above, or Man below,
> What can we reason, but from what we know?
> Of Man what see we, but his station here,
> From which to reason, or to which refer?
> Thro' worlds unnumber'd tho' the God be known,
> 'Tis ours to trace him only in our own.
>
> (I, 17–22)

Both Pope's present poem and his habits of mind generally are rootedly empirical. One need only recall the gloomy clerk in *The Dunciad*, Book IV, who 'nobly takes the high Priori Road' and then loses himself in a mist, to indicate Pope's consistent distrust of deductive habits of thought.

Pope certainly refers to the Great Chain of Being in *An Essay on Man*, but when he does so he is using the term to refer to empirically observed Nature. The chain and the ladder or scale become interchangeable terms for him:

> On superior pow'rs
> Were we to press, inferior might on ours:
> Or in the full creation leave a void,
> Where, one step broken, the great scale's destroy'd:
> From Nature's chain whatever link you strike,
> Tenth or ten thousandth, breaks the chain alike.
>
> (I, 241–6)

If we are to be asked to entertain, as in that closing couplet, the possibility of a breakable chain, then Pope must stand some way outside the strict Great Chain philosophy, as it is called, and be

121

using the terms *chain* and *scale* in his own fashion as interchangeable concepts. However, the underlying philosophy cannot be understood as so readily interchanged as this may sound. In the last analysis Pope remains critical of deductive methods of thought, preferring instead the empirical methods common in the eighteenth century that depend upon personal observation.

The order that Pope espouses in *An Essay on Man* is a paradoxical one based on integrated opposites. It is 'A Wild where weeds and flow'rs promiscuous shoot' (I, 7) and where 'ALL subsists by elemental strife' (I, 169). It is an order and harmony that Pope describes most powerfully in the opening lines of *Windsor-Forest* where,

> . . . Earth and Water seem to strive again,
> Not *Chaos*-like together crush'd and bruis'd,
> But as the World, harmoniously confus'd:
> Where Order in Variety we see,
> And where, tho' all things differ, all agree.   (12–16)

This harmony of opposites, or *concordia discors* (Horace, *Epistle*, I, xii, 19), comprehends both strife and antagonism, so that 'All Discord, [is but] Harmony, not understood' (*Essay on Man*, I, 291), and 'jarring int'rests of themselves create / Th'according music of a well-mixed State' (III, 293–4). As Pope says at the opening of the third epistle: '"The Universal Cause / Acts to one end, but acts by various laws"' (III, 1–2).

These ideas concerning the organization of the universe at large form a backdrop in the poem for a unifying concept of man that develops in complexity. The presumptuous creature, or 'vile worm' as Pope calls him, who dominates the first two epistles becomes through a proper regard for virtue and love of God the regenerate subject of Epistles III and IV. Maynard Mack, in his introduction to the Twickenham edition of *An Essay on Man* describes this fundamental pattern of development within the poem and its close relationship to Milton's great theme in *Paradise Lost* (see *Essay on Man*, I, 16) as follows: 'Beginning with a reminder of a paradise man has lost, the poem ends with a paradise he can regain'.[4]

Behind every philosophical idea in the first two epistles of *An Essay on Man* there lies the voice of the poet wittily, ironically and scornfully cutting man down to size. Two particular aspects of man come in for repeated attack, his pride and his dulness. The two qualities are inseparable, making him a being both 'darkly wise, and rudely great' (II, 4). They are given metaphorical force through the contrasted but connected motions of ascension and descension that run through both epistles. Thus Pope ironically describes man sightlessly soaring (I, 12), or upward soaring (I, 173), or soaring with Plato (II, 23) in his pride, at the same time as he contemptuously depicts him blindly creeping (I, 12) or dropping into himself to be a fool (II, 30) in his ignorance.

It is the contrast between our pride in our own potential and our actual dulness that makes us such as obvious target for ridicule. In Pope's view we are so presumptuous that we need to be forcibly reminded of our own weakness, littleness and blindness (I, 36). We may seem principal on earth, but in fact we are only a minute part of the greater whole. Our lives fill merely a moment in eternity and a point in infinity (I, 72), but we are so proud that we aspire to the power of angels, just as Satan aspired to the power of God:

> In Pride, in reas'ning Pride, our error lies;
> All quit their sphere, and rush into the skies.
> Pride still is aiming at the blest abodes,
> Men would be Angels, Angels would be Gods.
>
> (I, 123–6)

Man thinks he is the 'Great Lord of all things' and the 'Sole judge of Truth', but in fact he is a 'prey to all' and is hurled in 'endless Error' (II, 16–17). Even the wisest of men, Newton, is merely an ape when compared to the angels (II, 31–4). Again and again in these two epistles Pope brings us face to face with our feeble significance within the overall pattern of the universe.

Pope continually confronts readers with the brevity of human life and the imminence of death. As early as the third line of the poem he says that 'life can little more supply / Than just to look about us and to die'. Further on in the first epistle death is described as 'the great teacher' (I, 92), and we are reminded of the fact that we are helplessly subject to plagues, earthquakes and tempests (I, 142–4). At the beginning of the second epistle man is described as 'born but to die', as if this were the sole reason for life (II, 10). Next we are told that man, at the very moment of his birth, 'receives the lurking principle of death' (II, 134). The theme is continued in the third epistle where the brevity and insignificance of human life is compared to the transience and fragility of a bubble:

> All forms that perish other forms supply,
> (By turns we catch the vital breath, and die)
> Like bubbles on the sea of Matter born,
> They rise, they break, and to that sea return.
>
> (III, 17–20)

Seen from the almost godlike perspective and detachment that the speaker assumes for himself, man's existence is purely momentary.

What Pope urges in the first two epistles is a Christian humility before these facts. Pope's advice is the same as that of Raphael to Adam in *Paradise Lost*, Book VIII:

> Solicit not thy thoughts with matters hid,
> Leave them to God above, him serve and fear;
> Of other Creatures, as him pleases best,
> Wherever plac't, let him dispose: joy thou
> In what he gives to thee, this Paradise
> And thy fair *Eve*: Heav'n is for thee too high
> To know what passes there; be lowly wise:
> Think only what concerns thee and thy being;
> Dream not of other Worlds, what Creatures there
> Live, in what state, condition or degree,
> Contented that thus far hath been reveal'd
> Not of Earth only but of highest Heav'n.   (167–78)

According to Pope, too, we must be lowly wise, must recognize our limitations, know our 'own point' (I, 283), 'hope humbly' (I, 91), and learn to 'welcome Death' (II, 260). 'To reason right', he says, 'is to submit' (I, 164). This central directive comes again at the end of the first epistle:

> Submit – In this, or any other sphere,
> Secure to be as blest as thou canst bear.   (I, 285–6)

'I believe', Pope wrote to Caryll on 3 September 1718, 'that there is not in the whole course of the Scripture any precept so often and so strongly inculcated, as the trust and eternal dependence we ought to repose in that Supreme Being who is our constant preserver and benefactor' (I, 499). Mankind must submit to God's disposing power, and so far as Pope is concerned this means accepting traditional Christian explanations of the way the world is ordered.

Pope selects two main principles in human nature for special attention. These are Self-Love, which he sees as the 'urging' principle, and Reason, which he calls the 'restraining' principle. Thus the idea of a tension between opposites producing overall harmony (*concordia discors*), which we saw operating in the macrocosm, or world at large, is also seen operating in the microcosm of man. Shifting his imagery from that of horse-riding to that of watch-making, Pope calls self-love 'the spring of motion' and reason the 'comparing balance' (II, 59–60). Both qualities are necessary if mankind is to act to the best purpose, but self-love is naturally stronger, whereas reason must be developed through 'attention, habit, and experience' until it is capable of restraining self-love.

Pope then breaks self-love down into its different modes, or passions, which he groups into sets of opposites, such as love and hate, hope and fear, joy and grief, whose 'well accorded strife / Gives all the strength and colour of our life' (II, 121–2). It is at this point in the poem that Pope develops his theory of the ruling passion. This idea, developed further in the *Epistle to Cobham*, is that God gives each of us one particular passion which will operate as a 'strong direction', or focal point, that will enable us to cope with the complexity of our other passions. Whether we let this ruling passion lead us on to vice or virtue is entirely up to us and the way we use our restraining reason. As a result there are both vicious and virtuous people, and this becomes yet another part of the variety that goes to make the overall order.

Reason is the faculty that separates us from the animals, but this does not mean that we are superior to the animals. In a strict Great Chain of Being philosophy this would be so, but the *scala naturae* doctrine that Pope develops is descriptive rather than hierarchical. It is quite clear in *An Essay on Man* that reason has severe limitations. The point is worth insisting on, for many readers still come to Pope with unfavourable preconceptions of him as the great poet of 'an age of prose and reason'.[5] But for Pope reason is not as good a guide in man as instinct is in animals. Reason is 'cool at best', and 'cares not for service, or but serves when prest', whereas 'honest instinct', to continue the military metaphor, 'comes a volunteer' (III, 85–8). Where 'heavier reason' labours at happiness in vain, instinct gains it by 'quick Nature'; and where reason is merely a direction imposed by mankind, instinct is the direct power of God operating in animals. Reason, then, must learn from instinct. The idea is parallel to that expressed in *An Essay on Criticism* where art, which is made by man, must copy nature, which is made by God.

The fourth epistle deals with the possibility of human happiness. Pope takes the traditional Christian view that happiness has nothing to do with external goods or material wealth. For him the key to human happiness involves conforming to God's order, and the best way to do this is to fulfil the particular gifts that God has given one: 'Act well your part, there all the honour lies' (IV, 194). One acts one's part well when one leads a virtuous life – 'Virtue alone is happiness below' (IV, 310) – and one leads a virtuous life when one pursues humility, honesty, justice, truth, public-spiritedness and benevolence. These values, which emerge so strongly from the fourth epistle, form an important basis for an appreciation of Pope's later satires, for they are the positive criteria that underlie and inform his attacks on the corruptions of Hanoverian England.

The effect of self-love on the virtuous mind is like that of a pebble thrown into a peaceful lake. Just as the pebble creates perfect circles which grow in size and perfection until they finally merge into the lake itself, so self-love will stir the virtuous mind first into love for its friends, parents and neighbours, next for its country and finally for the whole human race:

> Self-love but serves the virtuous mind to wake,
> As the small pebble stirs the peaceful lake;
> The centre mov'd, a circle strait succeeds,
> Another still, and still another spreads,
> Friend, parent, neighbour, first it will embrace,
> His country next, and next all human race,
> Wide and more wide, th'o'erflowings of the mind
> Take ev'ry creature in, of ev'ry kind;
> Earth smiles around, with boundless bounty blest,
> And Heav'n beholds its image in his breast.
>
> (IV, 363–372)

Thus the poem that began with images of man's intellectual pride and physical mortality closes with images of man's spiritual regeneration and earth's boundless bounty. The vile worm becomes an image of Heaven, and the threat of damnation that dominated the first two epistles gives way to the possibility of redemption in the last two.

Religion

It would be absurd to call Pope a religious poet in the sense that one calls George Herbert or Gerard Manley Hopkins a religious poet. Religion is not the main concern or subject matter of his poetry, but his Christian belief is always assumed and in indirect ways shapes much of the structure of his poetry.

Pope inherited his faith from devoutly Catholic parents and a series of family priests who were appointed to educate him. 'The religion in which he lived and died', says Dr Johnson, 'was that of the Church of Rome to which in his correspondence with Racine [the poet's son] he professes himself a sincere adherent.'[6] As Johnson's use of the word 'professes' indicates here, he suggests that Pope was not always a totally devout Catholic, and it is certainly true that he was never as fervent a supporter of the Catholic Church as his parents. Indeed he clearly gave his friends some hope that they might persuade him to join the Anglican Church. When his father died suddenly on 23 October 1717, Bishop Atterbury wrote to Pope offering his condolences and suggesting that now was the time for him to make this change of allegiance. Pope's reply is worth quoting at length because it is one of the fullest statements we have of his religious and political position:

> Whether the change would be to my spiritual advantage, God only knows: this I know, that I mean as well in the religion I now profess, as I can possibly ever do in another. Can a man who thinks so, justify a change, even if he thought both equally good?

To such an one, the part of *joyning* with any one body of Christians might perhaps be easy, but I think it would not be so to *renounce* the other. . . . I'll tell you my politick and religious sentiments in a few words. In my politicks, I think no further than how to preserve the peace of my life, in any government under which I live; nor in my religion, than to preserve the peace of my conscience in any Church with which I communicate. I hope all churches and all governments are so far of God, as they are rightly understood, and rightly administered: and where they are, or may be wrong, I leave it to God alone to mend or reform them; which whenever he does, it must be by greater instruments than I am. (I, 453–4)

It would be misleading to take this statement as a lasting testament of his religious and political beliefs – his political views, especially, became much more definite as he grew older – but it does help to indicate his distinctly undogmatic feelings about Catholicism. His attitude to the Church he belongs to is similar to his attitude to the universe in *An Essay on Man*: it is not for man to presume to scan God's affairs. If there seems to be a certain lack of commitment to the Roman Catholic Church in this letter, there is certainly a firm avowal of Christian faith and not the slightest doubt about his belief in God.

Pope's type of Catholicism has been described as 'Erasmian'.[7] Erasmus (1466–1536), the great Renaissance theologian and scholar who tried to bring the Catholic and Lutheran churches together at the time of the Reformation by establishing a middle attitude to the religious conflicts of his day, was a lifelong hero for Pope. Like 'good Erasmus in an honest mean' (*Imitation of Horace, Satire II,i*, 66), Pope too believed in toleration and a middle way.

A Catholic priest himself, Erasmus wanted to see the Church cleansed of the ignorant hostility to classical learning of the monks and priests of the early sixteenth century, but he opposed the Reformation, introduced by Luther, which he saw as splitting rather than healing the Church. For this reason, as Pope says in *An Essay on Criticism*, he was both celebrated and reviled in his own day:

> At length, *Erasmus*, that *great, injur'd* Name,
> (The *Glory* of the Priesthood, and the *Shame*!)
> *Stemm'd* the *wild Torrent* of a *barb'rous Age*,
> And drove the *Holy Vandals* off the Stage. (693–6)

He was 'the Glory' of the priesthood because he was a priest who tried to save it from itself; its 'Shame' because of the way the Church treated him.

127

Erasmus was an apostle of common sense and an enemy of religious fanaticism. He was also a great ironic satirist whose *The Praise of Folly*, 1509, was one of the classic works of the Renaissance. For Pope, then, he became both a religious and literary role model of the highest order. When Pope's Catholic friend John Caryll wrote to him in June 1711 reporting the criticism of some zealous readers concerning a comparison he had made between wit and faith in *An Essay on Criticism*, he replied saying:

> If the heat of these disputants who I'm afraid, being bred up to wrangle in the schools, cannot get rid of the humour all their lives, should proceed so far as to personal reflections upon me, I do assure you notwithstanding, I will do or say nothing, however provoked . . . that is unbecoming the character of a true Catholic. I will set before me that excellent example of that great man and great saint, Erasmus, who in the midst of calumny proceeded with all the calmness of innocence, the unrevenging spirit of primitive Christianity!　　　　　　　　　　　　　　　　　(I, 118)

What Pope particularly admires about Erasmus here is his patience before the heat of disputants and wranglers. As a Catholic living in a country that barely tolerated Catholicism, and that had instituted harsh laws against it, Pope suffered throughout his life from zealous, bigoted and uninformed attacks, in the face of which he consciously strove, to keep to the model of a calm, sensible, 'honest mean' offered by 'that great man and great saint', Erasmus.

Pope lived at a time of important scientific discoveries concerning the universe. The development of the microscope had led to greatly increased knowledge of natural history in the latter part of the seventeenth century, and, most important of all, Newton had explained the gravitational basis of the universe in his *Principia Mathematica*, published in 1687, a year before Pope was born. These discoveries, unlike those of the nineteenth century, were taken as giving mathematical corroboration to God's majestic creation. What had before been a matter of faith was now regarded as a matter of scientific proof. Pope's epitaph intended for Sir Isaac Newton in Westminster Abbey sums up this attitude:

> Nature, and Nature's Laws lay hid in Night.
> God said, *Let Newton be*! and All was Light.

Pope's concept of a God who is both immanent and transcendent (*Essay on Man*, I, 267–80) is very close to Newton's concept in the *Opticks*, 1704, of a divine spirit who is omnipresent at the same time as he is a uniform Being.

Pope's poetry is rarely either explicitly Catholic, or even explicitly

Christian. His *Messiah*, 1712, is something of an exception, although even here one senses that the religious content is subservient to the carefully wrought display of grandeur. Nevertheless, his religious beliefs are deeply rooted in the general pattern of his thought and affect the structure and imagery of many of his poems. His delightful account of Belinda's toilet at the end of *The Rape of the Lock*, Canto I, for example, takes on a greater cogency when one sees it as a vain inversion of the Catholic mass:

> A heav'nly Image in the Glass appears,
> To that she bends to that her Eyes she rears;
> Th' inferior Priestess, at her Altar's side,
> Trembling, begins the sacred Rites of Pride.   (I, 125–8)

Similarly, the satiric description of Timon's banquet in the *Epistle to Burlington* gains additional force when one sees it as an Epicurean parody of the communion service:

> A solemn Sacrifice, perform'd in state,
> You drink by measure, and to minutes eat . . .
> Between each Act the trembling salvers ring,
> From soup to sweet-wine, and God bless the King.   (157–62)

And, to take one more example of implicit structural influence, Earl Wasserman has shown that the portrait of the Man of Ross in the *Epistle to Bathurst* is an '*imitatio Christi*', and that 'beneath the surface of the language there is a current of references to Christ's life and miracles'.[8]

Allusion to scripture is another way in which Pope's religious beliefs become a subsumed part of his poetry. Sometimes he uses such allusion to give emphasis to a point he is making, as in the following couplet from the *Epistle to Bathurst*:

> Riches like insects, when conceal'd they lie,
> Wait but for wings, and in their season, fly.   (171–2)

This is a rewriting of Proverbs 23:5 – 'Wilt thou set thy eyes upon that which is not? for *riches* certainly make themselves wings; they fly away as an eagle toward heaven'. At other times Pope uses allusion to the Bible for ironic purposes in order to create a deliberate contrast between a corrupt present and an idealized past. Nowhere does he do this to more effect than in the finale to *The Dunciad*, where the catastrophe of the 'Universal Darkness' that 'buries All' is heightened through the ironic allusion to the universal light that began all in Genesis. It is through the use of allusive and associative religious imagery, rather than through formally structured divine poems, that Pope's religion makes itself felt in his poetry.

Politics

Pope is perhaps better known than any other poet in our literature for his close involvement with politics, yet until the last ten years or so of his life he went out of his way to cultivate a publicly neutral position towards political parties. 'The general division of the *British* Nation is into Whigs and Tories', wrote Addison in *The Freeholder* of 25 June 1716, 'there being very few, if any, who stand Neuters in the Dispute, without ranging themselves under one of these denominations'. At the time of Addison's writing Pope was one of these few, and in order to understand both this early neutrality and his later commitment we need to take a brief look at the political scene in England during the early part of the eighteenth century.

The party warfare that so dominated early eighteenth-century English politics had its roots in the Exclusion Bill struggle of 1679–80 over whether the Duke of York, the future James II, should be allowed to succeed to the English throne as a Catholic. The term 'Tory' was used to describe those who supported the royal prerogative with regard to the succession, while the term 'Whig' was applied to those who supported the idea of a constitutional monarchy with Government by parliament. The question of succession was crucial in the development of the political parties and came to a head again in the Glorious Revolution of 1688 and the Hanoverian succession of 1714. Broadly speaking the Tories can be identified with the High Church and the landed gentry, while the Whigs can be identified with the Low Church and the commercial interest. The trouble with such a simplification, of course, is that the actual patterns of allegiance were very much more complex than this suggests. There were some Tories, for example, who supported the revolutionary settlement of 1688, and there were some Whigs who later betrayed its principles.

An additional difference between the two parties during the reign of Queen Anne was that the Whigs supported the war with France while the Tories increasingly looked for an end to it. At first Marlborough's victories were more than enough to keep the Whigs in power, but as war-weariness increased so did the pressure for peace, and in 1710 the Whigs were replaced in office by the Tory Ministry of Robert Harley. Harley's administration lasted for four years until the death of Queen Anne in 1714. The resulting establishment of the Hanoverian succession led to the total collapse of the Tory party and the impeachment of its leaders. Harley himself was committed to the Tower, where he remained for two years, while Bolingbroke fled to France where he joined the Jacobite cause. With the accession of George I there began a period of Whig hegemony in British politics that was to last for almost fifty years.

The Jacobite cause, (so named from 'Jacobus' the Latin for James) sought to have James II, or his son James Frances Edward Stuart (1688–1766), the 'Old Pretender', or *his* son, Charles Edward Stuart (1720–88), the 'Young Pretender', restored to the throne of England from which James II had 'abdicated' in 1688. The Jacobite Court in exile was a constant threat to political stability in England after the 'Glorious Revolution', though it was a threat that it also paid the Government of the day to publicize and exaggerate as a way of strengthening its own support. Walpole, in particular, played this card most deftly during the 1720s and 1730s, both to smear Tories as crypto-Jacobites dabbling in treason and to increase the allowances Parliament voted for his secret service.[9]

It is a debatable point amongst modern Pope scholars as to precisely what Pope's own position was with regard to the Jacobite cause.[10] It is certainly true that many of his closest friends were committed and confirmed Jacobites, most notably Bolingbroke, who became the Old Pretender's Secretary of State during the 1715 uprising, and Francis Atterbury, the Anglican Bishop of Rochester, who was arrested in 1722 for his part in a Jacobite conspiracy and tried, through political rather than legal procedures, before his peers in the House of Lords. Pope gave evidence on Atterbury's behalf at the trial, and always protested that he believed Atterbury to be innocent, although the latter's involvement in Jacobite machinations was well established by Walpole and his spies. In addition Lords Bathurst, Buckingham, Cobham, Lansdown, Oxford, and Peterborough, who were all good friends of Pope, were active Jacobites.

Windsor-Forest, published to celebrate the Treaty of Utrecht in 1713, and dedicated to Lord Lansdowne, is the poem of Pope's that comes closest to expressing Jacobite sympathies. Not only does it contain a veiled attack on William III as a tyrant, but it also contains the celebrated couplet:

> Rich Industry sits smiling on the Plains,
> And Peace and Plenty tell, a STUART reigns.   (41–2)

The capitals are Pope's. Although ostensibly a compliment to Queen Anne, this has undeniable Jacobite implications, since the only way a Stuart could continue to reign on Anne's death would be for the Old Pretender to return to the throne as James III.

Finally, the question of whether or not Pope was a Jacobite partly revolves around what precisely is meant by the word. If we use it in a general sense to refer to someone who was strongly pro-Stuart then Pope had clear Jacobite inclinations; but if we use it in a more exact sense to refer to someone who supported the restoration of the Stuart monarchy to the point of armed invasion, then there is no evidence whatsoever that Pope was Jacobite. My own view is that as a professed Catholic Pope may have secretly hoped for the restoration of a monarchy that would have repealed the oppressive laws against Roman Catholics, but as an Erasmian Catholic, believing in toleration and the middle way, he did not want to see, nor did he support, any sudden constitutional change, let alone armed insurrection and rebellion. In this he would have shared the views of the bulk of English Catholics of his day who were, on the whole, anti-Jacobite.[11]

Howard Erskine-Hill's view that Pope was not a Jacobite, 'but that he drew on what he must have known was part of the language and stance of Jacobitism', seems most in line with the available evidence. 'In a period of deceptive calm, treacherous currents and sudden storms, Pope navigated with skill. True he trimmed his sails at times, but he also sailed near the wind.'[12] In his public espousal of his politics, as in so much else, Pope walked on a very tight rope but was careful to steer clear of any too compromising a position.

The two most important figures in the political scenario as far as Pope is concerned are Henry St John, Viscount Bolingbroke, and Sir Robert Walpole. Apart from Harley, Bolingbroke was the most dominant personality in the Tory Ministry of 1710–14. Indeed it was the struggle for power between these two men that finally brought the Ministry down. Rather than face the impeachment proceedings about to be brought against him by the Whigs, Bolingbroke fled in 1715 to France, where he became involved in the Pretender's Court. He soon became disenchanted with the inefficiency of Jacobite plans, however, and dissociated himself from them in order to devote his time to the study of history and philosophy. In 1723 he was granted a pardon and returned to England where he eventually settled down at Dawley Farm near Twickenham. From 1725 until 1735, when he again left England for France, Bolingbroke led the opposition to Walpole. Since he had been deprived of the right to hold political office, as a condition of his pardon, he had to do this in an extraparliamentary way through the columns of his newspaper, *The Craftsman.* Two of Bolingbroke's major works, *Remarks on the History of England,* and *A Dissertation on Parties,* first appeared in the weekly pages of this paper. It was during these years of opposition to Walpole that he became such a close friend of Pope's, influencing him deeply in both philosophical and political matters. Pope's admiration for Bolingbroke, or 'all-accomplish'd St JOHN' as he calls him in the *Epilogue to the Satires,* was almost unlimited. In addition to his tribute to him in *An Essay on Man* as 'my guide, philosopher and friend' (IV, 390), there are references to him in the letters as 'a Being paullo minus ab angelis' (IV, 491),[13] and as 'the Greatest Man I ever knew' (IV, 173).

Sir Robert Walpole first came into prominence during the reign of Queen Anne, but he achieved his real fame under George I. From 1721 onwards he held power as First Lord of the Treasury for an unbroken period of twenty-one years. He was an even more dominant figure in the Whig party than we have just described Bolingbroke as being in the Tory opposition. He was an extremely skilful financier and an adroit manager of men. The main achievements of his long and successful administration were to give the country peace and prosperity. These were no mean achievements, but both were obtained at considerable cost in terms of personal principle. By the end of his period of supremacy he was widely considered to be a totally corrupt politician who had only managed to remain in office for so long because of the confused nature of the opposition.

Pope tried for a long time to keep on good terms with Walpole and in the summer of 1725 received a visit from him at his villa in Twickenham. During this and the next five years there are several references in Pope's correspondence to his having dined at Walpole's 'Sunday-Tables'. About 1730, however, his friendship with Sir Robert, which had only been diplomatic at the best of times, began to waver, and after 1733 it changed to scarcely veiled personal antipathy and overt political opposition.

But this is to anticipate an account of Pope's earlier position with regard to party politics. He first came to public notice as a promising poet during those years at the end of Queen Anne's reign in which party warfare was reaching its height of contention. In this situation Pope did all he could to maintain a neutral stance. Naturally drawn by his religious sympathies and friends in the Scriblerus Club to the Tory party, he nevertheless managed to retain acquaintances and friends among the leading Whigs. Not least of these was Addison who, as Pope later told Spence, advised 'me not to be content with the applause of half the nation. He used to talk much and often to me of moderation in parties, and used to blame his dear friend Steele for being too much of a party-man' (146). Addison was no doubt trying to win Pope over by stages to the Whig cause, but be that as it may, Pope seems to have accepted the advice. What he set out to do, as he later put it in his *Imitation of Horace, Satire II, i*, was to place all his glory in moderation with the result that 'Tories call me Whig, and Whigs a Tory'. It was a claim for neutrality that he repeated in the *Epilogue to the Satires: Dialogue I* (8), and that has a strong resemblance to his statement to Atterbury in 1717, already quoted in this chapter, that in politics he thought no further than how to preserve the peace of his life in any Government under which he lived. This overtly uncommitted position towards both political parties, which he maintained with considerable care over a long period of time, is clearly expressed in a letter he wrote to Swift on 28 November 1729:

> You know my maxim to keep clear of all offence, as I am clear of all interest in either party. . . . I have given some proofs in the course of my whole life, (from the time when I was in the friendship of Lord Bolingbroke and Mr. Craggs even to this, when I am civilly treated by Sir R. Walpole) that I never thought myself so warm in any Party's cause as to deserve their money; and therefore would never have accepted it.
>
> (III, 8)

Gradually during the 1730s, however, and especially after the defeat of Walpole's Excise Bill in 1733 which so raised Tory hopes for the 'Great Man's' downfall, Pope began to join forces with the Patriot opposition. This was not quite the same thing as joining the Tory opposition, and Pope would no doubt have defended himself by insisting that what he was fighting for was a resurgence of public spirit, not of a political party. Nevertheless we need to ask why he should have chosen at this stage in his career to get embroiled in political warfare after studiously cultivating public detachment to it over such a long period? There are perhaps two main reasons: the increasing personal influence over him exerted by Bolingbroke, and his growing dislike for Walpole.

Whatever the reason it is certainly true to say that the *Versifications of Donne* and *Imitations of Horace* written in the five years between 1733 and 1738 are full of pointed attacks on Walpole's administration that show a clear departure from Pope's earlier political neutrality. In *The Fourth Satire of Dr. John Donne, Dean of St. Paul's, Versifyed*, for example, he uses the character of an impertinent courtier to attack Walpole's graft:

> Then as a licens'd Spy, whom nothing can
> Silence, or hurt, he libels the *Great Man*;
> Swears every *Place entail'd* for Years to come,
> In sure Succession to the Day of Doom:
> He names the *Price* for ev'ry *Office* paid,
> And says our *Wars thrive ill*, because *delay'd*;
> Nay hints, 'tis by Connivance of the Court,
> That *Spain* robs on, and *Dunkirk's* still a Port. (158–65)

By putting the attack on Walpole into someone else's mouth Pope could always claim to be free of guilt. A few years later in the *Imitation of Horace, Epistle I, i*, addressed to Bolingbroke, he adopts a persona who talks about being a Patriot and battling for the State. In the same poem Walpole is referred to as a 'screen' and a 'wall of brass', and George II's Court is seen as a lion's den. Finally, in the

Imitation of Horace, Epistle II, i, Pope makes merciless fun of Walpole's peace policy while ironically praising George II:

> Oh! could I mount on the Maeonian wing,
> Your Arms, your Actions, your Repose to sing!
> What seas you travers'd! and what fields you fought!
> Your Country's Peace, how oft, how dearly bought!
> How barb'rous rage subsided at your word,
> And Nations wonder'd while they dropp'd the sword!
> How, when you nodded, o'er the land and deep,
> Peace stole her wing, and wrapt the world in sleep;
> Till Earth's extremes your mediation own,
> And Asia's Tyrants tremble at your Throne,   (394–403)

By the time one comes to the two dialogues of the *Epilogue to the Satires*, 1738, there is a new note of disillusion in Pope's attitude to party politics. His country's ruin makes him grave and he seems to be totally disenchanted with both parties. The attack on Walpole and the Court party is as strong as in the preceding five years, but there is a new dissatisfaction with both Tories and Patriots. The apocalyptic image of Vice corrupting the whole country that ends *Dialogue I*, for example, includes the Patriots:

> In Soldier, Churchman, Patriot, Man in Pow'r,
> 'Tis Av'rice all, Ambition is no more!   (161–2)

When we come to *Dialogue II* the same sort of attitude is present. It is Vice he attacks, not Whigs, and Virtue he praises, not Tories. His list of worthy men includes Sommers, Halifax and Shrewsbury (77–9), each of whom had been a leading Whig earlier in the century. Pope insists that he follows Virtue and praises her wherever she shines, whether she point to 'Priest or Elder, Whig or Tory' (95–6).

What we find in these later poems is a disillusioned return to his earlier moderation, with a strong suggestion of a plague on both your houses. In the rewritten *Dunciad* of 1743, Cibber asks Dulness in Book I whether she would have him take up party politics:

> Or bidst thou rather Party to embrace?
> A friend to Party thou, and all her race;
> 'Tis the same rope at different ends they twist . . .
>
> (I, 205–7)

Tories and Whigs are merely different sides of the same coin, and it is quite clear that for Pope fervent partisans of either party serve Dulness's cause equally well.

It is perhaps ironic that at the very time when Pope's own attitude to party politics should have become so disenchanted his reputation in the country should have risen to the point at which he was represented by the party hacks as the 'spiritual patron of the poetical opposition to Walpole'.[14] This emblematic significance attributed to his life can best be illustrated by the flurry of pamphlets printed at the end of 1740. The first of these, a savage denunciation of Walpole called *Are these things so?*, took the fictional form of an open letter from Alexander Pope, 'An Englishman in His Grotto', to Robert Walpole, 'A Great Man at Court'. In the two months between 23 October, when *Are these things so?* was first published, and 20 December, when *A Supplement to Are these things so?* appeared, no fewer than nine separate poems (four attacking Walpole and five defending him) were released, each directly related to one another and each written by an unnamed author. Though Pope had nothing whatever to do with this furious spate of party activity, it vividly illustrates the close relationship between literature and politics in the first half of the eighteenth century. While it is inconceivable that the publication of any poem in our own day, even by a major writer, should arouse such a response, it is reasonably typical of the first half of the eighteenth century that the publication of an occasional poem by a minor, indeed anonymous writer should do so.[15]

I have argued that there was nearly always a certain overt detachment from party politics in Pope's poetry. This should not however be confused with a lack of involvement in the society around him. Pope was deeply committed to the society of his day, but his commitment is to its state of morality not the state of the parties. What he really attacks in the satires of the 1730s is not party political issues but the deeper corruption, as he saw it, of the new moneyed society. This was a state of affairs that had repelled him since at least as early as 1723 when he wrote to Broome saying that:

> Every valuable, every pleasant thing is sunk in an ocean of avarice and corruption. The son of a first minister is a proper match for a daughter of a late South Sea Director, – so money upon money increases, copulates, and multiplies, and guineas beget guineas in *Saecula saeculorum*.   (II, 182)

It is this disgust for the new capitalism that rings most stridently through the poems of his later period. It perhaps gives an added perspective to our own views on the capacities and limitations of the capitalist system that Pope should challenge it not from a socialist point of view, but from a profoundly conservative one.

As Pope saw it his poetry was above all else a moral song. In January 1733 we find him writing to Caryll saying that his *Epistle to Bathurst* is, not the worst I have written, and abounds in moral example, for which reason it must be obnoxious in this age. God send it does any good! I really mean nothing else by writing at this time of my life. (II, 340)

As we read through Pope's correspondence this emphasis on the poet's moral duty strikes us again and again. It is there at the beginning of the 1730s and it is there at the end. He tells Warburton on 12 November 1741, that he 'has no other merit than that of aiming by his moral strokes to merit some regard from such men as advance Truth and Virtue in a more effectual way' (IV, 370).

In the satires of the 1730s we find Pope, driven desperate as he sees the critical condition of his country — the sons of Mammon in charge and public spirit nowhere — responding to that condition by creating the figure of a satirist who protests his outrage and disgust with increasing fervour. The persona Pope creates in the *Imitations of Horace* is not content simply to pass moral comment on his times. He feels he must join the battle and he therefore enters the public arena, but he does so in no narrow party political way. The urbane friend of the great who speaks through Horace's poems takes on an unrelentingly aggressive public-spiritedness that transforms him into something akin to a public prosecutor. Morality becomes militant.

Notes

1. The 'Man' of Pope's title refers to the collective human race or species, mankind, not the individual male member of the species. Pope mostly uses the third person singular male pronoun, 'he', to refer to mankind, though he also uses the non-gender-specific, second person singular, 'thou', and the inclusive first person plural possessive, 'our'. I follow Pope's procedure in this chapter.
2. A good summary of these ideas and a most useful introduction to the poem is to be found in *An Essay on Man*, ed. Maynard Mack, Twickenham Edition of *The Poems of Alexander Pope*, Vol. III, i (Methuen, London, 1950), pp. xi-lxxx.
3. See A. O. Lovejoy, *The Great Chain of Being: A Study of the History of an Idea* (Harvard University Press, Cambridge, Mass., 1936).
4. Mack, *An Essay on Man*, p. lxiii.
5. Matthew Arnold, 'The Study of Poetry', (1880), *Essays in Criticism, Second Series* (Macmillan, London, 1888).
6. Samuel Johnson, 'Pope', in *Lives of the English Poets* (1779–81); ed. G. B. Hill, 3 Vols (Clarendon Press, Oxford, 1905), Vol. III, p. 214.
7. See Brean Hammond, *Pope* (The Harvester Press, Brighton, 1986), pp. 21–3, and Maynard Mack, *Alexander Pope: A Life* (Yale University Press, New Haven, 1985), p. 81.

8. Earl R. Wasserman, *Pope's Epistle to Bathurst* (Johns Hopkins Press, Baltimore, 1960), pp. 41–3.
9. See J. H. Plumb, *The Growth of Political Stability in England 1675–1725* (Peregrine Books, Harmondsworth, 1969), pp. 170–2.
10. See especially Howard Erskine-Hill, 'Alexander Pope: The Political Poet in His Time', *Eighteenth-Century Studies*, 15 (1981–22), pp. 123–48; Mack, *Pope: A Life*, pp. 258–65 and *passim*; Hammond, *Pope*, pp. 23–8 and *passim*.
11. See Plumb, op. cit., p. 170.
12. Erskine-Hill, op. cit., pp. 138–41.
13. The Latin phrase means a Being 'only a little lower than the angels'.
14. Mack, *The Garden and the City: Retirement and Politics in the Later Poetry of Pope 1741–1743* (University of Toronto Press, Toronto, 1969), p. 190.
15. See my edition of two of these poems, *Are These Things So?* (1740), and *The Great Man's Answer* (1740), introduction by Ian Gordon, Augustan Reprint Society, Publication No. 153, William Andrews Clark Memorial Library (University of California, Los Angeles, 1972).

Part Two
Critical Survey

The winged Courser, like a gen'rous Horse,
Shows most true Mettle when you *check* his Course.
                                        (*An Essay on Criticism*, 86–7)

He gains all points, who pleasingly confounds,
Surprizes, varies, and conceals the Bounds.
                                        (*Epistle to Burlington*, 55–6)

The closed heroic couplet

All Pope's significant poetry is written in what is usually known as heroic couplets: five foot (pentameter) lines rhyming in pairs and with each foot containing the iambic structure of an unstressed syllable followed by a stressed syllable. There are occasional variations on this pattern, but they are rare and, when they do occur, Pope clearly expects us to measure them against this norm. It is a form of great compression that stretches a poet's resources with language to the utmost. When used by an unskilled poet it can easily result in a stiff and metronomic effect, but when handled by a poet as skilled as Pope its very limitations provide a challenge that concentrates the poet's mind and imagination, and results in a remarkable variety of contrapuntal effects being achieved.

At one point we may find Pope using the terse compactness of the heroic couplet to give punch to a satirical thrust, while at another we may find him exploiting its fundamental balance to evoke a lyrical scene. The immense variety of movement and tone that Pope achieves in his poetry is nearly always a matter of working within the bounds that the couplet imposes, rather than a matter of breaking away from them. His poetry illustrates the traditional paradox that one moves more easily for being in harness, or, to borrow the lines that Pope himself wrote in *An Essay on Criticism* when describing the strife between wit and judgment:

> The winged Courser, like a gen'rous Horse,
> Shows most true Mettle when you *check* his Course.   (86–7)

The heroic couplet had been used in English poetry long before Pope perfected it. Indeed, since each line is an iambic pentameter, its development is an integral part of the basic metrical tradition in English poetry. Chaucer had used the decasyllabic couplet in *The Canterbury Tales*, and two hundred years or so later John Donne had used it in his *Satires*. When he was still a young poet, Pope wrote 'modernizations' of parts of both these works as an exercise in developing his skill. But there is a crucial difference between Pope's couplets and those of Chaucer and Donne before him. Pope's poems are all written in the closed couplet form. This means that each couplet has a distinct element of self-enclosed completeness to it. This is not to say that each couplet is totally independent of those that surround it, but it does mean that there is a clear pause at the end of each line, and a more emphatic pause at the end of the second line. The open, or enjambed, couplet on the other hand, is one in which the meaning frequently flows across the line-end without any clear pause. It is so different in the expectations it creates in the reader, and in the demands that it makes on the writer, that it is easier to think of it as belonging to a separate tradition, though somewhat confusingly the open and closed couplets are frequently referred to under the same label of the heroic couplet.

It was in the second half of the seventeenth century and first part of the eighteenth that the heroic couplet reached its greatest popularity and, in the poetry of Dryden and Pope, its peak of performance. After Pope's death the heroic couplet continued to flourish in the poetry of Johnson, Goldsmith, Cowper and Churchill in the eighteenth century, and in that of Crabbe and Byron in the early part of the nineteenth. The development of the Romantic sensibility, however, saw a diminution in its popularity. Wordsworth used it in some of his earlier poems and Keats tried it in both *Endymion* and *Lamia*, but on the whole it is fair to say that the classical astringencies of the couplet form were unsuited to the more visionary nature of Romantic themes.

Dr Johnson tells us in his *Life of Dryden* that though 'some advances toward nature and harmony had been already made by Waller and Denham', it was to Dryden that the new versification owed its establishment.[1] Pope makes much the same point in his *Imitation of Horace, Epistle II, i*, when, through a rare use of the triplet, clearly intended as a compliment to Dryden's own fondness for it, he says:

> Waller was smooth; but Dryden taught to join
> The varying verse, the full resounding line,
> The long majestic march, and energy divine. (267–9)

Throughout his life Pope considered Dryden as his great master in the use of the couplet. His tributes to Dryden were many and unwavering. He told Spence, just before he died, that: 'I learned versification wholly from Dryden's works, who had improved it much beyond any of our former poets, and would probably have brought it to its perfection, had not he been unhappily obliged to write so often in haste.' Pope would have fully endorsed Dr Johnson's comparison of what Dryden did for English poetry to Augustus's boast of what he did for Rome: '*laeteritiam invenit, marmoream reliquit*: he found it brick and he left it marble'.[2]

There is not room here to give details of all the technical skills in the use of the couplet that Pope inherited from Dryden, but one particular development calls for mention since it is one of the chief things that distinguish the two poets from the mass of journeymen practitioners of the form. This is the quality, referred to by Pope above, as Dryden's 'long majestic march', or his ability to use the couplet cumulatively to gain great oratorical effects that sweep away the limitations of the couplet working by itself. This is not to say that Dryden and Pope do not frequently use individual closed couplets for variety and contrast when they need to, but it is to point out that the basic unit in their poetry is the carefully composed paragraph rather than the two line closed couplet. Traditional accounts, which still recur in literary handbooks where Pope's use of the closed couplet is defined as one in which the two lines form a completely separate and individual unit of meaning, should be treated with considerable scepticism. In very few of Pope's couplets is it possible to appreciate the complex allusiveness of the various parts, or the accumulation of rhythmical effects, without considering the couplets that precede and follow. One of the great advances in the development of the form made by Dryden and Pope is this incorporation of the individual closed couplet into the larger organizational unit of the verse paragraph.

Pope's use of the closed couplet form is ideally suited to his concept of a universe in which particular and observable disorder yields, in a larger perspective, to overall harmony. The component parts of Pope's couplets, whether it be the entire first line operating against the second line, or the first half of the line operating against the second half, or the first quarter operating against the second quarter, establish a tension that is heightened for being caught in an overall form of assured correctness, lucidity, and ease. Thus the final ironic paradox in *The Dunciad* is that, though the whole poem has illustrated in a thousand and one different ways the triumph of dread chaos and eternal night, that triumph is described by the poet in a medium of perfect order and clarity. We are enabled to see Universal Darkness burying all precisely because Pope's verse form creates so brilliant a light. Pope's couplets, like *Windsor-Forest* itself, are:

> Not *Chaos*-like together crush'd and bruis'd,
> But as the World, harmoniously confus'd:
> Where Order in Variety we see
> And where, tho' all things differ, all agree. (13–16)

The following essays are intended as introductions to some of Pope's major poems. The principle behind the choice of poems for discussion has been my desire to say something about the wide range of Pope's achievement in different 'kinds' of poetry throughout his writing life. For this reason I begin with one of his earliest publications, *An Essay on Criticism*, and end with his last, *The Dunciad* (in Four Books), and in between cover examples of each of the major 'kinds' that he attempted.

Each essay begins with a short commentary on the selected poem as a whole, and then moves into a more detailed discussion of part of that poem through consideration of an exemplary passage chosen for illustrative purposes. Finally it is only by looking in detail at Pope's poetry that the full force of his imaginative genius and expressive skill can be appreciated. It is my aim in this part of the book to demonstrate something of each of these qualities.

An Essay on Criticism

An Essay on Criticism does not have the critical topicality for the modern reader that it had for its contemporaries, but it remains, in many ways, a remarkable poem and one well worth careful study. It is as if a modern poet had written a poem discussing 'ancient' and 'modern' English criticism ranging from the Classical tradition and Humanism, through the New Criticism, up to Structuralism, modern forms of Feminist theory, Deconstruction, and reader-response criticism, reception theory and semiotics. Such a poet would have referred with informed familiarity to the writings of critics as varied as Johnson, Coleridge and Arnold; Richards, Eliot and Leavis; Saussure and Barthes; de Beauvoir, Millett and Showalter; Derrida and Lacan; de Man, Hillis Miller, Fish, Foucault . . . and so the list could go on. But perhaps most remarkable of all, our imagined poet would only have been a 'fearless youth' (220), of twenty or twenty-one, or possibly even younger, when he wrote the poem, and wrote it in a language of sharp gracefulness, in marked contrast to the frequently deliberate obfuscation of the language used by some of the theoreticians he discussed.

At its simplest level *An Essay on Criticism* is a didactic poem. It is conducted according to a broadly argumentative structure although it also contains more than a passing touch or two of Pope's burgeoning satiric impulse. Pope described the poem, in a letter to his friend John Caryll written on 19 July 1711, as 'a treatise . . . which not one gentleman in three score, even of a liberal education, can understand' (I, 128). What Pope meant by this, I think, is that the poem is rather more densely woven and subtly argued than may appear at first glance. It is not a 'treatise', however, to use Pope's word, that offers new critical insights or positions, but rather one that attempts a synthesis of a wide range of traditional and modern critical thought. The poem is what its title says it is, an 'essai', or attempt, or, as Pope calls it at the end of the poem, a 'short Excursion' (738), into a difficult and complex subject, the role and function of criticism. So although it is fair to call *An Essay on Criticism* a didactic poem, there is nothing staightforward about its didacticism.

One of the difficulties for the modern reader is that the synthesis of ideas concerning criticism that Pope develops is sufficiently concentrated not to be easily reducible to neat explication. The meaning is in the poem rather than a prose version of it. *An Essay on Criticism* is a poem in which a number of key words – Sense, Nature, Taste,

Judgment, Genius and Wit, to name the most important – play upon each other and are used in different ways in different contexts. No one definition alone suits any one of them. What Pope attempts to do in the poem is to reconcile the contemporary dispute between the proponents of ancient and modern learning. Then, as now, 'Critic Learning flourished most in France' (712). French critics had taken the lead in establishing a new aesthetics, and treatises dealing with such matters as the imitation of nature and the importance of the rules, by Bouhours, Boileau, Rapin, Le Bossu and Dacier, dominated the last quarter of the seventeenth century.[1] Pope was widely read in this 'modern' criticism, as well, of course, as in the 'ancient' criticism that preceded it, especially in such writers as Aristotle, Horace, Quintilian and Longinus. In *An Essay on Criticism* he ranges broadly over this extensive body of writing, although never with the methodical regularity many of the 'moderns' displayed, and comes up with a distillation of authoritative critical positions.

An Essay on Criticism is divided into three parts. According to the prefatory analytical summary (although it is not definite that Pope wrote this), Part I (1–200) deals with true Taste and Judgment in a critic, Part II (201–559) with some of the causes of false Taste and Judgment, and Part III (560–744) with the true conduct of Manners in a critic, concluding with a brief survey of the history of criticism. The overall organization, however, is never as neatly compartmentalized as this suggests. Pope moves across the stated demarcations, just as he moves backwards and forwards over ancient and modern criticism offering a polished conversational view of his conception of the critic's function and duty.

The poem is the nearest thing we have in eighteenth-century English writing to what might be called a neoclassical manifesto, but is never as definitively expounded as such a word implies. It comes closer to being a handbook, or guide, to the critic's and poet's art, very much in the style of Horace's *Ars Poetica*, or, to take the English models with which Pope was especially familiar, the Earl of Roscommon's translation of Horace, *The Art of Poetry*, 1680, and John Sheffield's (the Duke of Buckingham's) *Essay on Poetry*, 1682.[2] It is accordingly of great value to us today in understanding what Pope and his contemporaries saw as the main functions and justifications of criticism and poetry. I include poetry here because in discussing 'true' criticism Pope inevitably moves on to discussing 'true' poetry, and what sets out as *An Essay on Criticism* becomes, to a certain extent, *A Defence of Poetry*.

The poem is articulated through a more consciously epigrammatic style than that found anywhere else in Pope's writing. It is built upon a series of maxims, or pithy apothegms, such as 'To Err is

Human; to forgive, *Divine*' (525), and 'For *Fools* rush in where *Angels* fear to tread' (625). Pope's ability here, and at so many points in the poem, to sum up an idea tersely and memorably in a phrase, line or couplet of packed imaginative clarity is a hallmark of *An Essay on Criticism*. Few other poems in the language (Gray's *Elegy in a Country Churchyard* springs to mind as a possible contender) contain so many memorable lines or phrases that have gone on to achieve an independent proverbial existence in our culture. The polished couplets encapsulate points that reverberate on each other like conversational repartee. Pope's model, as already indicated, is Horace:

> *Horace* still charms with graceful negligence,
> And without Method *talks* us into Sense,
> Will like a *Friend* familiarly convey
> The *truest Notions* in the *easiest way*.   (653–6)

Pope, too, wants to charm with 'graceful negligence' and without apparent method 'talk us into Sense'.

One of Pope's greatest gifts, evident throughout his poetry, but particularly so in *An Essay on Criticism*, is his ability to make his ideas concrete and memorable through the graphic quality of his imagery. One can see this demonstrated either in a compact couplet:

> Some neither can for *Wits* nor *Critics* pass,
> As heavy Mules are neither *Horse* nor *Ass*   (38–9)

or developed, with equal facility and appropriateness, in a full analogy:

> Those half-learn'd Witlings, num'rous in our Isle,
> As half-form'd Insects on the Banks of *Nile*;
> Unfinish'd Things, one knows not what to call,
> Their Generation's so *equivocal*:
> To tell 'em, wou'd a *hundred Tongues* require,
> Or *one vain Wit's*, that might a hundred tire.   (140–5)

The allusive range of Pope's creative imagination is apparently boundless as he shifts the areas of reference from natural history to entomology, from science to theology, from sea-faring to equestrianism, from geography to meteorology, from politics to military and territorial campaigns, from medicine to law, to marriage, to dress . . . etc. The list seems without end as his fertile imagination draws on image upon image to secure his ideas and drive his points home.

The poem opens with a statement of the difficulty of the poet's task:

> 'Tis hard to say, if greater want of Skill
> Appear in *Writing* or in *Judging* ill;
> But, of the two, less dang'rous is th'Offence,
> To tire our *Patience*, than mis-lead our *Sense*:   (1–4)

Not only is it difficult to say whether bad poetry or bad criticism is the more dangerous, but significant expression itself is a struggle: ''Tis hard to say'. The poet and critic have to fight to articulate their ideas accurately. Both poetry and criticism, 'writing' and 'judging', are seen as acts that involve responsibilities and can lead to social judgment, to giving 'Offence'.

At an early stage in the poem Pope describes judgment as the distinguishing feature of the critic, and true judgment or taste (the words are interchangeable at this point) depends on nature as much as, if not more than, on nurture:

> 'Tis with our *Judgments* as our *Watches*, none
> Go just *alike*, yet each believes his own.
> In *Poets* as true *Genius* is but rare,
> True *Taste* as seldom is the *Critick's* Share;
> Both must alike from Heav'n derive their Light,
> These *born* to Judge, as well as those to Write.
> Let such teach others who themselves excell,
> And *censure freely* who have *written well*.
> *Authors* are partial to their *Wit*, 'tis true,
> But are not *Cricks* to their *Judgment* too? (9–18)

Both poets and critics need innate ability: they are born not made. 'Both must alike from Heav'n derive their Light' (13). Just as 'Wit' is seen as the crucial defining quality for the poet, so 'Judgment' is crucial for the critic. But the two terms are not easily separated (see chapter 4); they are interdependent, and the critic who develops true judgment will also develop at least a grounding in true wit.

A significant aspect of the poem as it unfolds is that Pope keeps drawing moral connections between criticism and ethics. Criticism, for Pope, cannot be separated from human conduct:

> Of all the Causes which conspire to blind
> Man's erring Judgment, and misguide the Mind,
> What the weak Head with strongest Byass rules,
> Is *Pride*, the *never-failing Vice of Fools*. (201–4)

This passage, with its emphasis on 'Man's erring Judgment' and the sinfulness of 'Pride', in many ways anticipates *An Essay on Man*. Indeed as we read on in the passage the injunctive syntax – 'Trust not your self' (213) – suggests it could easily fit into that poem. Even this early in his career Pope seems almost instinctively drawn to the authoritative, enjoining and hortatory voice.

Another foretaste of poems yet unwritten lies in the satiric elements that look forward to *The Dunciad*, and in particular to Pope's repeated attacks on Dulness. Dulness is seen by Pope, in *An Essay on Criticism*, as *the* great literary sin. Bad critics 'Write *dull* receits how poems should be made' (115); or admire poems where 'ten low words oft creep in one *dull* line' (347); or 'tune their own *dull* Rhymes' (358). Dulness carries the critic away to extremes; it leads to deception, overstatement and wrong proportion:

> As things seem large which we thro' Mists descry,
> *Dulness* is ever apt to Magnify. (392–3)

Dulness encourages some critics to judge a work according to the social rank of the author:

> Of all this *Servile Herd* the worst is He
> That in *proud Dulness* joins with *Quality*. (414–15)

Dulness is associated with Obscenity (532), and with those who have rank but no education or learning:

> Fear most to tax an *Honourable* Fool,
> Whose right it is, uncensur'd to be *dull*; (588–9)

The reference here to an 'Honourable Fool' is to someone who could have a degree conferred upon him by Oxford or Cambridge purely on account of his social status. Sometimes, says Pope, it is best to ignore bad writers: 'And charitably let the *Dull* be vain' (597). Such writers are impervious to criticism anyway:

> What Crowds of these, impenitently bold,
> In *Sounds* and jingling *Syllables* grown old,
> Still *run on* Poets in a raging Vein,
> Ev'n to the Dregs and *Squeezings* of the *Brain*;
> Strain out the last, *dull droppings* of their Sense,
> And Rhyme with all the *Rage* of *Impotence*! (604–9)

There are premonitions here, in the, as yet merely irritated, awareness of the gathering crowds of dunces and in the comparison of dulness to excrement, not just of *The Dunciad* but of the whole body of indignant satire that Pope wrote in the 1730s. A distinct satiric tone lies behind the conversational bonhomie, and shadows of foreboding already darken the shafts of epigrammatic wit that enlighten most of the poem. Images of schoolmen as spiders 'amidst their kindred cobwebs' (445) and of bad writers as insects 'still humming on their drowzy course' (600) are other omens of a similar mood. Although it functions as an authoritative synthesis of criticism, *An Essay on Criticism* announces Pope's engagement as a committed writer for whom bad writing and bad morals were inextricably linked.

Another aspect of *An Essay on Criticism* that it is important to acknowledge here is Pope's Longinian insistence that beauty cannot be limited by rules:

> Some Beauties yet, no Precepts can declare,
> For there's a *Happiness* as well as Care.   (141–2)

Longinus' treatise *On the Sublime* had been rediscovered in France and England during the last quarter of the seventeenth century and continued to grow greatly in popularity throughout the first half of the eighteenth.[3] Pope pays high tribute to Longinus in his brief survey of criticism towards the close of the poem:

> Thee, bold *Longinus*! all the Nine inspire,
> And bless *their Critick* with a *Poet's Fire*.
> An Ardent *Judge*, who Zealous in his Trust,
> With *Warmth* gives Sentence, yet is always *Just*;
> Whose *own Example* strengthened all his Laws,
> And *Is himself* that great *Sublime* he draws.   (675–80)

The spirited emphasis in these lines on boldness, fire, ardour, warmth, and on the 'great *Sublime*' itself is an important element, still too frequently overlooked, in Pope's aesthetic. It is this Longinian element that lies behind his espousal of the '*nameless Graces*' which no Methods teach' (144). 'Lucky LICENCE' (148) finally has an authority beyond the 'RULES' (88); indeed 'th'intent proposed, that *Licence* is a *Rule*' (149). Pope prefers irregular genius and 'brave disorder' to cold correctness and 'vulgar bounds':

> Great Wits sometimes may *gloriously offend*,
> And *rise* to *Faults* true Criticks dare not mend;
> From *vulgar Bounds* with *brave Disorder* part,
> And *snatch* a *Grace* beyond the Reach of Art,
> Which, without passing thro' the *Judgment*, gains
> The *Heart*, and all its End *at once* attains.   (152–7)

'True' critics will recognize the indefinable genius, 'the Grace beyond the Reach of Art' the *je ne sais quoi*, of great Art and shape their judgment and taste on that recognition.

Perhaps the most important consideration of all for Pope, and one that recurs at many points throughout his writing, especially in *An Essay on Man* and the *Epistle to Burlington*, is that the critic should 'Survey the Whole' (235):

> In Wit, as Nature, what affects our Hearts
> Is not th'Exactness of peculiar Parts;
> 'Tis not a *Lip*, or *Eye*, we Beauty call,
> But the joint Force and full *Result of all*.   (243–6)

The overall effect is what matters. 'All are but parts of one stupendous whole', as Pope puts it, in another context, in *An Essay on Man*

(I, 267), or 'Parts answering parts shall slide into a whole', as he says in the *Epistle to Burlington* (66). He says something very similar in *An Essay on Criticism*:

> No single Parts unequally surprize;
> All comes *united* to th'admiring Eyes.   (249–50)

The concern for the overall effect has merged here with the previously noted concern for 'nameless Graces'. The 'joint Force and full *Result* of all', and '*united*' effect on th'admiring eyes, are each more than the sum of their respective component parts. Ultimately they can only be described in deliberately indefinable phrases, such as the mystery that lies at the heart of art.

SELECTED EXCERPT

> First follow NATURE, and your Judgment frame
> By her just Standard, which is still the same:
> *Unerring Nature*, still divinely bright,   70
> One *clear, unchang'd*, and *Universal* Light,
> Life, Force, and Beauty, must to all impart,
> At once the *Source*, and *End*, and *Test* of *Art*.
> *Art* from that Fund each *just Supply* provides,
> Works *without Show*, and *without Pomp* presides:
> In some fair Body thus th'informing Soul
> With Spirit feeds, with Vigour fills the whole,
> Each Motion guides, and ev'ry Nerve sustains;
> *It self unseen*, but in th'*Effects*, remains.
> Some, to whom Heav'n in Wit has been profuse,   80
> Want as much more, to turn it to its use;
> For *Wit* and *Judgment* often are at strife,
> Tho' meant each other's Aid, like *Man* and *Wife*.
> 'Tis more to *guide* than *spur* the Muse's Steed;
> Restrain his Fury, than provoke his Speed;
> The winged Courser, like a gen'rous Horse,
> Shows most true Mettle when you *check* his Course.   (68–87)

CONTEXT   The passage is taken from Part I of the poem where Pope is describing the qualities necessary for true taste and judgment in a critic. It follows on from an introductory discussion of the poem's key terms – Taste, Judgment, Wit, Genius, Sense and Nature – and leads on to a discussion of the Rules (88–117).

CRITICISM   The excerpt falls into two sections: the first twelve lines (68–79), which focus on the importance of following 'Nature', and the last eight (80–7), which deal with 'Wit' and its relationship with 'Judgment'. The passage has been chosen for discussion here because it deals with ideas that come close to the heart of Pope's aesthetic concerns in the poem as a whole.

The critic is urged to 'First follow NATURE', a priority that Pope emphasizes through the use of capitals, only repeated at four other points in the poem — RULES, (88); ANCIENT's (119); LICENCE (148); and LEARN then what MORALS (560). The complex web of meanings attributed to 'nature' in the eighteenth century has already been discussed in Chapter 3 (see p. 69). The appeal to nature in eighteenth-century aesthetics is both one to an empirical reality, and one to the artist's perception of an ideal order and harmony revealed in God's creation. It is an appeal to that which is tangible and to that which is intangible, to the actual and to the ideal, and to the fusion and interplay between the two.

In the lines being considered here the imagery helps to establish the ways in which Pope is thinking of nature at this stage. Nature is first described as a fixed point in a turning world, as a 'just Standard', which is 'still', in both senses of the word, the same. 'Just' indicates both that which is morally right, or justified in the sight of God, and that which is aesthetically right in proportion. It also describes that which is exact and precise, as opposed to that which is approximate. The noun 'Standard', has a variety of possible meanings, but when attached to the verb 'frame' seems to suggest a level of excellence (cf. our use of the phrase 'academic standards'), or a uniform unit of measurement (cf. the gold standard), not a military flag or naval ensign. As a 'just Standard' nature offers the critic a right and exact criterion with which to build, or 'frame' his judgment: as a reliable measure for doing this it is a distinct improvement on the man-made watches, the image Pope introduced earlier in the poem, where none 'Go just *alike*, yet each believes his own' (11).

The imagery of the following lines is less open to ambiguity as nature is unequivocally associated with God and seen as part of his operation in the universe. Nature is 'Unerring', 'divinely' bright and a 'Universal' light, which is the 'Source' and 'End' and 'Test' of Art. There are allusions here to the descriptions of creation at the beginning of Genesis and the Gospel According to St John. Nature is presented as the beginning and the end of art, and just as mankind is made in God's image so art should be made in nature's. Nature is a 'Fund' (74), or permanent stock, that provides the true artist with exactly what is needed, a 'just Supply' based on her 'just Standard'. In the next line Pope uses chiasmus to emphasize the well-known maxim that the greatest art is the art to hide, *Ars est celare artem*: drawing on the 'fund' of nature, art 'Works *without Show*, and *without Pomp* presides' (75).

This section of the poem, appealing to the primacy of nature as a guide for the critic, ends with a third image for nature. This time she is seen as 'th'informing Soul' which feeds the 'fair Body' of art with spirits and fills it with vigour. Nature, as the soul, guides 'Each Motion' and sustains 'ev'ry Nerve'. As with the image of Nature as a 'fund' of light that enables art to work 'without Show' so nature as a soul works 'unseen' in the body but leaves its mark in 'th'Effects'. Again the greatest art is the art to hide.

The imagery used to describe nature has shown it, in turn, as a fixed standard, as an emanation of God's light, and as the soul in the body. The images give an ultimate authority to nature, whether measured on the observable scale of empirical reality or on the more elusive scale of Platonic ideas. The imagery establishes nature as tangible and intangible, as actual and ideal, those qualities already noted as characteristic of the eighteenth-century appeal to nature.

The last eight lines show a rather sudden shift in focus from 'Nature' to 'Wit', a change in direction typical however of the conversational structure and syntax of the poem. Pope first imagines critics who have been blessed with wit as a gift of heaven: 'Some, to whom Heav'n in Wit has been profuse'(80), implying that wit is an innate quality that critics either do or do not have. But the next line forces the reader to re-examine the word as Pope refers to it in an apparently contradictory sense: 'Want as much more, to turn it to its use' (81). Wit is now seen as only partly God given; it is equally important for man to nurture, and develop it. In his *Reflections Critical and Satyrical, Upon a Late Rhapsody, Call'd, An Essay Upon Criticism*, 1711, Dennis mocked Pope for this apparent contradiction, but Pope stuck with the paradox and, although he made several other revisions, did not change it. As with his discussion of nature Pope goes on to clinch his meaning through his imagery:

> For *Wit* and *Judgment* often are at strife,
> Tho' meant each other's Aid, like *Man* and *Wife*.   (82–3)

Ideally wit and judgment should work in a happy partnership, not be opposed to one another, as Hobbes and the members of the Royal Society had been arguing. By giving 'strife' the rhyme position however Pope implies that, only too often, it unfortunately predominates over the desired harmony.

The final image, running through the last four lines of the passage, describes Pegasus, the winged horse of mythology said to bear poets in flights of poetic inspiration. As with marriage, in which man and wife should be 'each other's Aid' (83), so in riding where horse and rider need to work, like wit and judgment, in close partnership:

> The winged Courser, like a gen'rous Horse,
> Shows most true Mettle when you *check* his Course.

The reined horse runs better than the wild stallion. Like liberty, Pegasus is a good horse to ride, but to ride somewhere.

This excerpt illustrates the range and visual precision of Pope's imagination. The abstractions of 'Nature', 'Wit', and 'Judgment' are made real to the reader through what Dr Johnson describes as 'a mind active, ambitious and adventurous, always investigating, always aspiring; in its widest searches still longing to go forward, in its highest flights still wishing to be higher; always imagining something greater than it knows, always endeavouring more than it can do'.[4]

Windsor-Forest

Windsor-Forest was originally written at two different periods in Pope's life and subsequently revised into a single poem.[1] The first part (1–290), was initially written in 1704, at the same time as his *Pastorals*, when he was only sixteen. The second part (291–434), was written eight years later, in 1712, to herald the 'Sacred Peace' and 'long-expected' (355) Treaty of Utrecht, the preliminaries for which had been agreed in London in October 1711, but which was not finally ratified until 11 April 1713. Pope worked on these two parts, altering and adding to them, throughout the summer, autumn and winter of 1712. The finished poem was then published on 7 March 1713, a few weeks before the Treaty was finally signed. Since the Treaty of Utrecht was supported by the Tories and opposed by the Whigs, Pope was publicly taking up an uncharacteristically clear party political position in publishing the poem, quite apart from the various pro-Stuart references it contained. All the evidence, especially that emerging from his correspondence, indicates that he did not simply join two separate pieces of composition together when he revised the poem in 1712, but that he endeavoured in all he did 'to make *Windsor-Forest* all of a piece'.[2] The result is a poem of acknowledged richness and complexity, working on many levels, drawing on mythology, history and prophecy, extending through time and space, and projecting a range of interconnected philosophical, political and visionary meanings.

Windsor-Forest is a descriptive-reflective poem, derived partly from the model of Denham's *Cooper's Hill*, 1642, which Dr Johnson described in his 'Life of Denham', as the work that conferred upon him the rank and dignity of an original author. 'He seems to have been . . . the author of a species of composition that may be denominated *local poetry*, of which the fundamental subject is some particular landscape, to be poetically described, with the addition of such embellishments as may be supplied by historical retrospection or incidental meditation.'[3] In *Cooper's Hill* Denham describes the prospect from the top of the hill, looking out over St Paul's, Windsor Castle, St Anne's Hill, Chertsey, the Thames and Runnymede. The poem is not so much one of landscape as of landmarks, in which the different objects spark off historical reflections. The prospect is seen as an allegorist or historian would see it: everything about it is emblematic or significant from an historical point of view.

Like Denham's poem, Pope's *Windsor-Forest* is initially organized around a landmark, Windsor Forest, that calls up historical and moral reflections, and like Denham Pope has as one of his informing themes the concept of *concordia discors*, the idea that harmony comes from a mixture of opposing forces.[4] Pope's poem also recalls Denham's in being written to defend and praise the ruling monarch; in Denham's case, Charles I, in Pope's, Queen Anne. Both poems were written against tense political backgrounds: Denham's at the outbreak of the Civil War and Pope's at a time of concern about the question of the royal succession. But, if Pope's poem resembles Denham's in these ways, it differs strongly from it in others. Pope takes poetic 'flight' (423) in *Windsor-Forest* in ways that Denham is not capable of doing. There is a visionary splendour and sweep to the language of Pope's poem that moves far beyond anything Denham attempts, despite Pope's admiring references to him as 'majestic' (271) and 'lofty' (280).

Pope presents us in *Windsor-Forest* with a series of contrasting scenes rather than a single framed view. There is brief acknowledgement, in the opening section, of the actual Windsor Forest as a starting point, but thereafter Pope rapidly undertakes a series of increasingly imaginative visionary excursions through seasonal, historical and mythological time. His yardstick is not empirical reality but, more than anywhere else in his poetry, literary and artistic allusiveness. *Windsor-Forest* is the most pictorial of all Pope's poems, the most influenced by his intense interest and involvement in painting. He wrote to John Caryll on 21 December 1712 complaining wryly about how much he was suffering in the very cold winter and describing his composition of *Windsor-Forest*:

My ill state of health ever since the cold weather began renders vain any such pleasing thoughts as of the enjoyments of your fireside: I cannot express how thoroughly I'm penetrated by the sharpness of it. I feel no thing alive but my heart and head; and my spirits, like those in a thermometer mount and fall through my thin delicate contexture just as the temper of air is more benign or inclement. In this sad condition I'm forced to take volatile drops every day: a custom I have so long continued, that my doctor tells me I must not long expect support from them, and adds that unless I use certain prescriptions, my tenement will not long last above ground. But I shall not prop it (as decayed as it is) with his rotten fulciments: if it falls, as the honest Hibernian said of the house, I care not, I'm only a lodger . . . What can be more ridiculous than that in the midst of this bleak prospect that sets my very imagination a shivering, I am endeavouring to raise up round about me a *painted scene* [my italics] of woods and forests in verdure and beauty, trees springing, fields flowering, Nature laughing. I am wandering thro' Bowers and Grottos in conceit, and

while my trembling body is cowering o'er a fire, my mind is
expatiating in an open sunshine. (I, 165–8)

Pope's comments to Caryll indicate both the conscious pictorialism
of his composition and the imaginative 'expatiation' involved. In an
attempt to protect himself against the actual cold he lets his imagination wander freely amongst 'painted scenes' of warmth and abundance. It is important to note, however, that these scenes are
conceived as imaginary, not observed ones: the fish, for example,
that he describes in such brilliant and shining colours (141–6), could
never be glimpsed, as Pope describes them, by someone actually
looking at the Thames.[5]

The 'painted scenes' Pope conjures up for the reader are frequently
Claudian, both in their composition and in their dreamlike and
idealistic quality. They are designed to evoke thoughts of a Golden
Age, as in the following lines:

> Oft in her Glass the musing Shepherd spies
> The headlong Mountains and the downward Skies,
> The wat'ry Landskip of the pendant Woods,
> And absent Trees that tremble in the Floods;
> In the clear azure Gleam the Flocks are seen,
> And floating Forests paint the Waves with Green.
> Thro' the fair Scene rowl slow the ling'ring Streams,
> Then foaming pour along, and rush into the *Thames*.
>
> (211–18)

The 'fair scene' is purified and elevated for the reader by being
viewed at a triple remove. Not only do we see it through the
distance of the poet's imagination, but the imagined landscape itself
is seen only through the 'musing Shepherd's' eyes, and he in turn
only sees it as a reflection in the Thames.

The other major literary model for *Windsor-Forest* is Virgil's *Georgics*.[6] Pope's poem, like Virgil's, is fervently patriotic:

> Fair *Liberty, Britannia's* Goddess, rears
> Her chearful Head, and leads the Golden Years. (91–2)

> Here cease thy Flight, nor with unhallow'd Lays
> Touch the fair Fame of *Albion's* Golden Days. (423–4)

Pope, in imitation of his Virgilian model, looks forward to a future
Golden Age. As in Virgil's *Georgics*, there is a roll call of national
poets inspired by the sense of place, Denham, Cowley, Surrey and
Granville; and of national rulers associated with Windsor Castle,
William I, II and III, Edward III and IV, Henry VI, Charles I
and most particularly Anne:

157

> At length great ANNA said – Let Discord cease!
> She said, the World obey'd, and all was *Peace*! (327–4)

Pope's praise for the Thames can also be seen as a Virgilian element looking back to Virgil's praise for the Tiber. The noticeably Latinate quality of much of the diction, particularly the epithets, e.g. 'verdant Isles' (28), 'fox obscene' (71), 'liquid sky' (186), and 'lucid globe' (395), is a further way in which Pope glances back to Virgil. Finally, just as Virgil completed his *Georgics* by quoting the opening lines of his *Eclogues*, so Pope completes *Windsor-Forest* by echoing the opening lines of his *Pastorals*.

Above all *Windsor-Forest* is a visionary poem. The England of Queen Anne is transformed into a mythological Albion ruled by the Goddess Britannia (91–2), with Anne sometimes present as 'Th' Immortal Huntress', Diana (159–64), and sometimes as Juno. The Loddon, a tributary of the Thames, is metamorphosed into a rural nymph, Lodona (171–210); and the Thames itself is converted to a river-god, Old Father Thames (329–54), whose majestic vision of the future (355–422) brings the poem to a triumphant close. Pope imagines a splendid future glowing with success:

> Behold! th'ascending *Villas* on my Side
> Project long Shadows o'er the Chrystal Tyde.
> Behold! *Augusta's* glitt'ring Spires increase,
> And Temples rise, the beauteous Works of Peace.
> I see, I see where two fair Cities bend
> Their ample Bow, a new *White-Hall* ascend!
> There mighty Nations shall inquire their Doom,
> The World's great Oracle in Times to come;
> There Kings shall sue, and suppliant States be seen
> Once more to bend before a *British* QUEEN. (375–84)

The elaborately patterned syntax and parallel structures give epic grandeur and rhetorical power to the vision of London transformed to a new Augusta.

Windsor-Forest is a political, patriotic and visionary poem conceived in strikingly pictorial terms. It is a poem that attacks despotism and champions liberty, and looks forward to a time when 'Conquest will cease and Slav'ry be no more' (408). It perhaps seems somewhat naively hopeful from the hindsight of later developments in Pope's lifetime, but it remains a noble conception projected in a language of majesty and splendour. Pope offers an idealized vision of the golden Augustan age he briefly hoped was about to begin. *Windsor-Forest* stands as a monument to Pope's positive feelings about the age of Queen Anne at an early period in his life, just as, in its very different way, *The Dunciad* stands as a monument to his negative feelings about the Hanoverian age at a late period in his life. To place the following excerpt alongside the last in this section of the book is to make a dramatic contrast between Pope's early hopes for 'Peace and Plenty' and his later fears of 'Universal Darkness'.

SELECTED EXCERPT

Thy Forests, *Windsor*! and thy green Retreats,
At once the Monarch's and the Muse's Seats,
Invite my Lays. Be present, Sylvan Maids!
Unlock your Springs, and open all your Shades.
Granville commands: Your Aid O Muses bring!
What Muse for *Granville* can refuse to sing?
   The Groves of *Eden*, vanish'd now so long,
Live in Description, and look green in Song:
These, were my Breast inspir'd with equal Flame,
Like them in Beauty, should be like in Fame.   10
Here Hills and Vales, the Woodland and the Plain,
Here Earth and Water seem to strive again,
Not *Chaos*-like together crush'd and bruis'd,
But as the World, harmoniously confus'd:
Where Order in Variety we see,
And where, tho' all things differ, all agree.
Here waving Groves a checquer'd Scene display,
And part admit and part exclude the Day;
As some coy Nymph her Lover's warm Address
Nor quite indulges, nor can quite repress.   20
There, interspers'd in Lawns and opening Glades,
Thin Trees arise that shun each others Shades.
Here in full Light the russet Plains extend;
There wrapt in Clouds the blueish Hills ascend:
Ev'n the wild Heath displays her Purple Dies,
And 'midst the Desart fruitful Fields arise,
That crown'd with tufted Trees and springing Corn,
Like verdant Isles the sable Waste adorn.
Let *India* boast her Plants, nor envy we
The weeping Amber or the balmy Tree,   30
While by our Oaks the precious Loads are born,
And Realms commanded which those Trees adorn.
Not proud *Olympus* yields a nobler Sight,
Tho' Gods assembled grace his tow'ring Height,
Than what more humble Mountains offer here,
Where, in their Blessings, all those Gods appear.
See *Pan* with Flocks, with Fruits *Pomona* crown'd,
Here blushing *Flora* paints th'enamel'd Ground,

Here *Ceres'* Gifts in waving Prospect stand
And nodding tempt the joyful Reaper's Hand,   40
Rich Industry sits smiling on the Plains,
And Peace and Plenty tell, a STUART reigns.

CRITICISM   The opening invocation to Windsor's 'Forests' and 'Retreats' indicates the central theme of the poem. This will be a poem about the coexistence of opposites; about 'Forests', used here in the plural to mean wooded areas (as opposed to the larger region, Windsor Forest, referred to in the singular, which describes land outside the common law and preserved for the Sovereign's hunting), and 'green Retreats', or clearings. Pope contrasts the woodland and the plain, monarchs and muses, kings and poets, for each is part of the 'Order in Variety' that he is going to celebrate in the poem. He mythologizes this setting from the outset, invoking the presence of wood spirits – 'Be present, Sylvan Maids' – and urging them to release the springs of inspiration. The Thames becomes, by implication, the Hippocrene, the ancient Greek fountain of poetic inspiration on Mt Helicon.

The repeated references to Granville in lines 5 and 6 brings us back to the present, however, for George Granville, Lord Lansdowne, was one of the twelve new peers created by Queen Anne, on 1 January 1712, to save the Tory Ministry and the peace treaty that he had helped to negotiate. *Windsor-Forest* opens, then, by fluctuating between the past and the present, appealing to classical and mythological times as well as reminding readers of current political realities. The movement between past and present, together with prophetic excursions into the future, becomes a marked feature of Pope's imaginative development throughout the poem.

One of the most striking things about the opening lines of the poem is the urbane movement of the verse. There is an assurance in the lines that makes itself felt through the fluctuating ease of the opening address. This is not simply a matter of a variety in the placing of the caesura, though that is certainly to be found, so much as of a flexibility that results from a careful and complex organization of the syntactical units. In the opening invocation there is both sufficient balance in the rhythm (e.g. line 2) to give a sense of harmony, and sufficient check (e.g. the double caesura of line 1) to give a slight contrast and avoid the dangers of mechanical harmony. The elaboration of the subject in the opening sentence that occurs in the first two lines contrasts with the brevity of the main verb and object at the beginning of the third line. The poem then takes a sudden change of direction as the poet moves from the indicative to the imperative mood. The changing pattern in the unfolding syntactical structure of the paragraph compels the reader to pay special attention. At the same time as the mood of the verb changes, however, an element of stability and continuity is retained by keeping the imperative clauses parallel to one another:

> Be present, Sylvan Maids!
> Unlock your Springs, and open all your Shades.   (3–4)

In the fifth and sixth lines Pope moves back to the indicative and emphasizes the compliment to Granville by inverting the verbs so that the couplet has a distinctly heroic quality. The first six lines form a conventional opening invocation and dedication, but they do so with an ease and charm that carry the reader into the poem proper in a relaxed and expectant frame of mind.

The description of Windsor Forest that forms the subject of the long second paragraph begins with a comparison to Milton's description of Eden in *Paradise Lost*. The actual locality that Pope knew so well is transformed through literary allusion into a modern paradise. Windsor Forest becomes a microcosm of the glory of God's creation throughout the world:

> Here Hills and Vales, the Woodland and the Plain,
> Here Earth and Water, seem to strive again,
> Not *Chaos*-like together crush'd and bruis'd,
> But as the World, harmoniously confus'd:
> Where Order in Variety we see,
> And where, tho' all things differ, all agree.   (11–16)

The couplet form, with its inherent structural duality, is ideally suited to the theme of *concordia discors* being expounded here. In the first line and a half, each quarter line is in opposition to the next quarter at the same time as it is bound to it by the parallel structure. In the next couplet each line is opposed to the other through the contrary ideas ('Not . . . But . . .'), while they are bound together by the repeating rhythm and connecting rhyme. The harmony that results despite the opposition of disparate elements in Pope's poetry is directly related to the harmony that results from the opposition of disparate elements in the physical world. The order in variety that exists in the handling of the couplet form helps to establish the 'Order in Variety' in Windsor Forest.

As Pope develops his description of the forest, so he introduces the technique of antithesis to capture the tension between opposites that is the source of the harmony he celebrates. The daylight in the forest is more enticing for being partly excluded by the trees, just as the lover's overtures are heightened for being partly repressed by the coy mistress. Sometimes the antithesis works within the couplet, with one line balanced against the other (23 and 24), and sometimes it works within the individual line, with one half of the line operating against the other (26 and 28). Ideas and images that would move in different directions if developed separately are thus fused together through the verse form to give an overall harmony.

The scene imagined between lines 7 and 42, and particularly that between lines 17 and 28, is organized like an idealized landscape painting, such as Claude Lorrain, or his English imitators John Wootton and George Lambert, might have painted. I have discussed this aspect of the poem in some detail in chapter 3, pp. 80–2. Particular features of a landscape painting developed in these lines include Pope's interest in the varying play of light throughout the scene, his arrangement of the whole composition into bands of merging perspective, and the gentle colouring that he gives to the entire imagined prospect.

The mood becomes increasingly patriotic and triumphant as the poem progresses. The rich luxuriance of eastern vegetation, 'the weeping Amber or the balmy Tree', becomes subservient to the sturdy strength of the English oak. Even 'proud Olympus' is seen as no more noble than the humble height of the English hills. The last comparison is clearly farfetched, but is has been sufficiently well prepared for to become playfully acceptable in its context. Thus Windsor Forest, which Pope began by comparing to the Christian Garden of Eden, is now compared to the home of the classical gods. It has become a mythological paradise with Queen Anne transformed, by implication, in the last sentence of the paragraph, into Juno commanding Roman gods on English soil. The opening command to attend, 'See', (37); the fullness of the rhythms; the affirmative force of the adjectival participles (blushing, waving, nodding and smiling); the alliteration and personification; and the continuing parallelism of the 'Here' clauses, all serve to reinforce this final panegyric effect.

The Rape of the Lock

The Rape of the Lock has long been regarded as Pope's best-loved and most charming poem. Dr Johnson called it 'the most airy, the most ingenious and the most delightful of all his compositions'.[1] It is a consummate achievement in which Pope glowingly evokes the luxurious world of sexual enticement associated with the rituals of eighteenth-century English high society courtship. While recent criticism has taken issue with Pope's attitude to women and his construction of the reader's expectations in the poem, neither of these critical perspectives has wanted to deny the elegant poetic quality of Pope's mock-epic masterpiece.[2] Pope's imagination was more inventive, exuberant and original, and his language more brilliantly responsive in this poem than in any other he wrote.

The work had its topical origins in a contemporary feud between two land-owning Catholic families, the Petres and the Fermors. The young Lord Petre had cut a lock of hair from the head of Arabella Fermor, a fashionable young society lady, and both she and her family had taken offence. Pope was told of the incident by his Catholic friend John Caryll, who asked if he could do anything to mend the division between the two families by making a jest of it and 'laughing them together again'.[3] *The Rape of the Locke* (with an 'e'), in two cantos, written in less than a fortnight in 1711, and published on 20 May 1712, was the result.

The Rape of the Lock, in five cantos, was not written till a year after the publication of the two canto version, and not published till two years later, on 4 March 1714. This was a much more considered and polished piece of work, over two and a half times as long as the first version, and containing the major addition of the supernatural elements that Pope refers to in his prefatory letter to the poem as the 'Machinery'. Then in 1717, in preparing the poem for the first edition of his *Collected Works*, Pope introduced 'grave Clarissa's' speech (Canto V, 9–34), 'to open more clearly the MORAL of the Poem', as he tells us in a footnote. Thus the poem went through three main stages of composition. It is the last version that we usually read today.

The prefatory letter, addressed to Mrs Arabella Fermor, which Pope wrote for the 1717 edition, illustrates well the measured ambivalence of his attitude to women in the poem as he insists that 'it was intended only to divert a few young Ladies, who have good Sense and good Humour enough, to laugh not only at their Sex's little unguarded Follies, but at their own'. Pope may have been inclined to argue that the emphasis was meant to fall on his intention to divert, but the diminutive is clearly there to disparage the 'few young Ladies' and the tone is self-consciously arch. He then goes on to say that 'the ancient poets are in one respect like many modern Ladies; Let an Action be never so trivial in itself, they always make it appear of the utmost importance', and that he knows 'how disagreeable it is to make use of hard words before a Lady'. The complimentary tone is none the less condescending for being disguised as a pleasantry.

The Rape of the Lock is what Pope calls on the title page 'An Heroi-Comical Poem', or what we now call a mock-epic. Since the poem oscillates between comicality and mockery both descriptions are helpful. A minor incident, in this case the cutting off of a young lady's side curl, is comically exalted and the brouhaha associated with it ridiculed, by being cast in the framework of the epic structure. There is a conscious disparity between content and form: 'Slight is the Subject, but not so the Praise' as Pope says in Canto 1, line 5. Pope deliberately turns the eighteenth-century concept of decorum upside down. He takes an insignificant subject matter and describes it in a grand style. Consider the opening lines of the poem:

> What dire Offence from am'rous Causes springs,
> What mighty Contests rise from trivial Things,
> I sing – This Verse to *Caryll*, Muse! is due;
> This, ev'n *Belinda* may vouchsafe to view:
> Slight is the Subject, but not so the Praise,
> If She inspire, and He approve my Lays.
>   Say what strange Motive, Goddess! cou'd compel
> A well-bred *Lord* t'assault a gentle *Belle*?
> Oh say what stranger Cause, yet unexplor'd,
> Cou'd make a gentle *Belle* reject a *Lord*?
> In Tasks so bold, can Little Men engage,
> And in soft Bosoms dwells such mighty Rage?   (I, 1–12)

The rhetorical proposition of the theme and the suspension of the main verb, as, for example, in the opening of *The Aeneid*, 'Arms and the man, I sing', give the reader epic expectations that are then brought down to earth with the address, in line 3, to Pope's friend Caryll, juxtaposed to the invocation to the Muse. The epic style is comically deflated through association with the familiar and the everyday. The polished compliments to Belinda's beauty and Caryll's judgment that follow in lines 5 and 6 are elaborations of the tongue-in-cheek tone. The introduction, in the second paragraph, of a 'well-bred *Lord*' and 'gentle *Belle*' extends this ironical tone, for such persons are not the most likely agents of epic action, far less does one look for good breeding and gentility to be involved in 'assault'. Pope builds his mock-epic tone on the comical incongruity of opposites: bold tasks and little men; mighty rage and soft bosoms. There is a mixture of comicality and mockery in these lines that is typical of the whole poem. The attitude behind the comic elements is friendly and affectionate; that behind the mock elements, not always easily separable, is more distanced and aloof. The overall tone of the poem is one of smiling ambivalence, of affection mixed with equivocation, with the poet's voice remaining continually elusive, carefully avoiding any single fixed stance.

There are levels of seriousness in *The Rape of the Lock*, particularly in the criticism of the social and the economic mores of eighteenth-century English life, that have been well elaborated by modern critics.[4] But there is also a joyousness in the poem very different from anything else in Pope's poetry. This is Pope's most delicate poem, as well as his most playful and urbane. It was written, like *Windsor-Forest*, during the period of his deepest involvement in painting, and, like that poem, is shot through with the influence of such practice. The description of the sylphs in Canto II, for example, has many of the qualities of a water colour:

> Transparent Forms, too fine for mortal Sight,
> Their fluid Bodies half dissolv'd in light.
> Loose to the Wind their airy Garments flew,
> Thin glitt'ring Textures of the filmy Dew;
> Dipt in the richest Tincture of the Skies,
> Where Light disports in ever-mingling Dies,
> While ev'ry beam new transient Colours flings,
> Colours that change whene'er they wave their Wings.
>
> (II, 61–8)

The whole poem is permeated with similar fluid and changing colours. Another way in which Pope establishes this transience is through the momentariness encapsulated in the use of present participles. Things are constantly 'trembling', 'floating', 'waving', 'fluttering', 'shining', 'sparkling', 'mingling', 'melting', and, above all, 'glittering'. This focus on the visual shimmer and attractiveness of Belinda's world is a recurring and central metaphor in the poem for the mutability of existence.

Pope's description of Belinda's progress up the 'Silver Thames' to Hampton Court at the beginning of Canto II (1–18) illustrates some of these qualities. Belinda is praised as the 'Rival' of the sun's 'Beams' (3). 'Every eye is fix'd on her alone' (6). On her 'white Breast' she wears 'a sparkling Cross' (7). Her looks are 'lively' (9), her mind 'sprightly' (9), and her eyes 'as bright as the sun' (13); she is the very picture of 'graceful Ease and Sweetness void of pride' (15). Yet, as she moves up the Thames, like Aeneas up the Tiber or

Cleopatra up the Nile, we are invited to note the flightiness of her context. Her looks may be lovely but they are unfixed; her smiles generous but unselective. Pope suggests her faults by ironically suggesting that belles have no 'faults' and by drawing a fine distinction between 'faults' and 'errors':

> If to her share some Female Errors fall,
> Look on her Face, and you'll forget 'em all.   (II, 17–18)

The two lines of the couplet are sharply counterbalanced. In the almost instantaneous transition from the first to the second line Pope shifts the focus from ethics to aesthetics, from considerations of morality to considerations of beauty, but in doing so he leaves both registers poised for consideration by the reader, while his own voice hovers deftly between the two. The speed of the shift in focus is enhanced by the elision at the end, and the chatty informality of the tone thereby established assumes the reader's agreement.

The place, time and action of *The Rape of the Lock* are each highly compressed. The action takes place in London on a single day, and the number of separate episodes are few. In Canto I Pope describes Belinda's dream and toilet; in Canto II her progress up the Thames to Hampton Court; in Canto III the game of cards, followed by coffee then the 'rape'; in Canto IV Umbriel's descent to the Cave of Spleen; and in Canto V the ensuing fracas and apotheosis of the lock. The relation of place, time and action in Pope's mock-epic to that found in true epic is one of diminution. The place is reduced from the extensive settings of the *Odyssey*, the *Aeneid*, or *Paradise Lost* to the narrow circumference of London; the time from the ten or twenty years of the *Iliad* or the *Odyssey* to a single day; and the action from the many heroic episodes of the classical epics to those listed briefly here. The length of the poem is diminished from the traditional twelve, or twenty-four, books to five cantos of about 150 lines each; and the Machinery, from the all powerful deities who act as shapers of Fate and guardians of the heroes in classical epic, to the tiny and fragile sylphs who vainly try to protect Belinda but can accidentally be cut in half if they don't take care. This process of reduction and diminution in the structure of the poem is an essential part of Pope's joke. The reader is delighted with each example of epic compression and reads on from incident to incident eager to see what will be parodically packed into the next nutshell.

In addition to its comic impact, *The Rape of the Lock* focuses powerfully on social mores. Pope satirizes the scale of values in upper-class eighteenth-century English society – male and female. The Baron and Sir Plume are no better than Belinda and Thalestris; the 'daring Sparks' (I, 73), no better than the 'melting Maids' (I, 71); the beaux no better than the belles. Pope ridicules the life of the

The Cave of Spleen, illustration for The Rape of the Lock, *Canto IV,*
designed by Louis Du Guernier and engraved by Claude Du Bosc, 1714

167

entire beaumonde in which moral values are as durable as the latest fashion. In such a world there are no fixed moral standards. Everything is fluid and changing:

> With varying Vanities, from ev'ry Part,
> They shift the moving Toyshop of their Heart;
> Where Wigs with Wigs, with Sword-knots Sword-knots strive,
> Beaus banish Beaus, and Coaches Coaches drive.
>
> (I, 99–102)

One fashionable item is no sooner in the ascendant than it is driven out by the latest. The human heart is a 'moving Toyshop', full of knick-knacks, trinkets, baubles and gewgaws.

On one level *The Rape of the Lock* is a lighthearted satire on the ritual surrounding eighteenth-century English high-society courtship. Human beings behave like animals while mating, erecting an elaborate ceremony of display before pairing off. Belinda preens and primps herself in front of her dressing-table in order to entice the Baron, but finally she over-displays and pays a penalty for doing so. Just as Belinda over-displays, the Baron obliges by over-responding. He as heartily acts the expected male role as she willingly performs the female. The poet observes the dalliance and pursuit of these courtship rituals as clearly and objectively as an anthropologist observing the mating habits of so-called primitive tribes in foreign lands.

At another level *The Rape of the Lock* is less lighthearted, touching on a world of violence and aggression beneath the dazzling surface of the world of society life. We find these darker threads not only in the occasional cutting asperity of a savage couplet like,

> The hungry Judges soon the Sentence sign,
> And Wretches hang that Jury-Men may Dine;
>
> (III, 21–2)

but also in the implications of sexual threat present both in the title and at various other points in the poem. Pope plays with *risqué* allusions, as in the notorious closing couplet of Canto IV:

> Oh hads't thou, Cruel! been content to seize
> Hairs less in sight, or any Hairs but these! (IV, 175–6)

The indecencies, however, are rarely self-indulgent. Here, as elsewhere, the *double-entendre* carries significance: in such a world outward appearance is all that matters. To a young society lady the reputation of chastity is more important than the reality.

The most disturbing section of the poem is Umbriel's visit to 'the gloomy Cave of Spleen', or descent to the Underworld, a virtually obligatory epic episode, in Canto IV. This is a 'dismal Dome' (IV,

18), and 'sullen Region' (IV, 19), where the 'dreaded East is all the Wind that blows' (IV, 20). It is a terrifying territory inhabited by 'glaring Fiends, and Snakes on rolling Spires' (IV, 43). Pope's imagination is at its most inventive here as he projects the neuroses of the human psyche into phantasmagoric patterns:

> Unnumber'd throngs on ev'ry side are seen
> Of Bodies chang'd to various Forms by *Spleen*.
> Here living *Teapots* stand, one Arm held out,
> One bent; the Handle this, and that the Spout:
> A Pipkin there like *Homer's Tripod* walks;
> Here sighs a Jar, and there a Goose-pye talks;
> Men prove with Child, as pow'rful Fancy works,
> And Maids turn'd Bottels, call aloud for Corks.
>
> (IV, 47–54)

The extraordinary metamorphosed forms, a 'fantastick Band' (IV, 55), present strikingly graphic formulations of the inner frustrations and torments that a person such as Belinda might have suffered as a result of having to lead such a limited social existence. The scene is nightmarish and comic at the same time, both looking back to the grotesque visions of Hieronymus Bosch and anticipating the blacker comedies of the twentieth century. The absurd shapes, the 'Unnumbered throngs on ev'ry side', are transformations emanating from darker regions of the human mind than the 'Transparent Forms' (II, 61), with their 'Thin glitt'ring Textures of the filmy Dew' (II, 64), that dominate most of the poem. It would be wrong to take the scene too seriously. The teapots, pipkin and goose-pie are highly comical, and meant to be so, as numerous illustrators of the poem have demonstrated; but it is also undeniable that Pope is dealing with disconcerting and troubling psychological forces in these shifting scenes. The final image in the lines quoted above overturns expected social norms in a brutally erotic way that betrays the poet's male complicity in the rape fantasy.

The Rape of the Lock's underlying subject is disintegration and flux. Matter constantly changes shape. Nothing remains stable for very long. The sylphs were themselves once human beings: as Ariel tells Belinda in the first canto, 'by a soft transition we repair / from earthly Vehicles to these of Air' (I, 49–50). Pope continually confronts the reader with the transience of human life and the mutability of female beauty. He does so most explicitly in Clarissa's speech in Canto V, warning that 'frail beauty must decay' and that 'painted or not painted, all shall fade' (V, 27), but the implication of such transience is present in much of the poem's imagery. As Pope says in describing Belinda's epic lamentation after the 'rape':

> Not louder Shrieks to pitying Heav'n are cast,
> When Husbands or when Lap-dogs breathe their last,
> Or when rich *China* Vessels, fal'n from high,
> In glittring Dust and painted Fragments lie!   (III, 157–60)

The 'China Vessels', like the 'living Teapots' in the Cave of Spleen, are images of human fragility, images moreover with a powerful sexual resonance. The insubstantiality of the fallen 'China Vessels', lying in 'glittring Dust and painted Fragments' is picked up and repeated in a different context at the end of the poem when Pope gently reminds Belinda that she too will be reduced to such a state:

> When those fair Suns shall sett, as sett they must,
> And all those Tresses shall be laid in Dust;   (V, 147–8)

There are liturgical and biblical echoes here, particularly from the Book of Job: 'Soon have I to lie down in the dust' (7:21); and 'They shall lie down alike in the dust, and the worms shall cover them' (21:26). But the poem is finally comic not tragic, and the closing image is one of dedication not disintegration:

> *This Lock*, the Muse shall consecrate to Fame,
> And mid'st the Stars inscribe *Belinda's* Name!   (V, 149–50)

SELECTED EXCERPT

> And now, unveil'd, the *Toilet* stands display'd,
> Each Silver Vase in mystic Order laid.
> First, rob'd in White, the Nymph intent adores
> With Head uncover'd, the *Cosmetic* Pow'rs.
> A heav'nly Image in the Glass appears,
> To that she bends, to that her Eyes she rears;
> Th'inferior Priestess, at her Altar's side,
> Trembling, begins the sacred Rites of Pride.
> Unnumber'd Treasures ope at once, and here
> The various Off'rings of the World appear;   130
> From each she nicely culls with curious Toil,
> And decks the Goddess with the glitt'ring Spoil.
> This Casket *India's* glowing Gems unlocks,
> And all *Arabia* breathes from yonder Box.
> The Tortoise here, and Elephant unite,
> Transform'd to *Combs*, the speckled and the white.
> Here Files of Pins extend their shining Rows,
> Puffs, Powders, Patches, Bibles, Billet-doux.
> Now awful Beauty puts on all its Arms;
> The Fair each moment rises in her Charms,   140

Repairs her Smiles, awakens ev'ry Grace,
And calls forth all the Wonders of her Face;
Sees by Degrees a purer Blush arise,
And keener Lightnings quicken in her Eyes.
The busy *Sylphs* surround their darling Care;
These set the Head, and those divide the Hair,
Some fold the Sleeve, whilst others plait the Gown;
And *Betty's* prais'd for Labours not her own.

CRITICISM   This is the closing paragraph of Canto I. In the preceding parts of the canto Pope has announced the theme of the poem (1–12), described Belinda first waking up before falling asleep again (13–26), recounted the warning dream put into her head by Ariel (27–114), and then shown Belinda completely forget the warning when she does finally wake up and her eyes light on a *billet-doux* (115–20). This last paragraph describes, in mock-epic terms, her preparation for the day's events as she dresses and puts on her make-up.

The paragraph is a fine example of Pope's mock-epic poetry at its most skilful. Belinda's toilet preparations are invested with all the mock solemnity of the epic hero going to worship before arming for battle. The dressing table is 'unveil'd', like an altar, and all the 'silver vases', containing various kinds of make-up, are transformed into religious chalices laid out 'in mystic order'. Belinda herself is 'rob'd in white' (a petticoat perhaps) like a priest, and she 'adores' (note the careful choice of religious language) the 'Cosmetic Pow'rs', which wittily suggest both cosmic forces and a new class of angels (Powers were an order of angels within the celestial hierarchy).

As Belinda first bows her head to the 'heav'nly Image' she worships (her own reflection), then raises her eyes in adoration, it becomes clear that what Pope is presenting in this passage is an inverted Mass in which all the ritualized ceremony that should be used to worship God is used instead to worship social and personal appearance. Catholic readers especially would be quick to realize the sacrilegious nature of Belinda's toilet. The touch is light enough on the surface, but the full implications of the scene are more far-reaching. What we have here is Pope's youthful response to a theme that consistently recurs in his poetry – the theme of mankind's presumption and pride. Belinda's vanity in worshipping her own image in *The Rape of the Lock* is only a more lighthearted version of man's pride in elevating his own importance in *An Essay on Man*. The difference is that whereas in 1714 Pope can jokingly see Belinda's vanity transforming her into a 'Goddess', in *An Essay on Man*, twenty years later, Pope describes man's pride transforming him into a 'vile worm'.

The parody of religious worship is of course a way of ridiculing Belinda's vanity not religion itself, just as the use of a mock-epic form in the poem as a whole is a way of diminishing trivial events not an attempt to make fun of epic poetry. The parody continues as Betty, 'the inferior Priestess', presents sacrificial oblations, 'the various Off'rings of the World', to the Goddess and decks Belinda with the 'glitt'ring Spoil'. Pope has moved now to the arming of the epic hero for battle. In terms of the toilet the word 'spoil' refers to the various jewels and perfumes used to make up Belinda, but in terms of the mock-epic the word describes the arms and armour seized from a defeated enemy. At the same time the word has a further ambiguity, for it also suggests a more general plunder and spoliation. Belinda's beauty depends on imported luxuries pillaged from India and Arabia. The economic criticism that lurks behind the description is an early indication of those concerns that Pope developed with such burning indignation in the satires of the 1730s. The touch here, however, is more jocular, and is perhaps typified by the comic unification of the small and the great as the shell of the tortoise and the ivory of the elephant are converted into combs for a lady's dressing-table. Distortions in scale are intrinsically funny as Swift shows so effectively in the Lilliputian and Brobdingnagian contrasts of *Guilliver's Travels*.

The comparison of Belinda to the epic hero arming for battle continues with the military allusion of the 'files of pins' extending their 'shining Rows' like columns of soldiers lined up in polished armour. Belinda's various items of armour are then listed: 'Puffs, Powders, Patches, Bibles, Billet-doux'. Alliteration gives precision to the catalogue and adds force to the telling juxtaposition of 'Bibles' and 'Billet-doux'. Belinda makes no distinction between spiritual and amatory scripture. As one by one she puts on all her 'arms', so she becomes a more redoutable protagonist for the epic contest with the Baron. Finally her Beauty is 'awful', and her eyes flash with 'keener Lightnings'.

The whole paragraph has a remarkable deftness of touch. The mock-epic allusions are playful without being heavyhanded, and the portrait of Belinda is sufficiently flattering to avoid giving offence. Indeed there is a sense in which Belinda emerges as a figure of praise rather than criticism. She is a heroine whose beauty, charms, smiles, face and eyes are each admired. The final image is one of pleasure in the overall effect she produces.

In terms of the complete poem, what Pope is doing is showing the fashionable young eighteenth-century lady making elaborate preparations to attract the foppish young eighteenth-century man. The scene is an integral part of the analysis of the ritual of courtship that runs through the whole poem. Pope's attitude to such over-display is essentially good-natured, even forgiving. If one puts this passage beside his description of Lady Mary Wortley Montagu's toilet preparations in *An Epistle to a Lady*, written twenty years later, one is immediately aware of a very different attitude. Although Belinda's beauty is transient, it is at least delicate and 'glittering' while it lasts. Lady Mary's toilet, on the other hand, is a 'greasy task'. She is compared to an insect rather than an epic hero:

> So morning Insects that in muck begun,
> Shine, buzz, and fly-blow in the setting sun. (27–8)

Pope's disgust for female vanity in general, and for Lady Mary in particular, has taken on a Swiftian dimension. The interested reader should compare Swift's *The Progress of Beauty*, 1719, or *A Beautiful Young Nymph Going to Bed*, 1731, a kind of anti-toilet poem which describes the process of stripping down rather than making up. The passage is also worth comparing to the opening of 'A Game of Chess' in *The Waste Land*. Eliot too satirizes the fragile world of extravagant luxury, but whereas Belinda is fully at ease in her world, the lady in Eliot's poem is as nervous and unsure of herself as the flickering flames that spring from the sevenbranched candelabra. Augustan confidence has given way to twentieth-century doubt.

Eloisa to Abelard

Pope's poem, written in 1716 and first published in his collected *Works* of 1717, is based on the well-known love story of Peter Abelard (1079–1142), the famous French philosopher, theologian and master scholar, and Heloise (1101–64), his erudite pupil with whom he fell in love when he was forty and she was eighteen. Abelard was the intellectual idol of Paris and had a large following of students, numbering many thousands. At the time of his affair with Heloise he was living in the house of her uncle and guardian, a man named Fulbert, who was one of the canons of Notre Dame Cathedral in Paris. When the affair was discovered and Heloise found she was pregnant, Abelard conveyed her to his family's chateau, in Brittany, where she gave birth to a son, whom she named Astrolabe. To appease her uncle, Abelard married Heloise (although she protested that she preferred to remain his mistress) on condition the marriage remained a secret, since he was bound to celibacy if he was to advance in the ecclesiastical world. Her uncle, however, was not satisfied with this arrangement, and the relationship between the two men deteriorated to such an extent that Fulbert hired two ruffians, one of whom was Abelard's own servant, who broke into his bedroom one night and castrated him.

Abelard then became a monk and Heloise a nun. He first sought the abbey of St Denis, just outside Paris and one of the most famous monasteries in Europe, for his home, but after a series of confrontations with his monastic superiors left the abbey for the solitude of a hermit's life. He built himself a small oratory, which he called the *Paraclete* (the Holy Ghost) near Troyes, about a hundred miles south-east of Paris. In spite of his chosen solitude students discovered him, flocked to his hermitage and urged him to continue teaching. The sheer number who came to hear Abelard eventually obliged him to leave the *Paraclete*, but not before he managed to install Heloise there as abbess of a community of nuns. In the early 1130s, a dozen years or so after their passionate love affair, they exchanged a series of seven letters which recounted their story. This correspondence, in which three of the letters, and those by far the most ardent, were written by Heloise and four by Abelard, was occasioned by a letter that Abelard wrote to a friend in trouble, intending to give him consolation through a comparison with his own sorrows. The letter, containing a history of the calamities of his life, fell by chance into Heloise's hands and prompted the first of her three letters.

This collection of letters became especially popular in seventeenth-century France when various translations and adaptations of the original Latin appeared. In England a version, translated from the French by John Hughes, which has been called 'largely a work of imagination' by Abelard's most authoritative biographer, was published in 1713.[1] It was this version of the story that Pope read and used to provide some of the details of his poem.

The exact narrative details of the love story vary, depending on the translation, and each version gives different perspectives on it. To what extent was the forty-year-old Abelard taking unfair advantage of an impressionable young girl? To what extent was she simply a 'tender lamb' and he a 'ravening wolf' as Abelard himself puts it, without apparent irony, in his autobiographical letter?[2] Was it pressure from Abelard or Heloise that the marriage should not be declared? How willing was Heloise to take the veil and forsake her child to the care of Abelard's sister? What matters, in considering Pope's poem, of course, is not the answer to these questions, but what Pope made of the story. How does he interpret a well-known love story in his poem? To what poetic uses does he put the story? What is his interest in it, and how does he view its significance?

Pope took Heloise's three letters and re-cast them as a single heroic epistle. Heloise, or Eloisa, as Pope calls her, is imagined speaking throughout a poem in which the main theme is the struggle within her between love for God and love for man, or, to use Pope's words from 'The Argument' that preceded the poem, 'the struggles of grace and nature, virtue and passion'. Passages presenting Eloisa's inner turmoil are mixed with passages describing the gloomy Gothic setting that Pope uses to heighten the poem's emotional intensity. The poem is loosely constructed around Eloisa's recollection of the development of her and Abelard's love for one another, but it is not really a narrative poem, for Pope assumes the reader's familiarity with the events of the story and sets out to give a particular interpretation of them, from the woman's point of view, rather than to recount them in a narrative way. The emphasis falls on Eloisa's present and deeply felt response to the events rather than on her relation of them.

The poem is modelled on Ovid's *Heroides*. Eloisa proclaims her plight in the grand style, and if we find this somewhat artificial today it is largely because we are no longer familiar with the heroic convention. Heroic epistles were rhetorical expressions of what women were meant to feel but not say. They were cast in the form of letters written by women to their absent lovers, expressing the anguish of their lost love. Since the object of their love was absent or lost the feeling expressed became magnified and even more painful.

175

The convention has been well described by a recent critic, quoting from Butler's *Hudibras*, as 'a way of putting into language the "unnatural No-voice" of silenced women'.[3]

Pope's epistle works in just such a way. As a nun Eloisa is a silenced woman, but she recalls events of at least twelve years earlier, 'a sad variety of woe' (36), with all the immediacy and fervour one might expect from someone to whom they had happened yesterday. She is totally immersed in the memory of her tragic love for Abelard, and cannot help reliving the experience of it as she struggles to suppress her passionate feelings and pours out all her heart. She knows that as a nun she should not allow love for man to gain precedence in her rational soul over contemplation of God, but she cannot control her human emotions:

> Yet, yet I love! – From Abelard it came,
> And *Eloisa* yet must kiss the name.   (7–8)

The repeated 'yets' express Eloisa's tumult and her inability to repress it. Pope uses such reiterative devices throughout the poem to establish her anguished feelings and passionate inner struggle.

Eloisa's heart moves impulsively to thoughts of Abelard, and, try as she will, she cannot restrain its 'stubborn pulse' (27). Despite all her misfortunes, she still proclaims her belief in 'true passion' (79), and majestically professes the all-encompassing quality of her love for Abelard:

> Should at my feet the world's great master fall,
> Himself, his throne, his world, I'd scorn 'em all: (85–6)

This is love on a grand scale. It is high passion expressed in high, rhetorical language. Pope gives utterance to Eloisa's tragic passion in heroic and declarative style.

Despite Eloisa's traumatic experiences, part of her still clings to an idealized belief in the bliss to be achieved 'when love is liberty, and nature, law' (92). She knows that she ought to grieve for her behaviour and 'repent old pleasures' (186), but it is an unequal task, and she cannot achieve it. Finally, in desperation, Eloisa imagines the moment of her own death. The thought of an after-life offers the only peace to which she can hope to aspire:

> I come, I come! prepare your roseate bow'rs,
> Celestial palms, and ever-blooming flow'rs.
> Thither, where sinners may have rest, I go,
> Where flames refin'd in breasts seraphic glow.   (317–20)

But even at this moment, when preparing her soul for everlasting rest, thoughts of Abelard intrude:

Thou, *Abelard*! the last sad office pay,
And smooth my passage to the realms of day:
See my lips tremble, and my eye-balls roll,
Suck my last breath, and catch my flying soul!   (321–4)

Her imagined death, like her buried life, becomes an erotic experience that she cannot suppress.

The intensity of Eloisa's emotional turmoil is given dramatic force through the shifting audience of her address. Sometimes she addresses herself, 'what means this tumult in a Vestal's veins?' (4); while at other times she addresses the physical surroundings of the cell that imprison her, 'Relentless walls!' (17). Sometimes she addresses Abelard, in name and memory, 'Oh name for ever sad! for ever dear!' (31); while at other times, and these the most frequent and urgent in the poem, she addresses him as if he were actually present, 'Come! with thy looks, thy words, relieve my woe' (119); or 'Come *Abelard*, for what hast thou to dread?' (257); or 'Come, thou dar'st, all charming as thou art!' (281). Sometimes she addresses Heaven, 'Assist me heav'n' (179); and at others she addresses an idealized concept of virtue, 'O grace serene!' (297). At times she addresses participants in the events, as, for instance, when she relives the assault on Abelard and cries out to one of his attackers, 'Barbarian stay!' (103); and at all times we, as readers, are admitted to intimacy with her fevered struggle. The insistency of the first person singular presentation gives added dramatic intensity to the passionate eloquence of her declaration, as, for example, when she briefly attempts to renounce her 'sinful' thoughts:

No, fly me, fly me! far as Pole from Pole;
Rise *Alps* between us! and whole oceans roll!
Ah come not, write not, think not once of me,
Nor share one pang of all I felt for thee.
Thy oaths I quit, thy memory resign,
Forget, renounce me, hate whate'er was mine.   (289–94)

The staccato movement within the lines, the short, desperate imperatives, the imaginative grasping for extremes of geographical distance, the accumulated prohibitions and the gasping interjections each augment the direct personal involvement of her dramatic apostrophe to create a poetry of ringing, exclamatory effect.

Pope concludes the poem with a coda in which Eloisa imagines a future time, 'ages hence' (345), when two lovers come by chance to her and Abelard's burial place at the *Paraclete*[4] and, 'with mutual pity mov'd' (351), shed a tear over their grave. In lines that reflect back on himself, Pope then has Eloisa close the poem by imagining that some future poet, who shares her anguished grief and enforced absence from the loved one, tells her and Abelard's sad story. The final lines seem to glance at Pope's own situation, perhaps at his feelings for Lady Mary Wortley Montagu, who had just left for a stay of at least five years in Constantinople where her husband had been appointed Ambassador.

In *Eloisa to Abelard* Pope presents us with a tragic heroine, trapped in her physical surroundings and emotional circumstances. She is imprisoned both by the 'relentless walls' of her cell and the hopelessness of her personal situation. She is torn between the dutiful devotions of the contemplative life, to which her spirit calls her, and the ardent desires of her heart, which her imagination constantly brings to her mind. Pope's depiction of Eloisa's anguished predicament is deeply felt, dramatic and packed with imaginative colouring. Perhaps not a little of the feeling he instills so powerfully into this depiction comes from his own experience as a person of heightened sensibility caged in a crippled body. Pope's deformed shape and dwarfed size made it difficult for him to establish reciprocal love relationships with women, as we know from the report of Lady Mary Wortley Montagu's laughing rejection of his declaration of love.[5] Although he did, later in life, develop deep bonds of affection with Martha Blount, those bonds had not been developed at the time he wrote *Eloisa to Abelard*, and it is reasonable to suggest that the intense feeling he presents so powerfully in this poem is related, at a certain level, to his own experience of thwarted romantic sentiment.

SELECTED EXCERPT

> How happy is the blameless Vestal's lot!
> The world forgetting, by the world forgot.
> Eternal sun-shine of the spotless mind!
> Each pray'r accepted, and each wish resign'd;   210
> Labour and rest, that equal periods keep;
> 'Obedient slumbers that can wake and weep';
> Desires compos'd, affections ever ev'n,
> Tears that delight, and sighs that waft to heav'n.
> Grace shines around her with serenest beams,
> And whisp'ring Angels prompt her golden dreams.
> For her th'unfading rose of *Eden* blooms,
> And wings of Seraphs shed divine perfumes;
> For her the Spouse prepares the bridal ring,
> For her white virgins *Hymenaeals* sing;   220
> To sounds of heav'nly harps, she dies away,
> And melts in visions of eternal day.
>   Far other dreams my erring soul employ,
>   Far other raptures, of unholy joy:

When at the close of each sad, sorrowing day,
Fancy restores what vengeance snatch'd away,
Then conscience sleeps, and leaving nature free,
All my loose soul unbounded springs to thee.
O curst, dear horrors of all-conscious night!
How glowing guilt exalts the keen delight!   230
Provoking Daemons all restraint remove,
And stir within me ev'ry source of love.
I hear thee, view thee, gaze o'er all thy charms,
And round thy phantom glue my clasping arms.
I wake – no more I hear, no more I view,
The phantom flies me, as unkind as you.
I call aloud; it hears not what I say;
I stretch my empty arms; it glides away:
To dream once more I close my willing eyes;
Ye soft illusions, dear deceits, arise!   240
Alas no more! – methinks we wandring go
Thro' dreary wastes, and weep each other's woe;
Where round some mould'ring tow'r pale ivy creeps,
And low-brow'd rocks hang nodding o'er the deeps.
Sudden you mount! you beckon from the skies;
Clouds interpose, waves roar, and winds arise.
I shriek, start up, the same sad prospect find,
And wake to all the griefs I left behind.

CRITICISM   The lines presented here contrast the peace of the true nun, 'the blameless Vestal's lot', with the tumult in Eloisa's 'erring soul', and are chosen to show how Pope's poetic range includes the expression of states of feeling not usually associated with him, and how he uses the heroic couplet to create differing effects within the same poem.

In the first paragraph Pope uses all the resources at his command to create a sense of the heavenly tranquillity of the perfect nun's life. Whereas the natural balance of the couplet's movement is frequently used by Pope to enact a sense of conflict, it is used here to enact an even and serene mood. A single caesura falls in the middle of each line, and the two halves are carefully balanced against one another. The imagery of 'eternal sunshine' and grace that 'shines around her with serenest beams' connects the nun's perfection with the light of God. Indeed the imagery of the paragraph connects her with the perfection of various senses. There is brilliant colour in her 'golden dreams', sweet smell in 'th'unfading rose' and 'divine perfumes', and soft music in the 'sounds of heav'nly harps'. The description of the nun's life mounts to a climax in the last six lines. The rhetorical pattern of this closing sentence, with its parallel introductory 'For her . . .' clauses leading into the gentle release of the last line, gives a final heroic elevation to the perfect harmony of her life.

By contrast the second paragraph, in which Eloisa describes her own dreams, is broken in movement and menacing in its imagery. The change is immediately apparent from the opening couplet where the repetition of the phrase 'Far other' prepares the reader for the shift in mood that follows. Once Eloisa's 'conscience' (227) rests 'at the close of each sad sorrowing day', then her 'Fancy' is free to assert all her 'loose soul' in her dreams. The adjective is significant and shows her conscious awareness of where her contemplative soul should be focused. The inner tumult that disturbs her during her sleep, 'all-conscious night' (229), is established through a poetry of great intensity and drama. Eloisa tells us what her dreams are like and to this extent the poetry is descriptive, but she makes us feel so much part of her dreams that it is also extremely dramatic. The movement of the verse becomes unpredictable as the short phrases act out the struggle between 'grace' and 'nature' going on within her. The use of a series of oxymorons ('dear horrors', 'glowing guilt', 'keen delight', 'dear deceits', and 'soft illusions') is not simply a rhetorical device for heroic embellishment, but a way of compressing the opposite forces that create the inner turmoil. The constant reiteration of the first person singular pronoun heightens our sense of the degree to which Eloisa, in recounting her dreams, has become immersed in their actuality.

In the last eight lines she awakes from this dream of guilty pleasure with Abelard, only to find herself plunged into a nightmare of sharper pain in which they wander together through a dreary, Gothic landscape. The gloomy details of the scene heighten the sublimity of Eloisa's grief. She and Abelard traverse a melancholic waste land that contains a 'mouldering tower', covered in 'pale ivory', and 'low-brow'd rocks' that hang threateningly over the ocean. Then, as Abelard leaves her, in Christ-like ascension, images of wild nature further heighten her uncontrollable feelings: 'Clouds interpose, waves roar, and winds arise.' She wakes, shrieking, from this nightmare to a world that is no less painful even if less frightening:

> I shriek, start up, the same sad prospect find,
> And wake to all the griefs I left behind.

The setting of this passage looks back to the Miltonic gloom of *Il Penseroso* and forward to the ideas and images found in the Gothic novels of Walpole and Mrs Radcliffe, or in the poetry of Keats (e.g. *The Eve of St Agnes*). It is an indication of the range of Pope's sensibility and of the dangers of any too narrow conception of what it means to label him a neoclassical writer.

Epistle to Burlington

This poem, now known as 'Epistle IV' of the *Moral Essays*, was the first of the four to be written. It was published, in December 1731, before *An Essay on Man* which Pope initially intended it should follow as part of his *opus magnum*. It was the first poem Pope had published since his attack on his enemies in *The Dunciad* of May 1728, and *The Dunciad Variorum* of April 1729, but if he hoped that his critics might have quietened down in the intervening two and a half years he was to be sadly disappointed. A large number of persons satirized in *The Dunciad* were more than eager to get even with him, and the *Epistle to Burlington* was received with renewed, if not increased, hostility.

The outcry against the poem was instant. Immediately on its publication his critics fastened on the character of Timon and the description of his villa, which takes up nearly half the text, and declared that Pope meant his acquaintance, James Brydges, first Duke of Chandos, to be portrayed and that this was a typical example of his ingratitude and treachery. Pope was greatly upset by the accusation, and first wrote privately, and then publicly, to Burlington denying it: 'For nothing is so evident ... as that character of Timon is collected from twenty different absurdities and improprieties, and was never the picture of any one human creature.' Despite his denial the charge stuck, and for almost two centuries Timon was popularly supposed to be a caricature of Chandos. More recent scholarship, however, has supported the accuracy of Pope's statement to Burlington.[1] Many contemporary examples of conspicuous consumption are clearly satirized in Timon's Villa, and if the portrait is part Cannons (Chandos's house), it is also part Chatsworth (the Duke of Devonshire's house), part Blenheim (the Duke of Marlborough's house), and part Houghton Hall (Robert Walpole's house), to name only three others.

The *Epistle to Burlington* was the first poem Pope wrote in the Horatian style which then became the dominant model for the rest of his poetic career. It is based on the method and tone of Horace's *Epistles* generally, rather than on any one in particular. Lord Burlington, the addressee, is worked into the text at various points (23–6, 39–40, 178, 191–4) and always addressed in a complimentary manner. The poem fluctuates between these complimentary passages addressed directly to him, and bitingly satiric ones describing the 'Imitating Fools' who fill 'half the land' (26). The most powerful and extended of these passages is the satiric description of

Timon's gardens and villa, discussed in detail at the end of this introduction.

Pope's subject matter in the *Epistle to Burlington* concerns good and bad taste in architecture and landscape gardening, and his central theme the proper use of wealth with regard to both. The poem's addressee, Lord Burlington, is held up as an outstanding example of good taste in these matters. He was currently involved in publishing *The Designs of Inigo Jones*, and his villa and gardens at Chiswick were amongst the earliest and finest examples of the contemporary fashion for Palladianism and landscape gardening. (See chapter 3 for a contextualized discussion of his circle and ideas.) But, Pope argues, half the land is full of pretenders to good taste who think, like Timon, that it can be acquired by wealth rather than sense. The Earl of Squanderfield, in Hogarth's *Marriage à la Mode*, 1745, is satirized for holding similar assumptions over a decade later. In Plate I of that comic history cycle Squanderfield is seen marrying his son off to a rich city alderman's daughter in order to acquire a settlement with which to pay off a mortgage on his estate and finish building his Palladian mansion, glimpsed, already under construction, through the window.

The *Epistle to Burlington* falls into three main sections: lines 1–98, in which the speaker discusses the general principles of good and bad taste in architecture and landscape gardening; lines 99–176, in which he describes Timon's Villa and gardens, as a detailed example of bad taste in both; and line 177–end, in which he imagines a future when men of wealth spend it in ways that bring Peace to 'happy Britain'.

In the first section Pope develops his aesthetic ideas which are based on reason and nature. They are in close accord with Lord Burlington's and show that there is something that comes before riches, that is prior even to good taste itself:

> Oft have you hinted to your brother Peer,
> A certain truth, which many buy too dear:
> Something there is more needful than Expence,
> And something previous ev'n to Taste – 'tis Sense: (39–42)

Good sense cannot be bought and sold. It is a 'gift of Heav'n' (43); a 'Light, which in yourself you must perceive' (45); and not something which can be acquired, even from the finest of architects and landscape gardeners, such as Jones and Le Notre. This is the whole point of the portrait of Timon, who has no gift from Heaven, no light within himself, and tries to make amends by buying such qualities. But he buys all wrong.

In this respect Timon's Villa is the exact opposite of Mr Darcy's

Pemberley in *Pride and Prejudice*. Consider Jane Austen's description of Elizabeth Bennett's response on first seeing Pemberley House:

> It was a large, handsome, stone building, standing well on rising ground, and backed by a ridge of high woody hills; – and in front, a stream of some natural importance was swelled into greater, but without any artificial appearance. Its banks were neither formal nor falsely adorned. Elizabeth was delighted. She had never seen a place for which nature had done more, or where natural beauty had been so little counteracted by an awkward taste.[2]

At Pemberley the house is in perfect harmony with its natural location. The setting has no 'artificial appearance' or 'false adornment'. At Timon's Villa, by contrast, natural beauty is everywhere 'counteracted by an awkward taste'. Instead of consulting 'the Genius of the Place' (57), and drawing that out, Timon has forced his own extravagant vanity on his surroundings. He has inverted nature and ignored the human scale. A fixed regularity and massive over-elaboration have reduced Timon himself to appearing as no more than a 'puny insect shiv'ring at a breeze' (108).

Pope's guiding principle for architecture and landscape gardening is the same as that for poetry:

> To build, to plant, whatever you intend,
> To rear the Column, or the Arch to bend,
> To swell the Terras, or to sink the Grot;
> In all, let Nature never be forgot.   (47–50)

I have already discussed the appeal to nature here, in some detail, in an earlier part of the book (see p. 69). Pope felt that the artist should encourage nature's underlying forms to emerge so that its essential features would be able to speak for themselves, rather than impose artificial patterns upon it. Furthermore, the artist makes a stronger impression through imaginative suggestiveness than explicit statement:

> Let not each beauty ev'ry where be spy'd,
> Where half the skill is decently to hide.
> He gains all points, who pleasingly confounds,
> Surprizes, varies, and conceals the Bounds.   (53–6)

The lines, ostensibly describing the art of the architect and landscape gardener, are equally appropriate to Pope's own poetry. As Pope put it in the *Epistle to Mr Jervas*, 'images reflect from art to art' (20).

The crucial point in landscape gardening is to 'consult the Genius of the Place' (57), and to allow that to shape the setting and prospect. This is what Mr Darcy has done so outstandingly well at Pemberley, and what Timon has singularly failed to do at his estate. The overall effect should be the result of a careful integration of the component parts. No single feature, whether lake, or temple, or wood, should be allowed to draw attention to itself alone. Each feature should be part of a harmonious whole:

> Still follow Sense, of ev'ry Art the Soul,
> Parts answ'ring parts shall slide into a whole. (65–6)

The verb indicates the gradual, unobtrusive nature of the fusion to be aimed at.

The Timon's Villa section of the poem (99–176), is one of the most sustainedly witty and effective pieces of satire Pope wrote. It is deservedly well known and receives detailed attention after this introduction. There is a marked change of tone, however, at the close of the section, that is not entirely commensurate with the rest of the poem. The epistle, which has fluctuated between serious discussion of the visual arts and satiric attack on those who falsely espouse them, suddenly moves into high panegyric strain. The closing twenty-eight lines (177–204) show Pope in the patriotic and visionary vein of *Windsor-Forest*. He imagines future kings, following Burlington's example, building harbours, churches, flood-barriers, roads and bridges; demonstrating an admirable concern for what we would now call the country's infrastructure. It is a splendid vision of public-spiritedness, but whereas in *Windsor-Forest* it grows naturally out of the visionary nature of the poem, it seems strangely placed in the *Epistle to Burlington* and marks a sudden shift of tone in a poem that has established a firm focus on actual buildings and landscape as its central concern. It makes for a somewhat uncomfortably rhapsodic end to a carefully argued work that has mainly dealt with the present. The epic strain, with its images of 'Imperial Works', sits uneasily with the discursive mode, and its images of 'huge heaps of littleness'. But if the ending seems, to this reader, somewhat off-key, it is only a small detraction in the overall structure of a poem containing passages of compelling satiric force and persuasive aesthetic conception.

SELECTED EXCERPT

> My Lord advances with majestic mien,
> Smit with the mighty pleasure, to be seen:
> But soft – by regular approach – not yet –
> First thro' the length of yon hot Terrace sweat,   130
> And when up ten steep slopes you've dragg'd your thighs,
> Just at his Study-door he'll bless your eyes.

His Study! with what Authors is it stor'd?
In Books, not Authors, curious is my Lord;
To all their dated Backs he turns you round,
These Aldus printed, those Du Suëil has bound.
Lo some are Vellom, and the rest as good
For all his Lordship knows, but they are Wood.
For Locke or Milton 'tis in vain to look,
These shelves admit not any modern book.   140
   And now the Chapel's silver bell you hear,
That summons you to all the Pride of Pray'r:
Light quirks of Musick, broken and uneven,
Make the soul dance upon a Jig to Heaven.
On painted Cielings you devoutly stare,
Where sprawl the Saints of Verrio or Laguerre,
On gilded clouds in fair expansion lie,
And bring all Paradise before your eye.
To rest, the Cushion and soft Dean invite,
Who never mentions Hell to ears polite.   150
   But hark! the chiming Clocks to dinner call;
A hundred footsteps scrape the marble Hall:
The rich Buffet well-colour'd Serpents grace,
And gaping Tritons spew to wash your face.
Is this a dinner? this a Genial room?
No, 'tis a Temple, and a Hecatomb.
A solemn Sacrifice, perform'd in state,
You drink by measure, and to minutes eat.
So quick retires each flying course, you'd swear
Sancho's dread Doctor and his Wand were there.   160
Between each Act the trembling salvers ring,
From soup to sweet-wine, and God bless the King.
In plenty starving, tantaliz'd in state,
And complaisantly help'd to all I hate,
Treated, caress'd, and tir'd, I take my leave,
Sick of his civil Pride from Morn to Eve;
I curse such lavish cost, and little skill,
And swear no Day was ever past so ill.
   Yet hence the Poor are cloath'd, the Hungry fed;
Health to himself, and to his Infants bread   170
The Lab'rer bears: What his hard Heart denies,
His charitable Vanity supplies.
   Another age shall see the golden Ear
Imbrown the Slope, and nod on the Parterre,
Deep Harvests bury all his pride has plann'd,
And laughing Ceres re-assume the land.

CRITICISM   The lines presented above are taken from the Timon's Villa section of the poem in which Pope conducts the reader on a guided tour of an imaginary eighteenth-century house and gardens that typify bad taste. The complete description of Timon's Villa (99–176) is too long to include here, so the tour of the park and gardens (99–126) has been omitted in favour of the description of the house (127–68) and Pope's concluding thoughts on the extravagant expenditure displayed (169–76).

The excerpt begins with a short transitional paragraph that connects the walk round the garden with the tour through the house. Timon's garden has been notable for its complete absence of proportion. 'Huge heaps of littleness' dwarf the human scale, so that Timon himself appears as no more than a 'puny insect'. And yet this insect is puffed up with pride and pomposity, 'smit with the mighty pleasure, to be seen'. Just as his garden lacks all pleasing intricacy and variety, so the approach to his house is rigid and formal:

> But soft – by regular approach – not yet –
> First thro' the length of yon hot Terrace sweat,
> And when up ten steep slopes you've dragg'd your thighs,
> Just at his Study-door he'll bless your eyes.

The deliberate, broken movement of the opening line, and the slow, drawn-out length of the next two lines, culminating in the ten monosyllables and three elisions of the third line, carefully enact the exhausting process of climbing the 'ten steep slopes' and entering the house.

The description of Timon's study is a satire on false learning. Timon is interested in the outside not the inside of books, in their monetary not their intellectual value. Old books represent a good financial investment for him (much as paintings by old masters do in the modern market) rather than a source for learning and enjoyment. Pope first lets Timon show the reader round the room, pointing out the books' great age and fine bindings, and then smartly undercuts the display with his own acid comment saved up for the end of the sentence:

> Lo some are Vellom, and the rest as good
> For all his Lordship knows, but they are Wood.

The timing is perfect, and leads quite naturally into the scornful dismissiveness of modern writing, contained in the last two lines in the paragraph.

When we are led into the chapel and the dining-room we find a total inversion of appropriate values. All the ceremony and ritual that belong in a chapel are found instead in the dining-room, and all the geniality and comfort that belong in a dining-room are found in the chapel. Timon has no sense of propriety or decorum, no idea of what is proper for what purpose. The chapel is an extravagantly ornamented room indicating material rather than spiritual concern. The music that is performed is more suited to a ballroom than a place of worship, and there is something grossly obscene about the paintings on the ceilings. The verb 'sprawl', used to describe the painted saints, picks up the disgust that Pope feels for the Cupids that 'squirt' in the garden, and the Tritons that 'spew' in the dining-room. Pope's scorn for Timon's religious complacency is given a final satiric twist in his comparison of the 'soft Dean' to a 'cushion' in the closing couplet of the paragraph.

The guests are then called to the dining-room by 'chiming Clocks' that ring out like church bells summoning a congregation. Such a summons directly contrasts to the soft melodious sound that was suggested by the chapel's 'silver bell'. The dining-table itself is ornamented with 'well-coloured Serpents' and 'gaping Tritons' that are quite inappropriate to meal-time, while the dinner that the poet receives is a travesty of what dining should be – 'The feast of Reason and the flow of Soul' as Pope describes it in his *Imitation of Horace: Satire II, i* (128). At Timon's house dining is an occasion for ostentatious show not relaxed conviviality. It is, like Belinda's toilet, a 'sacred rite of pride'. The guests drink and eat in time with the chiming clocks: 'You drink by measure, and to minutes eat'. The silver plates ring out in a grotesque parody of the bells at the communion service:

> Between each Act the trembling salvers ring,
> From soup to sweet-wine, and God bless the King.

The last line is a brilliant example of the deftness and speed of Pope's satiric touch. The whole meal is crammed into one line. The elaborate banquet is reduced to skeletal simplicity, while the toast to the King is presented as an afterthought to be got over and done with as soon as possible.

At this point in the poem the satirist brings himself directly into the account of Timon's Villa for the first time. Up to now Pope has kept himself out of things as much as possible. He has conducted the reader round the house, making cruel fun of Timon's bad taste, but he has not allowed the scene to affect him directly. In the last six lines of the paragraph he can no longer control his revulsion and scorn for what he is witnessing:

> In plenty starving, tantaliz'd in state,
> And complaisantly help'd to all I hate,

Treated, caress'd, and tir'd, I take my leave,
Sick of his civil Pride from Morn to Eve;
I curse such lavish cost, and little skill,
And swear no Day was ever past so ill.

The personal pronouns ring out the more impressively for being introduced for the first time, while the negative force of the verbs – 'hate', 'take my leave', 'curse', and 'swear' – steadily heightens the poet's rejection of such lavish cost and little skill.

In the last two paragraphs of the excerpt there is a crucial change in tone. Pope the irate participant becomes Pope the objective commentator. He has condemned Timon's false taste but he now shows that he is philosophically resigned to it. Borrowing perhaps from Bernard Mandeville's *The Fable of the Bees: or, Private vices, Publick benefits*, he tries to justify Providence by arguing that Timon's charitable vanity at least keeps the labourer employed and his family healthy. The lines ring somewhat hollow to a modern reader. They are full of general benevolence but lacking in detailed feeling for the poor. They are also a clear reminder of Pope's political position. What he sees wrong with Timon's prodigality is probably not what most readers today would see wrong with it. Timon is an object of attack not because he has too much money, but because he misuses it. Pope celebrates Christian humility but he is in no way a socialist.

Finally, in four of the finest lines he ever wrote, Pope reminds us of Timon's total insignificance in a larger perspective. In a beautifully modulated sentence, full of rich images of triumphant nature, he calmly enacts the inevitable victory of time. Timon's villa and gardens become a transient plaything that quietly dissolves before a vision of almost paradisal nature.

The Timon's Villa episode gives us Pope at his satirical best. His wit and scorn in dealing with what is rotten, and his lyrical defence of what he believes in, show a mind at full imaginative stretch. He is writing about a subject – the country house and its setting – that has vital implications for the whole structure of his society. For Pope the ideal country house is one in which man and nature exist in mutual harmony. Such a relationship is described by Ben Jonson in his poem *To Penshurst*, written over a hundred years earlier. It is helpful to see Jonson's ideal of the country house, the organic centre of community life, hovering in the background of Pope's poem as an implied ideal against which to measure the aberrations and enormities of the eighteenth-century entrepreneurs he is satirizing.

An Essay on Man

Pope originally wrote *An Essay on Man*, which comprises four separate epistles, as part of a work that was planned to be very much larger, his grand poetical enterprise, or *'opus magnum'* as he called it in a letter to Swift, which was to offer a 'system of Ethics in the Horatian way' (III, 81). The overall design was initially for a group of moral poems, or 'Ethic Epistles', that dealt with Human Life and Manners in a wide variety of aspects, including a Book on 'The Nature and State of Man' (*An Essay on Man*) and one on 'The Use of Things' (such as the 'Limits of Human Reason', the 'Principles of Civil and Ecclesiastical Polity' and the 'Use of Education, Learning, Riches'). However, Pope adapted this grand design as he worked on it, and told Spence, in 1734, that he had drawn it in 'much narrower than it was at first' (300). In its final version the work contained the four epistles of *An Essay on Man*, plus the four epistles to several persons, to which Warburton later gave the collective title, *Moral Essays*. It is possible that some of the *Imitations of Horace* were originally intended as part of the planned *opus magnum*, and even some passages that were later included in *The New Dunciad*, but the grand design, as it was originally conceived, was never completed, and *An Essay on Man*, or *The First Book of Ethic Epistles*, to use the subtitle Pope gave it in his *Works*, Volume II, of 1735, was the only fully cohesive part he finished. Although complete in itself, the poem remains part of an incomplete whole.[1]

The first three epistles of *An Essay on Man* were published successively in February, March and May of 1733. After the hostile reviews given to the *Epistle to Burlington*, Pope published them anonymously in order to try to establish an impartial reception. His manoeuvre was successful and several of his enemies reviewed the epistles most favourably without realizing their authorship. As Pope said in a letter to Swift:

> The design of concealing myself was good, and had its full effect; I was thought a divine, a philosopher, and what not? and my doctrine had a sanction I could not have given to it.   (III, 433)

He published the fourth epistle in January 1734, and all four appeared together, as a complete poem, for the first time in April 1734.

In the prefatory note, headed 'The Design', that Pope added to the poem in 1734, and to all subsequent editions, he outlined his overall intention:

What is now published, is only to be considered as a *general Map* of MAN, marking out no more than the *greater parts*, their *extent*, their *limits*, and their *connection*, but leaving the particular to be more fully delineated in the charts which are to follow. Consequently, these epistles in their progress (if I have health and leisure to make any progress) will be less dry, and more susceptible of poetical ornament. I am here only opening the *fountains*, and clearing the passage. To deduce the *rivers*, to follow them in their course, and to observe their effects, may be a task more agreeable.

An Essay on Man, then, was conceived as 'a general Map of Man', leaving the particular parts to be more fully delineated in 'the charts which are to follow'. That Pope saw himself as 'only opening the fountains and clearing the passage' is perhaps one of the reasons why some readers have found the work lacking in specificity.

The poem is didactic and philosophical, formally modelled, partly on Horace's *Epistles*, but above all on Lucretius's *De Rerum Natura*.[2] Lucretius's poem, written sometime around 60 B.C., almost 1,800 years before Pope's, was an exposition of Epicurean philosophy and an explanation of natural phenomena leading to speculation about the nature of the universe. Although the Christianity that guides Pope's poem is very different from the Epicurianism that guides Lucretius's, the overall structure of the two has much in common. Just as Lucretius addresses his poem to his friend Memmius, so Pope addresses his to his 'guide, philosopher and friend' (IV, 390), Henry St John, Lord Bolingbroke:

> Awake, my ST JOHN! leave all meaner things
> To low ambition, and the pride of Kings.   (I, 1–2)

The allusion to Lucretius becomes clearer when we compare this opening couplet with an earlier, unpublished, manuscript version of it:[3]

> Awake my Memmius, leave all meaner things
> To working Statesmen & ambitious Kings.   (I, 1–2)

But Bolingbroke's fictive role as addressee is not very thoroughly sustained. Having introduced it at the beginning of the first epistle, Pope then ignores it, except for a fleeting moment at the beginning of the fourth, till the famous encomium to him at the end:

> Come then, my Friend, my Genius, come along,
> Oh master of the poet, and his song!   (IV, 373–4)

Pope's poem can be seen as an early eighteenth-century response to Lucretius's espousal of Epicurus's belief that the world was a result of an accidental collision of atoms. Drawing on contemporary scientific discoveries, and particularly on those of Newton, for whom he had the highest respect, Pope set out to 'vindicate the ways of God to Man' (I, 16) and to demonstrate a strongly Christian cosmogony, or theory of the creation of the universe, in which:

> All are but parts of one stupendous whole,
> Whose body, Nature is, and God the soul; (I, 67–8)

Lucretius's tone as he addresses Memmius is majestic and assertive, and the stance Pope adopts is similarly elevated and assured. The speaker addresses Bolingbroke, and through him the reader, with a conviction in his own correctness that brooks little or no dissent. The tone fluctuates somewhat within the poem, 'from grave to gay, from lively to severe' (IV, 380), as he says to Bolingbroke; but the gay and lively passages are very much less in evidence than the grave and severe ones, and the preponderant quality of the speaker's tone is magisterial, peremptory and exhortatory. The role of the public lecturer, or preacher, soon takes over from that of the private conversationalist who begins the poem and the reader often feels that he or she is on the receiving end of a public dressing-down rather than listening in on a companionable address to a friend.

The subject matter of *An Essay on Man* marked a new turning in Pope's career. He was aware that it was not easy to make philosophy poetical, that his poem was, as he says in his preface, 'To the Reader', 'mixt with Argument, which of its Nature approacheth to Prose'. He chose to write in verse, not prose, however, both because 'principles, maxims or precepts so written . . . strike the reader more strongly at first, and are more easily retained by him afterwards', and because 'I was unable to treat this part of my subject more in detail, without becoming dry and tedious; or more *poetically*, without sacrificing perspicuity to ornament, without wand'ring from the precision, or breaking the chain of reasoning'. Pope felt that the heroic couplets helped him strike a valued balance between prolixity of subject matter on the one hand and over-elaboration of language on the other. He felt the verse form was a discipline that enabled him to express his ideas 'more *shortly* . . . than in prose itself'.

An Essay on Man is an uneven poem and it is easier to focus on, and discuss, individual epistles than the whole poem. Epistle I deals with the nature and state of man in relation to the universe; Epistle II with his nature and state in relation to himself; Epistle III with his nature and state in relation to society; and Epistle IV with his nature and state in relation to happiness. The sequence is careful and ordered, and grows out of Pope's central premise that the world man lives in may be a mighty maze, but is not 'without a plan'.

That plan, which forms the backdrop to the poem, is the inherited Medieval and Renaissance belief in the Great Chain of Being. This gives the basic order into which everything else fits, and has already been elaborated in some detail in chapter 5 (see pp. 121–22). What Pope set out to do in *An Essay on Man* was to 'vindicate' the ways of God to Man, not through myth, as Milton had done in *Paradise Lost*, but through rational argument. It is not that Pope disagrees with Milton, from whom he inherits a great deal, but that he attempts to arrive at a similar end through different means. *An Essay on Man* is a poem relying on empirical argument and scientific proof rather than on revealed religion and unsupported faith.

Pope's position is rootedly empirical throughout the poem:

> Say first, of God above, or Man below,
> What can we reason, but from what we know?
> Of Man what see we, but his station here,
> From which to reason, or to which refer?
> Thro' worlds unnumber'd tho' the God be known,
> 'Tis ours to trace him only in our own.   (I, 17–21)

Pope scorns deductive logic. Our reasoning must be based on our experience. Those who begin with *a priori* assumptions, such as Epicurus with his claim to have pierced through 'vast immensity' and returned with godlike knowledge, are mere visionaries who have no understanding of the world we actually inhabit. They are presumptuous in the extreme, and Pope's speaker has nothing but disdain for such pride and dulness. Indeed the poem is packed with contempt for mankind's presumption, and he is variously excoriated as 'Presumptuous Man!' (I, 35); 'Vile Worm! – oh Madness, Pride, Impiety!' (I, 258); 'vile Man' (I, 277); 'Fools!' (II, 211); 'thou Fool!' (III, 27); 'this lord of all' (III, 42); 'Weak, foolish Man!' (IV, 173); and 'Oh fool!' (IV, 189). Pope stresses mankind's insignificance, 'his time a moment, and a point his space' (I, 72).

Humanity's abiding weakness is Pride: 'In Pride, in reas'ning Pride, our error lies' (I, 123). The speaker includes himself in the accusation. His voice becomes, to a certain extent, that of Everyman. As the charge is repeated, forty lines further on, the recommended response is Christian submission:

> From pride, from pride, our very reas'ning springs;
> Account for moral as for nat'ral things:
> Why charge we Heav'n in this, in these acquit?
> In both, to reason right is to submit.   (I, 161–4)

The speaker exhorts the individual reader to 'Know thy own point' (I, 283) and 'Submit' (I, 285). Pope has arrived, via a different route, at the same advice Milton proffers, through Raphael, in Book VIII of *Paradise Lost*: 'be lowly wise'.

An Essay on Man is a compendium of contemporary philosophical and ethical ideas, drawing on Hobbes and Shaftesbury as well as Bolingbroke and Whiston. Pope says in his introductory 'Design' to the poem that if he could flatter himself the *Essay* has any merit, 'it is in steering betwixt the extremes of doctrines seemingly opposite, in passing over terms utterly unintelligible, and in forming a *temperate* yet not *inconsistent*, and a *short* yet not *imperfect* system of Ethics'. *An Essay on Man* is, finally, a very positive poem. Despite its prevailing tone of contempt for man, and its insistence on cutting humanity down to size, it offers hope, especially through the possibility of a virtuous life developed in Epistle IV, for spiritual regeneration. Maynard Mack puts it more poetically: 'Beginning with a reminder of a paradise we have lost – the "Garden, tempting with forbidden fruit" – the poem ends with a paradise to be regained.'⁴ Compared to the dissolution and darkness described in the final version of *The Dunciad*, *An Essay on Man* represents an optimistic vision, however guarded, for the future of the human race.

SELECTED EXCERPT

Epistle II

> Know then thyself, presume not God to scan;
> The proper study of Mankind is Man.
> Plac'd on this isthmus of a middle state,
> A being darkly wise, and rudely great:
> With too much knowledge for the Sceptic side,
> With too much weakness for the Stoic's pride,
> He hangs between; in doubt to act, or rest,
> In doubt to deem himself a God, or Beast;
> In doubt his Mind or Body to prefer,
> Born but to die, and reas'ning but to err;   10
> Alike in ignorance, his reason such,
> Whether he thinks too little, or too much:
> Chaos of Thought and Passion, all confus'd;
> Still by himself abus'd, or disabus'd;
> Created half to rise and half to fall;
> Great lord of all things, yet a prey to all;
> Sole judge of Truth, in endless Error hurl'd:
> The glory, jest, and riddle of the world!

CRITICISM This often-quoted opening paragraph of Epistle II of *An Essay on Man* is a fine example of the way Pope establishes his philosophical content through the poetical structure of his verse. Each element of expression here, and especially the couplet form itself, reinforces Pope's presentation of the concept of humanity's paradoxical, dual nature. Following the curt, imperative force of the self-contained opening couplet, Pope develops his extended definition of 'Man', spanning sixteen lines, and yet never for one moment losing direction as the clauses gather towards the memorable, epigrammatic conclusiveness of the paragraph's closing line. For the purposes of this analysis, I will refer to 'Man' much as Pope does in the epistle, while noting that the generic, or all-inclusive, use of 'Man' for humanity is not unambiguous and contains strongly gendered implications, as Shakespeare wryly points out in Hamlet's soliloquy quoted towards the end of this critical analysis.

Pope's focus on the contradictory duality of human nature draws on a long tradition of philosophical writing, and particularly on Blaise Pascal's *Pensées*, written about sixty years earlier, which Pope had recently read. He wrote to Caryll in February 1731 saying 'Your recommendation of Pascal's *Pensées* is a good one, though I have been beforehand with you in it'. (III, 173). As we shall see, Pascal's influence is especially strong in this passage.

The opening injunction not to 'scan' God is carefully selected. Pope does not say that we should not worship God, but that we should not presume to measure him in a mathematical way. To 'scan', whether in its prosodic or in its scientific sense, involves measuring according to a fixed standard; to attempt to do that in relation to the Divine Creator would be, Pope suggests, presumptuous. Scientific enquiry is only justified, in Pope's view, if carried out 'with Modesty thy guide' (I, 43). As far as the speaker is concerned the foundation of all knowledge is self-knowledge, in the sense of coming to know the human species through a knowledge of the self. It is towards this kind of knowledge that the rest of the passage, and indeed the whole poem, is directed. It is worth noting here that Pope's views do not reflect a fragmented understanding of knowledge, or of human nature, nor a subjective view. We are not being exhorted to a course of introspection, but to an understanding of other people through a knowledge of ourselves.

'Man' is placed on an 'isthmus' of a middle state. The geographical image carries a range of interrelated associations. It suggests a temporal position, with the present seen as a narrow strip of land connecting the vast continents of the past and the future; it suggests a spatial position, with this world seen as a narrow passage joining Heaven and Hell; and it suggests a social position in God's hierarchy of creation, with the higher life of the angels above and the lower life of the animals beneath. The essential point is the ambiguity of mankind's position, an ambiguity given further force by the oxymorons of the next line. 'Man' is wise and great compared to the brutes beneath, but dark and rude compared to the angels above.

Suspended, like a pendulum, and oscillating in opposite directions, 'He hangs between'. He is torn with doubt by a series of philosophical dilemmas, and his whole life is merely an expanded paradox summed up by the fact that he is 'born but to die'. The confusion and contradiction of the choices confronting humanity are embodied in the constant see-saw motion of the verse. Sometimes this movement operates within the couplet, as in lines 5 and 6; sometimes within the line, as in line 4; and sometimes within the half line, as in the second half of line 7.

The dual aspects of human nature are established through the duality of the metrical and syntactical organization. Nouns, phrases and clauses are repeatedly coupled together to enact the double-sided quality of the various components of mankind's nature. The syntactical elements italicized in the following six lines illustrate this:

> Chaos of *Thought* and *Passion*, all confus'd;
> Still by himself *abus'd*, or *disabus'd*;
> Created *half to rise* and *half to fall*;
> Great *lord of all things*, yet *a prey to all*;
> *Sole judge of Truth, in endless Error hurl'd*:
> The *glory, jest*, and riddle of the world! (13–18)

Each of the characteristics italicized is immediately brought into conflict with a contradictory force that results in chaos, confusion and ultimate enigma. The last line is a taut and ringing summary of the whole passage: the 'glory' encapsulates man's potential nobility, the 'jest' his potential absurdity, and the 'riddle' his actual confusion.

There is nothing new in the content of what Pope is saying about mankind here. The ideas expressed were commonplace in Renaissance thought. This can be demonstrated by putting Pope's lines alongside Hamlet's famous soliloquy in Act II, ii:

> What a piece of work is man, how noble in reason, how infinite in faculties, in form and moving how express and admirable, in action how like an angel, in apprehension how like a god: the beauty of the world, the paragon of animals; and yet to me, what is this quintessence of dust? Man delights not me; nor woman neither, though by your smiling you seem to say so.

Pope had expressed a similar idea in a letter to Caryll written on 14 August 1713:

> Good God! what an Incongruous Animal is Man? how unsettled in his best part, his soul; and how changing and variable in his frame of body? The constancy of the one, shook by every notion, the temperament of the other, affected by every blast of wind.

195

> What an April weather in the mind! In a word, what is Man
> altogether, but one mighty inconsistency.   (I, 185–6)

In composing these opening lines of Epistle II, memories of Hamlet's
soliloquy, and his own letter to Caryll written twenty years earlier,
seem to have reverberated in Pope's mind, whether consciously or
unconsciously, with his own recent reading in Pascal's *Pensées*. These
had been translated into English by Basil Kennet in 1704, and in
chapter 21, on 'The strange Contrarieties discoverable in Human
Nature', Kennet had translated Pascal's conclusion as follows:

> What a Chimaera then is Man! What a surprizing Novelty! What
> a confused Chaos! What a subject of Contradiction! A profess'd
> Judge of all Things, and yet a feeble Worm of the Earth; the great
> Depositary and Guardian of Truth, and yet a meer Huddle of
> Uncertainty; the Glory and the Scandal of the Universe!

There are clearly interrelated echoes in each of the three prose
passages quoted here. Pope turned these different versions of a
similar idea over in his mind and precipitated, through his expressive
imagination, the pointed resonance and crafted music of the couplets
he produced. The originality of these lines does not lie in the ideas
they contain but in the way Pope expresses them. This is a basic
Augustan position. Pope believed that there were only a few
irrefutable truths in human nature. 'There are not *many certain truths*
in this world,' as he says in 'The Design', and the duty of the poet is
to express those truths in a fresh, contemporary light:

> True Wit is Nature to Advantage drest,
> What oft was Thought, but ne'er so well Exprest.
>   (*An Essay on Criticism*, 297–8)

An Epistle to Dr Arbuthnot

In *An Epistle to Dr Arbuthnot* Pope gives an account of his poetic career, and particularly of his role as a satirist. The poem belongs to a long tradition of poems in which the satirist defends his art. It is Pope's *Apologia pro sua Satura*, or 'Defence of his Satire'. All previous masters of formal verse satire had written at least one poem in which they explained why they felt it necessary to attack the persons and objects they did, in the way they did. Horace and Juvenal had each written poetic self-defences, so when Pope's good friend from Scriblerian days, John Arbuthnot, wrote to him, as he was dying, on 17 July 1734, making it his 'Last Request that you continue that noble Disdain and Abhorrence of Vice, which you seem naturally endu'd with, but still with a due regard to your own Safety' (III, 417) Pope seems to have felt that the time had come for him too to publish such a poem. He replied to Arbuthnot, two weeks later, on 2 August, saying that he would indeed, as Arbuthnot had urged, 'continue to manifest a disdain and abhorrence of vice' in his writings, and would prefer to do so 'with more restrictions, and less personally', which was more agreeable to his nature:

> But General Satire in Times of General Vice has no force, and is no Punishment: People have ceas'd to be ashamed of it when so many are join'd with them; and tis only by hunting One or two from the Herd that any Examples can be made. If a man writ all his Life against the Collective Body of the Banditti, or against Lawyers, would it do the least Good, or lessen the Body? But if some are hung up, or pilloryed, it may prevent others. And in my low Station, with no other Power than this, I hope to deter, if not to reform. (III, 423)

If this exchange of correspondence with his dying friend, in the summer of 1734, was one of the spurs to the final composition of *An Epistle to Dr Arbuthnot*, the poem's full genesis is rather more complex. In the 'Advertisement', which prefaced the completed work's first publication, on 2 January 1735, Pope tells the reader that:

> This Paper is a sort of Bill of Complaint, begun many years since, and drawn up by snatches, as the several Occasions offer'd. I had no thoughts of publishing it, till it pleas'd some Persons of Rank and Fortune to attack in a very extraordinary manner, not only my Writings (of which being publick the Publick judge) but my

> Person, Morals and Family, whereof to those who know me not, a
> truer Information may be requisite.

Pope emphasizes the poem's composite construction, pointing out
that it was 'drawn up by snatches', as the appropriate occasions
presented themselves, but that he only published it when 'some
Persons of Rank and Fortune', namely Lord Hervey and Lady
Mary Wortley Montagu, attacked him personally. An early draft of
a lengthy section of the poem (260 lines) already existed in an
unpublished version he had started in 1730 addressed to his Scots
friend, William Cleland.[1] Some of these lines had, in turn, been
written, and published, even earlier: those on Addison (193–14), for
instance, were probably written about 1715 and first appeared in
print, without Pope's permission, in 1722. A further example still of
lines that must have been written some considerable time before the
poem was published concerns the moving lines (406–13), near the
end of the poem, that pray for the continued life of his mother.
Editha Pope had in fact died in June 1733, eighteen months before
the poem's final publication.

An Epistle to Dr Arbuthnot, then, was compiled from previous verses
Pope had written, and what is more, compiled in some haste since
Dr Arbuthnot was so very ill. He eventually died on 27 February
1735, just under two months after the poem was published. Not only
was it put together in some haste, but a variety of motives went into
its assembly, particularly Arbuthnot's ill health and the recent
vicious attacks on Pope in published verses by Lord Hervey and
Lady Mary Wortley Montagu. One of the questions that has caused
critics most debate, and to which I shall return at the end of this
introduction, concerns the degree to which Pope succeeded in binding these separate, and haphazardly composed, 'snatches' together
into an unified whole.

An Epistle to Dr Arbuthnot is the most Horatian of Pope's original
works, fusing the style of Horace's *Satires* and *Epistles*. Although
Pope calls the poem *An Epistle*, Dr Arbuthnot, the fictional addressee,
is imagined not simply receiving a letter, but speaking, in lively and
direct speech, much as might one of the dramatic interlocutors
in Horace's *Satires*. Arbuthnot becomes addressee and adversary,
listener and talker, rolled into one. In this sense Pope draws on both
Horace's *Epistles* and *Satires* in his composition.

The poem's most interesting dramatic creation, however, is that
of Pope himself. The besieged poet who speaks in the poem, and
vigorously defends his life and art, is clearly, on one level, the voice
of the actual, living poet, Alexander Pope. But the poet speaker
comes to us through a series of filters. He is, after all, only one of the
poem's voices. Pope, the author, embraces the 'Pope' who speaks in

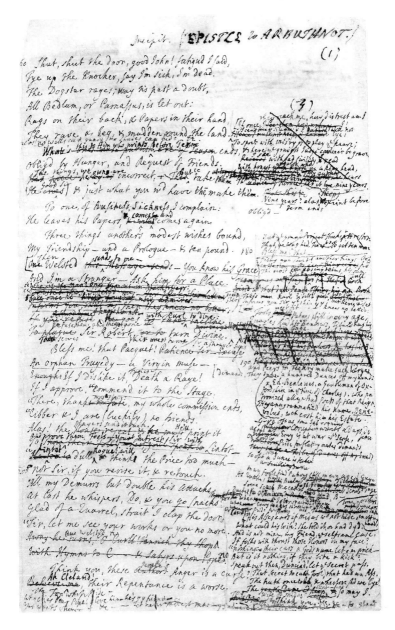

'*Paper-sparing Pope*'. *Pope's handwriting from the manuscript of* An Epistle to Dr Arbuthnot

it, as well as the 'Dr Arbuthnot' with whom he speaks. The Pope who speaks in the poem is Pope as he would like the public to think of him; Pope without warts. He is also a speaker who consciously absorbs a long tradition of satiric verse speakers. He sees himself in a direct line with both Horace and Juvenal, as the references, for example, to Bavius (99) and Codrus (85) respectively show.[2] The voice of the poet who speaks in *An Epistle to Dr Arbuthnot* comes as close as any in Pope's poetry to being an authentically autobiographical one, but it is important to recognize that it is a dramatic projection; just as much a construct, in one way, as that of Dr Arbuthnot is in another.

The epistle falls into three main sections. From lines 1–124 the satirist expresses his annoyance at being disturbed by an ever-increasing horde of poetasters and scribblers who make his life intolerable. Then at line 125 he begins an account of his life, punctuated by the three character sketches of Atticus, Bufo and Sporus, arranged in ascending order of scorn, which leads into a final section, of contrasting peace, starting at line 388 and continuing to the end of the poem, built around an epitaph to his father. A poem that opens in exasperation, and moves through varying stages of disgust, closes in a mood of serene composure. The epistle passes from storm to calm, suspended between an opening command to Pope's servant, John Serle, and a closing prayer that Heaven may preserve Dr Arbuthnot's and his mother's lives.

The poem begins more dramatically than any of Pope's poems, as the speaker impatiently cries out for his servant to close the door:

> Shut, shut the door, good *John*! fatigu'd I said,
> Tye up the knocker, say I'm sick, I'm dead,
> The Dog-star rages! nay 'tis past a doubt,
> All *Bedlam*, or *Parnassus*, is let out:
> Fire in each eye, and Papers in each hand,
> They rave, recite, and madden round the land.   (1–6)

The poet is not merely tired, he is angry. The trochaic opening and repeated caesuras of the first two lines act out his indignation. Through the juxtaposition of *Bedlam* and *Parnassus*, in line 4, the pretenders to reason become inseparable from the pretenders to poetry; both 'rave, recite, and madden round the land'. The poet feels, and is, besieged by second-rate poets who come to him for approval and patronage. Pope is, by implication, demonstrating his own pre-eminent literary position. The varying boundaries to his property each fail to protect him; whenever he goes out he is surrounded. He has no privacy; his pursuers don't even leave him alone on Sundays. The poetasters and scribblers become a plague of insects who 'pierce' his thickets, 'glide' through his grotto, and 'renew the charge' by land and water:

> All fly to *Twit'nam*, and in humble strain
> Apply to me to keep them mad or vain.　　　　(21–2)

In desperation he appeals to Arbuthnot for some medical remedy to this disease-carrying swarm:

> Friend to my Life, (which did not you prolong,
> The World had wanted many an idle Song)
> What *Drop* or *Nostrum* can this Plague remove?
> Or which must end me, a Fool's Wrath or Love?　　　(27–30)

But his plea is to no avail. This eighteenth-century version of the paparazzi is no more easily put off than its twentieth-century counterpart. Pope is put upon from all sides and can no longer ignore the hostility and folly he is forced to witness:

> Seiz'd and ty'd down to judge, how wretched I!
> Who can't be silent, and who will not lye;　　　(33–4)

Pope sustains and re-enacts the scribblers' attack for a further hundred lines or so. The verse is packed with interjection and response, with thrust and counter-thrust, but the poet has finally to admit that it is impossible to defeat a scribbler:

> Who shames a Scribbler? break one cobweb thro',
> He spins the slight, self-pleasing thread anew;
> Destroy his Fib, or Sophistry; in vain,
> The Creature's at his dirty work again;
> Thron'd in the Centre of his thin designs;
> Proud of a vast Extent of flimzy lines.　　　(89–94)

Pope's comparison of the scribbler to a spider, looking back to Swift's famous image in *The Battle of the Books*, comes to a brilliantly timed climax in the closing pun on his verses.

Pope stresses his own outspokenness, honesty and sobriety. He develops the stance of the man of honour, guiltless of causing undeserved, or even deserved, harm:

> Whom have I hurt? has Poet yet, or Peer,
> Lost the arch'd eye-brow, or *Parnassian* sneer?　　　(95–6)

The author allows Arbuthnot to attempt to restrain him, much in the way he had urged in his letter of 17 July 1734:

> 'Hold! for God-sake – you'll offend:
> No Names – be calm – learn Prudence of a Friend:
> I too could write, and I am twice as tall,
> But Foes like these!'　　　(101–4)

But, predictably perhaps, the restraining voice only acts as further impetus to the speaker's peremptory anger:

> —One Flatt'rer's worse than all;
> Of all mad Creatures, if the Learn'd are right,
> It is the Slaver kills, and not the Bite.   (104–6)

The fulsome flattery of fools is like the spittle of mad dogs, and equally dangerous.

The unremitting, personal attacks of the 'mad Creatures' upon him forces Pope to publicly defend his position, and leads into the most clearly autobiographical section of the poem:

> Why did I write? what sin to me unknown
> Dipt me in Ink, my Parents', or my own?
> As yet a Child, nor yet a Fool to Fame,
> I lisp'd in Numbers, for the Numbers came.   (125–8)

There is an echo here of his comments to Spence that 'I began writing verses of my own invention further back than I remember'. These lines introduce an indubitably idealized account of Pope's life. He tells us how many discerning, and great, people encouraged him, and how longsuffering he was before all jealous attackers:

> Did some more sober Critic come abroad?
> If wrong, I smil'd; if right, I kiss'd the rod.   (157–8)

He protests his love of the quiet life and his discomfort in the corridors of power. He presents himself as a law-abiding, Christian citizen who has no desire to interfere in other people's lives:

> I was not born for Courts or great Affairs,
> I pay my Debts, believe, and say my Pray'rs,
> Can sleep without a poem in my head,
> Nor know, if *Dennis* be alive or dead.   (267–70)

He proclaims his affronted innocence – 'Poor guiltless I!' (281). He is a friend to all worthy men and to Virtue, but a foe to all who love lies and affectation:

> A Lash like mine no honest man shall dread,
> But all such babling blockheads in his stead.   (303–4)

This leads into the scathing portrayal of Sporus (Lord Hervey) discussed in detail after this introduction. In contrast to Lord Hervey, Pope depicts himself as rational, calm, modest, independent and, with a dig at Hervey's bisexuality, 'manly':

> Not Fortune's Worshipper, nor Fashion's Fool,
> Not Lucre's Madman, nor Ambition's Tool,
> Not proud, nor servile, be one Poet's praise
> That, if he pleas'd, he pleas'd by manly ways;   (334–7)

In his mature and graver years he has turned away from all frivolity, and with the single-minded determination of a falcon dropping on its prey, has 'stoop'd to Truth and moraliz'd his song' (341). He wants to be remembered for having stood up for 'Virtue's better end' (342), even to the extent of being willing to die for it:

> Welcome for thee, fair Virtue! all the past:
> For thee, fair Virtue! welcome even the *last*!   (358–9)

Shortly after this the tone changes as Pope moves into a defence of his parents' virtuous lives. His father is portrayed as the antithesis of the corrupt scribblers and 'hireling Peers' who have peopled most of the poem and so pestered his existence:

> No Courts he saw, no Suits would ever try,
> Nor dar'd an Oath, nor hazarded a Lye:
> Un-learn'd, he knew no Schoolman's Subtle Art,
> No Language, but the Language of the Heart.
> By Nature honest, by Experience wise,
> Healthy by Temp'rance and by Exercise:
> His Life, tho' long, to sickness past unknown,
> His Death was instant, and without a groan.
> Oh grant me thus to live, and thus to die!
> Who sprung from Kings shall know less joy than I.   (396–406)

Recollections of his father's honesty, wisdom and goodness restore the poet's composure and lead him to wish similar blessings on Dr Arbuthnot and his mother. The final paragraph sees Pope reversing his established relationship to these two persons of such great importance to him. In his imagination he becomes physician to his own doctor, hoping to 'preserve him social, cheerful, and serene' (416), and parent to his own mother, longing to be allowed to continue tenderly 'to rock the cradle of reposing Age' (409). Images of his dying friend and dying mother, both of whose final illnesses actually occurred at different times, are conflated in his sympathetic imagination into a single moment, on which he prays Heaven may bestow its blessing, that acts as a ritual release for his personal concern and as poignant conclusion to the poem.

The concept of the satirist that emerges from the poem is highly moral and deliberately self-conscious. Pope describes himself as a satirist who does not attack someone for the sake of it, or for revenge, or even for fun, but because the person attacked embodies Vice in some form. He takes Arbuthnot's cue that he 'continue that noble Disdain and Abhorrence of Vice, which you seem naturally endu'd with', and uses it to create a satirist who sees himself as the watchman of the public weal, as self-appointed prosecutor of those who transgress the accepted moral codes of society.

Against the rather earnest, somewhat defensive, tenor of this persona's voice needs to be set the clear comicality and vigour of so much of the poem. *The Epistle to Dr Arbuthnot* is both very serious and very funny. The transformation, for example, of Pope's scholarly critics, such as Bentley and Tibbald, into weird kinds of foraging animals – 'Each Word-catcher that lives on syllables' (166) – or, worse still, into strange collector's items:

> Pretty! in Amber to observe the forms
> Of hairs, or straws, or dirt, or grubs, or worms;   (169–70)

preserved only because of the enduring genius of writers, like Milton or Shakespeare, that they presumed to tamper with, shows, regardless of its justice, comic and satiric imagination of the highest order. The same, is true, in different ways, of the withering destruction of Atticus (193–214), Bufo (231–48) and Sporus (305–33). The swiftness of the satiric jabs, the range of imaginative repulse and the sustained inventiveness of derision mark some of the wittiest and most devastating satiric verse in the English language.

And so, to return to the question raised at the beginning, does Pope succeed in binding these different elements of composition together into a unified whole? We need to ask how we are to measure that whole. What expectations of unity can we legitimately make? A patchwork quilt has the unity expected of it if it is the right shape and size to cover a bed, or whatever it has been designed to cover. In the same way Pope's poem has the unity expected of the kind of poem he has chosen to write. In a familiar Horatian epistle the topic of conversation ebbs and flows, in fits and starts, according to the writer's, or speaker's, mood. As I have shown, this mood shifts, in Pope's *Epistle*, from opening frustration to closing composure. The poet, who begins in a mood of provoked aggravation, works out his anger in the course of the epistle, particularly through the portrait of Sporus, and comes, finally, to a position in which he is at peace with himself. Our recognition of unity in the poem depends upon our recognizing the developing stages of the speaker's character.

Let *Sporus* tremble – 'What? that Thing of silk,
Sporus, that mere white Curd of Ass's milk?
Satire or Sense alas! can *Sporus* feel?
Who breaks a Butterfly upon a Wheel?'
Yet let me flap this Bug with gilded wings,
This painted Child of Dirt that stinks and stings;   310
Whose Buzz the Witty and the Fair annoys,
Yet Wit ne'er tastes, and Beauty ne'er enjoys,
So well-bred Spaniels civilly delight
In mumbling of the Game they dare not bite.
Eternal Smiles his Emptiness betray,
As shallow streams run dimpling all the way.
Whether in florid Impotence he speaks,
And, as the Prompter breathes, the Puppet squeaks;
Or at the ear of *Eve*, familiar Toad,
Half Froth, half Venom, spits himself abroad,   320
In Puns, or Politics, or Tales, or Lyes,
Or Spite, or Smut, or Rymes, or Blasphemies.
His Wit all see-saw between *that* and *this*,
Now high, now low, now Master up, now Miss,
And he himself one vile Antithesis.
Amphibious Thing! that acting either Part,
The trifling Head, or the corrupted Heart!
Fop at the Toilet, Flatt'rer at the Board,
Now trips a Lady, and now struts a Lord.
Eve's Tempter thus the Rabbins have exprest,   330
A Cherub's face, a Reptile all the rest;
Beauty that shocks you, Parts that none will trust,
Wit that can creep, and Pride that licks the dust.

CONTEXT   Pope's long-standing antagonism to Lord Hervey came to a head almost two years before the publication of *An Epistle to Dr Arbuthnot* with Lord Hervey's and Lady Mary Wortley Montagu's joint authorship of *Verses Address'd to the Imitator of the First Satire of the Second Book of Horace*, published in March 1733. This, perhaps the most sophisticated of the many attacks on Pope, concluded with a ferocious curse on him and a savage depiction of his deformity:

Like the first bold Assassin's be thy Lot,
Ne'er be thy Guilt forgiven, or forgot;
But as thou hate'st, be hated by Mankind,
And with the Emblem of thy crooked Mind,
Mark'd on thy Back, like *Cain*, by God's own Hand,
Wander like him, accursed through the Land.

Hervey was to find that some of the jibes he and Lady Mary made against Pope in these verses, and in another pamphlet, *An Epistle from a Nobleman to a Doctor of Divinity*, that he published nine months later, in November 1733, were to be far more wittily and pointedly turned back on him in the Sporus passage.

CRITICISM   'Sporus' was the name of one of Nero's favourite eunuchs, whom he later married. In applying this name to Hervey, Pope makes a double strike from the outset, commenting not only on his bisexuality, but also on his role as a closet favourite at Court. No sooner has he announced his intention of putting the fear of God into Hervey – 'Let *Sporus* tremble' – than Arbuthnot intervenes in an attempt to restrain him. Sporus isn't worth the effort, he's already contemptible, quite trivial, a flimsy silken thing spun from a worm, a sickly coagulation of thin milk,[3] a being incapable of feeling; and so, implies Arbuthnot, one could go on, but why waste one's time and breath? You don't need a steamroller to crack a nut, or a torture wheel to crush a butterfly.

Arbuthnot's attempted restraint only provokes Pope to move up a gear. If he's not allowed to 'break' Sporus, then he will at least give him the beating of his life:

> Yet let me flap this Bug with gilded wings,
> This painted Child of Dirt that stinks and stings;
> Whose Buzz the Witty and the Fair annoys,
> Yet Wit ne'er tastes, and Beauty ne'er enjoys,   (309–12)

The insect imagery connects Hervey directly with the swarm of scribblers which so persistently plagued Pope earlier in the poem. This particular insect may appear glossier than the others, but the glitter is superficial; 'gilded' not truly golden; a cosmetic, 'painted' on to conceal the grubby reality beneath. Anyway, says Pope, Hervey is more like a gadfly than a butterfly, with a capacity to irritate the witty and the beautiful but lacking one to appreciate either. He's more of a nuisance than anything else; a yes-man doing as he's told, and yet always fussing around and getting in the way. In fact he's like a submissive, cringing spaniel who does exactly what he's been trained to do, while drooling over that which he would dearly love, but lacks the courage, to do for himself:

> So well-bred Spaniels civilly delight
> In mumbling of the Game they dare not bite.
> Eternal smiles his Emptiness betray,
> As shallow streams run dimpling all the way.   (313–16)

He's obedient and smooth mannered, but his constant smiling demonstrates his superficiality, like a river of no depth that seems always to ripple gently along on the surface. He's like the perfumed popinjay, who so enrages Hotspur after the battle of Holmedon, in *Henry IV* (*i*) – 'and still he smil'd and talk'd' (I, iii, 40) – or like Malvolio, in *Twelfth Night*, who in an attempt to impress Olivia, 'does nothing but smile' (III, iv, 11). And yet, in Hamlet's words, 'one may smile, and smile, and be a villain' (I, v, 108).

Pope next changes the line of attack from Sporus's looks to his speech. Hervey was Walpole's spokesman in the Commons as well as being Queen Caroline's favourite at Court. In his *Memoirs of the Reign of George II*, Hervey tells us that Queen Caroline had arranged that when she went hunting 'he might ride constantly by the side of her chaise and entertain her'.[4] What is remarkable about Pope's satire of Hervey, as about all his poetry, is the speed and compression at which his imagination works. Sporus is first attacked as a ventriloquist's dummy for Walpole – 'And, as the Prompter breathes, the Puppet squeaks' – and then as the Devil, in the guise of a toad, at Queen Caroline's side – 'Or at the Ear of *Eve*, familiar Toad'. What is common to both images is the act of manipulation: Sporus is equally despicable whether being manipulated or doing the manipulating. There's no honesty or openness; everything is a matter of string-pulling and manoeuvring. Sporus is puppet and puppeteer, controlled and controller, deceived and deceiver.

Pope develops the image of Sporus as a toad quite brilliantly and mercilessly as he acts out, through the staccato movement of the verse and alliterative monosyllables, the spitting poison of his ways:

> Or at the Ear of *Eve*, familiar Toad,
> Half Froth, half Venom, spits himself abroad,
> In Puns, or Politics, or Tales, or Lyes,
> Or Spite, or Smut, or Rhymes, or Blasphemies.
> His Wit all see-saw between *that* and *this*,
> Now high, now low, now Master up, now Miss,
> And he himself one vile Antithesis. (319–25)

The rhyming triplet of the last three lines is as foreign to Pope's poetry generally as Sporus is to the human race. Sporus is neither one thing nor another; he's always acting different parts, now that of a man, now that of a woman, and the result is an abominable confusion, a 'vile Antithesis', an 'Amphibious Thing', a creature of two worlds and a being of ambiguous composition.

The disgust mounts to a final crescendo:

> Fop at the Toilet, Flatt'rer at the Board,
> Now trips a Lady, and now struts a Lord.
> *Eve's* Tempter thus the Rabbins have exprest,
> A Cherub's face, a Reptile all the rest;
> Beauty that shocks you, Parts that none will trust,
> Wit that can creep, and Pride that licks the dust. (328–33)

Again alliteration and parallelism reinforce the abuse. He may look pretty with his 'Cherub's face', but the remainder of his body is that of a serpent. There's no art to find the mind's construction in the face. The final image is drawn from the Old Testament as, like Satan cursed, he 'creeps' along the ground on his belly and 'licks the dust' of the earth.

From butterfly to bug, to dog, to toad, to snake, has been a rapid and furious transformation indeed. The character sketch of Lord Hervey as Sporus is the most savage portrait anywhere in Pope's writing, and possibly the most devastating caricature in English poetry. From a fictional and poetic point of view its fairness as a portrait of the actual Lord Hervey is neither here nor there. It is satiric destruction of the first order. Pope has converted his living enemy into the archetype of the fawning courtier and sycophantic hanger-on to power whose heart is full of millions of mischiefs. He has given Hervey a kind of immortality he never dreamt of.

Epilogue to the Satires

Swift wrote enthusiastically to Pope on 8 August 1738, saying: 'I take your second Dialogue that you lately sent me, to equal almost anything you ever writ'.[1] Swift was referring to the *Epilogue to the Satires: Dialogue II*. The two dialogues which comprise the *Epilogue to the Satires* had initially been written and published as separate poems in 1738, *Dialogue I* in May, and *Dialogue II* in July. They were then brought together and published under a single title in 1740. Although written and published at two month intervals, the two poems were conceived in the same spirit of political disillusion, shaped in the same formal poetic structure and written from a cohesive moral standpoint.

Throughout the 1730s Pope had become increasingly involved in the Patriot opposition to Robert Walpole's Whig Government. *Dialogue I* represents the most overt and eloquent statement of his political commitment to that opposition, but by *Dialogue II* he is beginning to show disillusion with the opposition as well as with the Government. The strength and depth of Pope's indignation at the political corruption of the age can be felt by considering the footnote that he appended to the last line of *Dialogue II*:

> This was the last poem of the kind printed by our author, with a resolution to publish no more; but to enter thus, in the most plain and solemn manner he could, a sort of PROTEST against that insuperable corruption and depravity of manners, which he had been so unhappy as to live to see. Could he have hoped to have amended any, he had continued those attacks; but bad men were grown so shameless and so powerful, that Ridicule was become as unsafe as it was ineffectual.

In referring to 'the last poem of the kind printed by our author', Pope is drawing attention to the poetical, as well as the political, nature of these poems. They constitute a kind of finale, or signing off, to his long sequence of *Imitations of Horace*, going back to his *Imitation of Horace, Satire II, i,* published five years earlier in February 1733. The two dialogues that comprise the *Epilogue to the Satires* share, with *An Epistle to Dr Arbuthnot,* the distinction of being the most Horatian of Pope's original works; but where the latter poem is modelled on a fusion of Horace's style in his *Epistles* and *Satires*, the two dialogues are modelled more directly on the dialogue form that Horace used in Book II of his *Satires*. Indeed the first dialogue was originally entitled *One Thousand Seven Hundred and Thirty Eight: A*

209

Dialogue Something Like Horace. As the subtitle indicates, however, there are differences as well as similarities to Horace; the dialogue is only '*something* like Horace'. As with *An Epistle to Dr Arbuthnot* the Horatian model has been assimilated within the Popean creation. The biggest difference to Horace is that the figure of the satirist, which Pope projects through his own persona, in these two dialogues takes on a far more outspokenly militant position than any that is taken on by Horace's satirist.

Indeed, as a correspondent of Pope's at the time commented, the tone of the *Epilogue to the Satires* is as Juvenalian as the form is Horatian. Writing to Pope about *Dialogue II*, on 31 July 1738, Aaron Hill, the poet and dramatist, said:

> I find, in this satire, something inexpressibly daring and generous. It carries the acrimony of *Juvenal*, with the *Horatian* air of ease and serenity. It reaches heights the most elevated, without seeming to design any soaring. It is raised and familiar at once. It opposes just praise to just censure, and, thereby, doubles the power of either. (IV, 112)

Pope ironically refers to the adversary, or interlocutor, he establishes in the two dialogues as '*Fr.*' (Friend), but the person who assumes such impertinent familiarity with the poet is anything but a true friend. He has much in common with the importunate poetasters who besiege Pope in *An Epistle to Dr Arbuthnot*. He seems, like Lord Hervey, both to come from the Court (see, for example, I, 2 and I, 20) and to have, or want to be thought of as having, connections with Sir Robert Walpole (I, 26–7). He is a time-serving place seeker who lives for gossip and favour. In *Dialogue I* Pope counters his effrontery with a polite and tolerant irony, but by the time he gets to *Dialogue II* Pope seems to have realized that irony is wasted on fools and he quite simply crushes him beneath the weight of his indignation.

The two dialogues demonstrate the fine assurance of Pope's handling of the couplet form in his later poetry. The cut and thrust of argumentative exchange between Pope's presentation of himself and his 'Friend' operates within the boundaries of the closed couplet so easily that the reader is hardly aware of the formal bondage that exists. Further, the poems are amongst the most dramatic Pope wrote, with sudden interventions and 'Interruption smart' from both speakers, and yet Pope never loses control, for a single moment, of the rhymed decasyllabic couplets. The dramatic friction between the disputing speakers is increased by being contained in so tight a form.

Dialogue I opens with the 'Friend' criticizing Pope for becoming too moral in his writings and for failing to emulate Horace's 'sly, polite, insinuating, stile' (I, 19), which could please 'at Court and make AUGUSTUS smile' (I, 20). Pope cleverly uses the 'Friend' to begin his attack on Robert Walpole's corruption. The 'Friend' is allowed to describe Horace in terms that compare him to Sir Robert himself. He is described as an 'artful Manager' (I, 21) and 'a kind of Screen' (I, 22). This was a well-established metaphor in the late 1730s for referring to Walpole's policy of opposing all Parliamentary enquiries into public frauds. The 'Friend's' criticism gives Pope an opportunity to declare his own position:

> Come, come, at all I laugh He laughs, no doubt,
> The only diff'rence is, I dare laugh out.   (I, 35–6)

The poet is proud of his political independence. It has been hard fought for over the years, and will not be lightly surrendered.

The 'Friend' continues in hearty vein. By all means laugh at old-fashioned things, like Religion, Honesty, Principle, Patriotism and Virtue, and ensure that you 'charitably comfort Knave and Fool' (I, 62). Pope uses the adversary's jovial and breezy dismissal of traditional values to bring out his own positive beliefs. He next tries heavy-handed irony on his frivolous 'Friend', and, asking forgiveness for his youthful impetuosity, mockingly invokes general satire that hurts no one:

> *P.* Dear Sir, forgive the Prejudice of Youth:
> Adieu Distinction, Satire, Warmth, and Truth!
> Come harmless *Characters* that no one hit,
> Come *Henley's* Oratory, *Osborn's* Wit!   (I, 63–6)

But the mock invocation quickly turns to strong sarcasm as he cannot sustain such empty politeness:

> The Honey dropping from *Favonio's* tongue,
> The Flow'rs of *Bubo*, and the Flow of *Y–ng!*
> The gracious Dew of Pulpit Eloquence;
> And all the well-whipt Cream of Courtly Sense
>   (I, 67–70)

Pope maintains the sarcastic vein through much of the remainder of *Dialogue I*, proclaiming, 'Satire is no more' (I, 83), and there is 'No Gazeteer more innocent than I!' (I, 84).

There's no need to go as far as that, interjects the 'Friend', so long as you only attack persons who are not in positions of influence or power. A technique Pope uses to great effect in the *Epilogue to the Satires* is to damn persons or concepts by falsely praising them. Thus it is with the 'Friend's' praise for the Earls of Selkirk and De La Warr (I, 91–104), and with the poet's own ironic vindication of the 'Dignity of *Vice*' (I, 114), at the end of *Dialogue I*. In this powerful passage (I, 141–70), Pope moves into an epic strain that anticipates the moral urgency and reach of *The New Dunciad*.

The satirist ironically defends the allegorical figure of Vice against the corruption of being associated with the low-born:

> *Vice* is undone, if she forgets her Birth,
> And stoops from Angels to the Dregs of Earth:
> But 'tis the *Fall* degrades her to a Whore;
> Let *Greatness* own her, and she's mean no more
>
> (I, 141–4)

One of Walpole's nicknames, on account both of his position and size, was the 'Great Man'. Pope is making a scarcely veiled allusion here, and in the lines that follow, to Walpole's mistress, Molly Skerrett. She merges with the allegorical description of Vice as she,

> Mounts the Tribunal, lifts her scarlet head,
> And sees pale Virtue carted in her stead!   (I, 149–50)

Pope describes a triumphal procession through the streets of London, in which all those things he most believes in are denigrated, and all those he most despises, celebrated. A patriotic appreciation of England's historical liberties is 'Dragg'd in the Dust', like Hector being dragged round Troy. The young, dressed in the latest continental fashions, dance before Vice, while the old are left to 'crawl' behind. Family and marital loyalties are bartered, or ignored, as all are caught up in a mad idolatrous rush. Vice's 'black trumpet' pronounces her message through the land that 'Not to be corrupted is the Shame' (I, 160). It is a highly visual and pictorial scene drawing on Pope's acquaintance with similar tableaux in grand history paintings.

Dialogue I ends with a ringing proclamation of the ascendancy of Vice, in which the high- and low-born aspire, with equal admiration, to a life of avarice and crime:

> All, all look up, with reverential Awe,
> On Crimes that scape, or triumph o'er the Law:
> While Truth, Worth, Wisdom, daily they decry –
> 'Nothing is Sacred now but Villany.'   (I, 167–70)

The image of Vice triumphant in England is similar in its power, tone and pictorial composition to that of Dulness on her throne at the end of *The Dunciad*. The final, relegated, couplet brings us down to earth, as Pope quietly reminds the reader that his own voice is not to be confused with that which celebrates this apocalyptic vision:

> Yet may this Verse (if such a Verse remain)
> Show there was one who held it in disdain.   (I, 171–2)

212

Dialogue II begins with the 'Friend' making a typically niggling comment. He accuses Pope of writing libel, and yet pretends the accusation is not his but that of the Solicitor to the Treasury, Nicholas Paxton, who was in charge of reporting all libels to the Government. Thus he conceals his criticism beneath a pretended objectivity coupled with an obsequious politeness – note the interpolated 'Sir'. But Pope has no intention of letting the 'Friend' develop his position in this poem in the same leisurely way he did in *Dialogue I*, and firmly interrupts him after only one line. When the 'Friend' breaks in again at line 10, and accuses Pope of being too personal in his satire, the satirist again replies with great vigour. The shifts in tone, as the argument sways first one way then another, are skilfully handled. The dramatic intensity increases as Pope first makes a lively but direct defence of his position: 'How Sir! not damn the Sharper, but the Dice?', and then promptly moves into a heavily ironic invocation to general satire:

> Come on then Satire! gen'ral, unconfin'd,
> Spread thy broad wing, and sowze on all the Kind.
>
> (II, 14–15)

Pope uses the same image for the satirist here, that of the falcon, that he used in *An Epistle to Dr Arbuthnot* (340–1), and mockingly pretends that the satirist swoops like a bird of prey on 'all the kind' (15) rather than on particular victims. The 'Friend' is naturally inquisitive and cannot bear the suspense of not knowing who is being attacked. This, of course, is precisely Pope's point, and from lines 18 to 27 there is a rapid exchange between the two in which Pope manipulates the closed couplet with extraordinary flexibility to create the frenzied rhythms of their argument. The chopped movement of line 18, for example, in which there are three distinct caesuras, as the 'Friend' fiercely questions the poet, is followed by the sudden speed of line 19 in which there is no caesura at all between the tripping monosyllables of which the line is composed. Then, at line 22, the staccato movement returns as the satirist and his adversary bandy words and furiously contradict each other four times in the single line. Again this is contrasted by the release of the line that follows. At line 26 Pope drops his ironic stance as a general satirist, and returns, in his own voice, to a series of questions (26–33) whose urgency is heightened by the contrast with what has gone before. The image of the satirist as a bird of prey gives way to that of the satirist as hunter; both images which show Pope's essentially militant concept of his role. The satirist's victims are seen as 'Game' (27) to be shot at, or deer to be 'run down' (29). The argument between the two men continues throughout the poem, but not always at the same hectic speed established in this opening section.

Pope slows down the pace and changes direction, for instance
when he introduces examples of worthiness and honesty, particularly
celebrating those of his friends who suffered as a result of it:

> But does the Court a worthy Man remove?
> That instant, I declare, he has my Love:
> I shun his Zenith, court his mild Decline;
> Thus SOMMERS once, and HALIFAX were mine.
> Oft in the clear, still Mirrour of Retreat,
> I study'd SHREWSBURY, the wise and great:
> CARLETON's calm Sense, and STANHOPE's noble Flame,
> Compar'd, and knew their gen'rous End the same:
> How pleasing ATTERBURY's softer hour!
> How shin'd the Soul, unconquer'd in the Tow'r!
>
> (II, 74–83)

As Maynard Mack demonstrated many years ago, in an essay
that remains the best introduction to Pope, names take on a metaphorical colouring in his poetry. The poetry does not require that
we identify them too closely: 'they become vehicles of an aura of
associations'.[2] Thus the name 'SHREWSBURY', in the lines above,
suggests a certain shrewdness to go with his wisdom and greatness,
the name 'CARLETON', reinforces the calmness of his sense; the name
'STANHOPE' acts as a standard of hope for his 'noble Flame'; and the
gentle sound of 'ATTERBURY' enacts the saintliness associated with
him.

Furthermore, says Pope, I praise Virtue wherever I see it and not
only in my own friends. I never knew the Man of Ross, but that
didn't stop me praising him in the *Epistle to Bathurst*. Indeed, to
continue the hunting imagery,

> To find an honest man, I beat about,
> And love him, court him, praise him, in or out.
>
> (II, 102–3)

The debate between Pope and the 'Friend' rages on from this point:

> *Fr.* Then why so few commended? *P.* Not so fierce;
> Find you the Virtue, and I'll find the Verse.   (II, 104–5)

Sometimes there are set piece exchanges, sometimes repeats of the
rapid altercation that we saw at the beginning. Pope allows the
satirist to make much more of the rhetorical running in *Dialogue II*
than in *Dialogue I*. He has adopted the policy of attack being the
best means of defence. The 'Friend' tries, like a modern-day current
affairs television interviewer, to control the dialogue and ask difficult
questions, but the satirist, like an accomplished politician, brushes

him aside. The figure of the satirist dominates the dialogue: 224 of the poem's 255 lines are put into his mouth, and only 31 into that of the 'Friend'. Furthermore, those 31 lines include 19 separate interventions, of which the longest is only 11 lines and several are only a half or quarter line. Pope, as satirist, never allows the 'Friend' time to develop his objections. He subjugates the adversary with the intensity and fervour of his protestation. As the dialogue develops he becomes increasingly irate, first trying scatological imagery to shock the 'Friend' (168–84), and then moving on to the final ringing defence of his satire and indictment of a world that is financially, politically and spiritually rotten.

SELECTED EXCERPT

> Ask you what Provocation I have had?
> The strong Antipathy of Good to Bad.
> When Truth or Virtue an Affront endures,
> Th'Affront is mine, my Friend, and should be yours.   200
> Mine, as a Foe profess'd to false Pretence,
> Who thinks a Coxcomb's Honour like his Sense;
> Mine, as a Friend to ev'ry worthy mind;
> And mine as Man, who feel for all mankind.
>   *Fr.* You're strangely proud.
>   *P.* So proud, I am no Slave:
> So impudent, I own myself no Knave:
> So odd, my Country's Ruin makes me grave.
> Yes, I am proud; I must be proud to see:
> Men not afraid of God, afraid of me:
> Safe from the Bar, the Pulpit, and the Throne,   210
> Yet touch'd and sham'd by *Ridicule* alone.
>   O sacred Weapon! left for Truth's defence,
> Sole Dread of Folly, Vice, and Insolence!
> To all but Heav'n-directed hands deny'd,
> The Muse may give thee, but the Gods must guide.
> Rev'rent I touch thee! but with honest zeal;
> To rowze the Watchmen of the Publick Weal,
> To Virtue's Work provoke the tardy Hall,
> And goad the Prelate slumb'ring in his Stall.
>   Ye tinsel Insects! whom a Court maintains,   220
> That counts your Beauties only by your Stains,
> Spin all your Cobwebs o'er the Eye of Day!
> The Muse's wing shall brush you all away:
> All his Grace preaches, all his Lordship sings,
> All that makes Saints of Queens, and Gods of Kings,
> All, all but Truth, drops dead-born from the Press,
> Like the last Gazette, or the last Address.

When black Ambition stains a Publick Cause,
A Monarch's sword when mad Vain-glory draws,
Not *Waller's* Wreath can hide the Nation's Scar,   230
Nor *Boileau* turn the Feather to a Star.
   Not so, when diadem'd with Rays divine,
Touch'd with the Flame that breaks from Virtue's Shrine,
Her Priestess Muse forbids the Good to dye,
And ope's the Temple of Eternity;
There other *Trophies* deck the truly Brave,
Than such as *Anstis* casts into the Grave;
Far other *Stars* than * and ** wear,
And may descend to *Mordington* from *Stair:*
Such as on HOUGH's unsully'd Mitre shine,   240
Or beam, good DIGBY! from a Heart like thine.
Let Envy howl while Heav'n's whole Chorus sings,
And bark at Honour not confer'd by Kings;
Let Flatt'ry sickening see the Incense rise,
Sweet to the World, and grateful to the Skies:
Truth guards the Poet, sanctifies the line,
And makes Immortal, Verse as mean as mine.
   Yes, the last Pen for Freedom let me draw,
When Truth stands trembling on the edge of Law:
Here, Last of *Britons!* let your Names be read;   250
Are none, none living? let me praise the Dead,
And for that Cause which made your Fathers shine,
Fall, by the Votes of their degen'rate Line!
   Fr. Alas! alas! pray end what you began,
And write next winter more *Essays on Man.*

CRITICISM: The initial appeal is to fundamental morality, to the plain opposition of virtue and vice. Pope, as satirist has moved into a strongly rhetorical mode. The 'Friend' has not, in fact, asked him what provocation he has had, but Pope invents the question as a rhetorical device for telling him anyway. All irony and sarcasm is temporarily cast aside as the satirist asserts his defence of virtue. The speaker's rhetorical fervour is established through repetition, first of the noun 'affront', and then of the possessive pronoun 'mine', which rings through lines 200–4, gathering force as it progresses from identification with the single speaker to representation of all mankind.

The 'Friend's' interruption is a further rhetorical device that allows the satirist to proclaim his defence of liberty and patriotism in even more resounding tones. He reverts to heavy-handed irony, as being the only kind that the 'Friend' might understand. If it shows pride to be independent-minded, then I am proud; if it is impudent to be honest, then I am impudent; if it is odd to love one's country then I am odd. The rhetorical patterning of the repeated adverb, 'so', and first person present indicatives establish a rising rhythm that comes to a climax in the concluding emphasis on the power of ridicule.

This leads into one of the most fervent defences of his satiric art in Pope's poetry. It is invoked in crusading and classical terms. Satire is a 'Weapon' (212) given by 'the Muse' (215) but guided by 'the Gods' (215). Pope's classical distancing associates his own satiric persona with those of Horace and Juvenal. The language is religious – 'Rev'rent I touch thee!' (216) – as Satire takes on a hallowed, but specifically non-Christian, aspect. Satire is presented as a fighting tool to be used for public-spirited purposes to galvanize, motivate and urge others into defending Virtue.

The satirist then mockingly addresses all superficial hangers-on to place and power linking them, through the imagery, with those who importuned him in *An Epistle to Dr Arbuthnot*. They are insects or spiders, and the Muse of Satire is imagined sweeping them away with her wing. As at the end of *Dialogue I* the verse takes on an epic dimension. Equivocation and evasion against virtue and honour is collected together through the accumulating 'all's, and envisaged dropping still-born 'from the Press' (226). The verb dismisses such generation as bestial.

The satirist, ideally, hopes that panegyric cannot conceal Truth. Waller cannot cover up Cromwell's overweening ambition, nor Boileau that of Louis XIV (228–31). It is different, however, with satire whose muse, enobled by informing virtue, celebrates true and lasting worth. An imagery of light and splendour takes over from the darkness and injury associated with Ambition. Virtue's shrine sends out 'Rays divine' (232) and a 'flame' (233). Stars 'shine' (240) on Hough's 'unsully'd Mitre' (240) and 'beam' from Digby's heart.

The poem closes with another imagined allegorical tableau. There are buried memories of Spenser's figure of Error, as an ugly monster from Canto I of *The Faerie Queene*, and of Milton's description of Sin, in *Paradise Lost*, Book II, in Pope's visualization of Envy howling and barking at Honour, and Flattery sickening before true praise. The satirist robustly associates himself with Truth:

> Truth guards the Poet, sanctifies the line,
> And makes Immortal, Verse as mean as mine.   (246–7)

Although there is a pretence at modesty in referring to his own verse as 'mean', the satirist has no hesitation in believing that he represents 'Truth'. The religious imagery has returned: the poet's lines are consecrated and his verses, if not himself, given everlasting life.

In the final paragraph the satirist takes on the role of moral standard-bearer of Truth and heroic defender of Freedom as he faces up to the perceived threatened censorship of the press:[3]

> Yes, the last Pen for Freedom let me draw,
> When Truth stands trembling on the edge of Law: (248–9)

He returns to the image of satire as a weapon to be 'drawn' in defence of freedom, and rather self-consciously casts himself as its 'last' defender. When he comes to read the names of fellow spirits there are none remaining. Pope shows here a disillusion with the Patriot opposition to Walpole as well as with the Government itself. The disenchantment is reinforced by giving the 'Friend' the final word and allowing him to suggest that Pope would be better employed keeping out of politics:

> Alas! alas! pray end what you began,
> And write next winter more *Essays on Man*.   (254–5)

The Dunciad

The Dunciad is Pope's most ambitious, deeply felt, contentious and, some would say, seriously flawed poem. It is imaginative and allusive as well as being remorselessly analytical, compressed and comic. Pope's care and concern about the state of English society and civilization in his day is nowhere more evident than in the final version of this poem. *The Dunciad* was a continuing part of Pope's imaginative life in a way that no other of his compositions were although some of them, particularly *An Epistle to Dr Arbuthnot*, can be seen as expressions of cognate concern. The poem had a long gestation, appearing in different versions over a fifteen-year period.

The first version was published in May 1728 and the fourth, and last, in October 1743, just six months before Pope's death. Pope lived with the increasingly nightmarish fear of dulness as an annihilating force within civilization, and of those whom he considered to be dunces, as an unendurable provocation, for at least the last fifteen years of his life. The terror of cultural mediocrity had obsessed him, and was developing in his mind long before the publication of the first version in 1728. The idea of converting this fear into a satirical anti-epic began as an attempt to destroy his critics, but what began as a personal feud and something of a literary joke, however savage, gradually grew into a cosmic metaphor for the future. Pope's abiding fear is of a dissolving cultural inheritance in which there is no continuity with the past. He is haunted by the prospect of humankind's lost possession of a shared birthright.

When we study *The Dunciad* we are confronted with four separate versions of the poem, and it is as well to begin with an account of the genesis and growth of the final version. As early as 1717, in the Preface to his collected *Works*, Pope had remarked that 'the life of a Wit is a warfare upon earth', and nothing had happened since then to make him change his view. His writings had been constantly attacked, and his person sniped at, since the date of his first publication, the *Pastorals*, 1709. Those attacks had not lessened as the result of tolerance on his part. He had tried, as he told Swift in a letter of 14 December 1725, 'to put an end to Slanders only as the Sun does to Stinks; by shining out, exhale 'em to nothing' (II, 349); but ignoring insults had not worked and although, as he went on to say in the same letter, he did not have much anger against the great ones of the world his spleen was roused by 'the little rogues of it':

It would vexe one more to be knockt o' the Head by a Pisspot,
than by a Thunderbolt. As to great Oppressors (as you say) they
are like Kites or Eagles, one expects mischief from them: But to be
Squirted to death (as poor Wycherley said to me on his deathbed)
by *Potecaries Prentices*, by the under Strappers of Under Secretaries,
to Secretaries, who were no Secretaries – this would provoke as
dull a dog as Philips himself.   (II, 350)

When, in 1726, Lewis Theobald, published *Shakespeare Restored: or,
A Specimen of the Many Errors, As Well Committed, as Unamended by Mr
Pope in his Late Edition of this Poet*, Pope seized on this example of
what he considered to be pedantic nit-picking of the dullest kind as
the final provocation. He resolved to scourge his numerous detractors
and enemies, critics and poets alike. On 18 May 1728, he anonymously published *The Dunciad*, in three books, with Theobald as
anti-hero. The poem was modelled on Dryden's *MacFlecknoe*. But
where Dryden's poem was a lampoon of 217 lines attacking a single
person, Thomas Shadwell, Pope's was a more fully developed satirical anti-epic attacking a host of those he was passionately convinced
were bad writers in a poem of three books and over 1,000 lines.
Pope in fact left many of the dunces' names blank in the first version
and others were effectually concealed by the use of their initial letter
alone, but this only exacerbated the furore its publication brought
about, for much nervous curiosity and energy was expended in
attempting to identify the targets. The crowning of Theobald as
King of the Dunces was the main action. The fear of Universal
Darkness engulfing the world was as yet only a private nightmare
vision, not reality, which finally passed through the ivory gates of
false dreams at the end of Book III.

Although *The Dunciad* had been published anonymously there was
never much doubt as to its authorship. As one might expect, far
from silencing his enemies, the publication brought numerous new
attacks on Pope. The war with the dunces was now fully joined and
he decided to republish the poem in amplified form that would
further burlesque contemporary scholarly and critical practice. He
wrote to Swift a month after its publication, in June 1728, describing
his plans for a new edition and in particular his intention to
dedicate *The Dunciad* to him:

The Dunciad is going to be printed in all pomp, with the
inscription, which makes me proudest. It will be attended with
Proeme, Prologomena, Testimonia Scriptorum, Index Authorum, and Notes
Variorum. As to the latter, I desire you to read over the Text, and
make a few in any way you like best, whether dry raillery, upon
the stile and way of commenting of trivial Critics; or humorous,
upon the authors in the poem; or historical, or persons, places,

times; or explanatory, or collecting the parallel passages of the
Ancients. (II, 503)

Swift replied two weeks later saying that he 'never . . . saw so much
good satire, or more good sense, in so many lines' (II, 504) and
urging Pope to fill in the asterisks 'with some real names of real
Dunces' (II, 505). Swift also suggested that Pope create imaginary
commentators to amplify the satire. Pope acted fully on his advice
and, according to the modern editor of his letters, 'it led him to
annotate recklessly so far as true facts were concerned' (II, 505).
Pope's notes partly extend the personal satire on the duncesthrough
direct attack, but they are also an elaborate spoof intended to
parody the paraphernalia surrounding much contemporary scholarship. A twentieth-century parallel would be T. S. Eliot's footnotes to
The Waste Land, another protest against the cultural devastation of
an age. *The Dunciad Variorum*, with the names of the duncesprinted
in full and their biographies sketched in through the notes, was
published in April 1729.

The poem then lay more or less dormant for thirteen years, except
for one or two minor changes for its inclusion in Volume II of
Pope's collected *Works* (1735), until, in March 1742, he published
an entirely new fourth book, entitled *The New Dunciad*, in which he
finally realized the dire predictions of the earlier three books. The
threatened reign of Dulness now became a reality. Where in *The
Dunciads* of 1728 and 1729 the Goddess Dulness merely 'tries' (I, 15)
to confirm her empire, she now succeeds in putting Britannia to
sleep: 'And pour'd her Spirit o'er the land and deep.' (I, 8) Attempt
has become accomplishment, foreboding fact. *The New Dunciad* is an
altogether more serious and universal satire than the first three
books, much as Book IV of *Gulliver's Travels* has a greater seriousness
than the first three books. Pope is concerned now not with his
individual enemies, but with decay, loss and folly, in both cultural
and intellectual matters. The state of public entertainment and of
education, both in the schools and universities; the behaviour of
young gentlemen at home and abroad; the intellectual horizons of
scholars and collectors; the development of free-thinking and deist
ideas in religious thought; these are the graver and wider concerns
that now command his satiric attention.

Then, in July 1742, Colley Cibber published *A Letter from Mr
Cibber to Mr Pope*, one of the most scurrilous personal attacks ever
made on Pope, in which Cibber fictitiously pretends to rescue him
from a brothel:

> But I (forgive me all ye mortified Mortals whom his fell Satyr has
> since fallen upon) observing he had staid as long as without
> hazard to his Health he might, I, 'Pricked to it by foolish Honesty

and Love,' as *Shakespeare* says, without Ceremony, threw open the Door upon him, where I found this little hasty Hero, like a terrible *Tom Tit*, pertly perching upon the Mount of Love! But such was my Surprize that I fairly laid hold of his Heels, and actually drew him down safe and sound from his Danger.

The libel came supported with a graphic illustration showing Cibber pulling Pope off a prostitute by tugging at one of his heels. The unintended irony is that by putting these particular words from Shakespeare's Iago into his own mouth, Cibber was, without apparently realizing it, comparing himself to one of the greatest fictional villains of all (*Othello*, III, iii, 418).

Cibber's attack stung Pope into a final revision of *The Dunciad*. In the autumn and winter of 1742 he set about rewriting all four books with Cibber replacing Theobald as hero. *The Dunciad, in Four Books* was published in October 1743. The restoration of the Empire of Dulness becomes the principal action, and the mother, not the son, the principal personage. This last version of *The Dunciad* is undoubtedly a richer, more fully developed poem than the earlier three versions. It is this version that is normally read by students today, and which the remainder of this introduction will discuss.

The Dunciad has always been a controversial poem. It was, as we have seen, written as such: Pope set out to destroy his enemies. Many readers have felt, however, that in attacking those persons who had attacked him, Pope sank to their level. There is undeniably a strong element of personal revenge in *The Dunciad*, but it is important to recognize that the poem also grew out of the most deep-rooted of Pope's feelings about literature. At its base is the firmly held belief that bad literature, indeed bad art generally, is immoral, and if allowed to spread unchecked will corrupt and eventually nullify civilization. The writer's duty is perceived as a moral one: to defend the validity of the written word at a time when it is being defiled, and, in doing so, to preserve the living bond between idea and language.

The Dunciad is not a mere personal brawl, or unseemly public display of private hostility. Pope has done what any artist does: he has taken the experiences he lived through and transformed them into a fictional account. Pope converts the dunces' writings into weird forms of rudimentary life that parody the biblical account of Creation:

> Here she beholds the Chaos dark and deep,
> Where nameless Somethings in their causes sleep,
> 'Till genial Jacob, or a warm Third day,
> Call forth each mass, a Poem, or a Play:
> How hints, like spawn, scarce quick in embryo lie,

How new-born nonsense first is taught to cry,
Maggots half-form'd in rhyme exactly meet,
And learn to crawl upon poetic feet.
Her one poor word an hundred clenches makes,
And ductile dulness new meanders takes;
There motley Images her fancy strike,
Figures ill pair'd, and Similies unlike.   (I, 55–66)

The inhabitants of Grub Street seem to merge with the primitive shapes of their own malcreation. Their amorphous offspring seem infinitely malleable as their spinelessness takes on literal biological meaning.

The War of the Dunces has been described by Aubrey Williams, in his excellent study, as an extension of the traditional conflict between the medieval humanists and schoolmen: 'At the heart of the struggle is the concern with the means, use, ends and limits of human knowledge'.[1] To the humanist, to the supporter of the Ancients, to Pope, knowledge is of no value in itself; what matters is the use to which it is put. Pope felt that the dunces valued knowledge for its own sake but failed to put it to constructive use. They have 'learning without wisdom'.[2] Williams reminds us that the origin of the word 'dunce' lies in the name of John *Duns* Scotus, the celebrated scholastic theologian whose followers became known for their imperviousness to the new humanist learning. Pope presents the dunces of his own day as similarly obstinate. They are shown fastening on to factual knowledge of flowers, or butterflies, or words, and being trapped within that knowledge. As Dr Busby, the notorious head-master of Westminster, says about his charges:

We ply the Memory, we load the brain,
Bind rebel Wit, and double chain on chain,
Confine the thought, to exercise the breath;
And keep them in the pale of Words till death.
                                          (IV, 157–60)

Language taught in this way becomes an imprisoning boundary which restricts and excludes, rather than an enabling vehicle for opening up knowledge and including new ideas. An instrument that should allow human beings increased control over their own lives and greater freedom to determine their future becomes instead a straitjacket for restraining thought.

A similar theme invests *Gulliver's Travels*, Book III. There too, scholars, pedants, scientists, projectors and academicians misuse and misapply human knowledge. Pope and Swift fear a second flood in which a morass of printed matter, the pulp production of their day, swamps all they value and regard as truly wise. Their own writings become an ark for preserving the best that can be rescued. It is an elitist fear, but none the less powerfully realized for that.

The Dunciad is both mock- and anti-epic. It has comic elements, such as the ribald games of Book II, which have a sportive mock-epic quality; but also it has passages of high seriousness, such as the description of Dulness's awesome triumph that closes Book IV, giving an epic grandeur to a negative vision and not well described as mock anything. The distinction can clearly be seen by comparing the close of *The Dunciad* with the close of *MacFlecknoe*. Where Dryden's poem ends in farce, as Flecknoe disappears through a trap door and his robe floats upwards to settle on Shadwell, Pope's poem ends in tragedy with the cataclysmic vision of the Goddess Dulness letting the curtain fall on the theatre of the world, engulfed by Universal Darkness.

The two epic poems that lie most directly behind *The Dunciad* are Virgil's *Aeneid* and Milton's *Paradise Lost*. As Pope has Martinus Scriblerus tell us in his preface to the poem, 'the Action of the Dunciad is the Removal of the Imperial seat of Dulness from the City to the polite world; as that of the Aeneid is the Removal of the empire of Troy to Latium'. Thus the poem begins with 'the Smith-field Muses' (I, 2), just outside the city of London, and ends with Dulness's mighty yawn reaching the Court at St James's and the House of Commons at Westminster (IV, 605–18). Particular episodes in *The Dunciad* allude more closely to particular episodes in the *Aeneid*. The description of the games held to celebrate Dulness's greater honour in Book II, for instance, parodies the funeral games held in the *Aeneid* Book V; while Cibber's descent to the Underworld in Book III parodies Aeneas's visit to Hades in Book VI. Virgil's poem acts as both a model for the parodically comic fun and as a vehicle for heightening the seriousness of the satiric vision.

Paradise Lost lies behind *The Dunciad* in similar ways. Pope sees Dulness as an evil force, and the 'great Anarch' (IV, 655) shares much with Satan, the great Adversary. Her followers, Colley Cibber and his cohorts, parallel Satan's fellow devils, crowding the streets of London as Satan's supporters crowd Hell, and performing grotesque games in Book II as the devils writhe in anguish in Books I and II of *Paradise Lost*. Cibber, too, takes on a Satanic dimension at places, especially at the beginning of Book II, where he is described as 'the Antichrist of Wit' (II, 16) sitting:

> High on a gorgeous seat, that far out-shone
> Henley's gilt tub, or Flecknoe's Irish throne,   (II, 1–2)

in a way that compares him directly with Satan exalted 'High on a Throne of Royal State', at the beginning of *Paradise Lost*, Book II. In addition to a range of similar specific allusions to *Paradise Lost* a more generally allusive contrast imbues the poem. Pope ironically celebrates the approaching darkness, as light dies before Dulness's uncreating word, in contrast to Milton's invocation of God as Light.

One of the more telling criticisms of *The Dunciad*, from the time of its first publication, has been that it lacks action. Pope's original bête noire, John Dennis, remarked that 'there is no such Thing as Action in his whimsical Rhapsody ... The Hero of the Piece does nothing at all.'[3] It is worth noting that a poem with over twice as many lines as *The Rape of the Lock* has far fewer identifiable episodes. Book I describes Dulness's habitation and the annointing of Cibber as Poet Laureate; Book II the games held in Dulness's honour; Book III Cibber's descent to the Underworld and vision of the glories of his reign to come; and Book IV the restoration of Dulness's Empire. Apart from the crowning of Cibber in Book I and the dunces trekking out of the city and back again in Book II, very little happens in terms of measurable action. The anti-hero, Cibber, does not undertake any great adventure in the poem – even his visit to the Underworld only occurs while he is asleep in Dulness's lap – and he does not participate in the final book at all. One response to such criticism is to point out that the main action is not meant to be about Cibber but about the 'Removal of the Imperial seat of Dulness from the City to the polite world'. The point is valid but it remains true to say that the strength of *The Dunciad* lies more in the satiric resourcefulness and imaginative transformations of its language than in the overall design of its line of action.

But if it is a poem with little directed action, it is at the same time a poem packed with activity. It is an essential part of Pope's central metaphor that a multitude of business leads nowhere. Dulness is described at the beginning of the poem as 'Laborious, heavy, busy, bold and blind' (I, 15), and her followers are presented as involving themselves in similarly pedestrian, leaden-footed, cumbersome and painstaking pursuits. They too are 'busy' and 'bold' but in undirected, or self-inflated, ways. There is much bustle but no goal. The dunces flounder around in fogs and mists, in dirt and filth and mud, amidst shouting and roaring and braying, but the result of such hectic activity and noise is only greater confusion.

The Dunciad, in Four Books is Pope's disillusioned response to the civilization of his day. It is his final protest at what he saw as the decay of cultural inheritance in Britain, a decay that he associated directly with the Hanoverian rule of George I and George II:

> Say you, her instrument the Great!
> Call'd to this work by Dulness, Jove and Fate;
> You by whose care, in vain decry'd and curst,
> Still Dunce the second reigns like Dunce the first;

Say how the Goddess bade Britannia sleep,
And pour'd her Spirit o'er the land and deep.   (I, 3–8)

Hanoverian corruption has replaced the Augustan ideal pictured so glowingly, thirty years earlier, in *Windsor-Forest*. In *The Dunciad* images of darkness and chaos take over from the images of peace and plenty that shone so brightly in the earlier poem.

The Dunciad makes an interesting comparison with a poem written nearly two hundred years later, T. S. Eliot's *The Waste Land*. Eliot, too, protests the cultural, moral and spiritual devastation that he thought his age had undergone, but where Eliot finds that the very means of communication themselves have become fragmented, so that all man knows is 'a heap of broken images'; Pope's vehicle of expression retains a cutting lucidity and coherence. This paradox lies at the heart of the poem and is the root cause of its power to engage us. Pope describes intellectual chaos and decay through a medium of penetrating clarity. The great Anarch's fogs and mists and clouds are described in poetic language and couplets that defy their opacity and illumine the darkness.

SELECTED EXCERPT

More she had spoke, but yawn'd – All Nature nods:
What Mortal can resist the Yawn of Gods?
Churches and Chapels instantly it reach'd;
(St James's first, for leaden Gilbert preach'd)
Then catch'd the Schools; the Hall scarce kept awake;
The Convocation gap'd, but could not speak: 610
Lost was the Nation's Sense, nor could be found,
While the long solemn Unison went round:
Wide, and more wide, it spread o'er all the realm;
Ev'n Palinurus nodded at the Helm:
The Vapour mild o'er each Committee crept;
Unfinish'd Treaties in each Office slept;
And Chiefless Armies doz'd out the Campaign;
And Navies yawn'd for Orders on the Main.
  O Muse! relate (for you can tell alone,
Wits have short Memories, and Dunces none)   620
Relate, who first, who last resign'd to rest;
Whose Heads she partly, whose completely blest;
What Charms could Faction, what Ambition lull,
The Venal quiet, and intrance the Dull;
'Till drown'd was Sense, and Shame, and Right, and
  Wrong –
O sing, and hush the Nations with thy Song!

  *   *   *   *   *   *

In vain, in vain,– the all-composing Hour
Resistless falls: The Muse obeys the Pow'r.
She comes! she comes! the sable Throne behold
Of *Night* Primaeval, and of *Chaos* old!   630
Before her, *Fancy's* gilded clouds decay,
And all its varying Rain-bows die away.
Wit shoots in vain its momentary fires,
The meteor drops, and in a flash expires.
As one by one, at dread Medea's strain,
The sick'ning stars fade off th'ethereal plain;
As Argus' eyes by Hermes' wand opprest,
Clos'd one by one to everlasting rest;
Thus at her felt approach, and secret might,
Art after *Art* goes out, and all is Night.   640
See skulking *Truth* to her old Cavern fled,
Mountains of Casuistry heap'd o'er her head!
Philosophy, that lean'd on Heav'n before,
Shrinks to her second cause, and is no more.
Physic of *Metaphysic* begs defence,
And *Metaphysic* calls for aid on *Sense!*
See *Mystery* to *Mathematics* fly!
In vain! they gaze, turn giddy, rave, and die.
Religion blushing veils her sacred fires,
And unawares *Morality* expires.   650
Nor *public* Flame, nor *private*, dares to shine;
Nor *human* Spark is left, nor Glimpse *divine!*
Lo! thy dread Empire, Chaos! is restor'd;
Light dies before thy uncreating word:
Thy hand, great Anarch! lets the curtain fall;
And Universal Darkness buries All.

CONTEXT   These are the last fifty-two lines of *The Dunciad, in Four Books*, first published in October 1743. Although the first part of the passage (605–26) had been written for the close of *The New Dunciad* (i.e. Book IV), published in March 1742, and certain lines from the second part (627–56) had first appeared at the close of *The Dunciad*, Book III, published in 1728, the whole passage has been so carefully reworked as a fit conclusion to the revised *Dunciad, in Four Books* that we can justifiably see it as an expression of Pope's final poetic vision.

At the beginning of Book IV Pope had ironically appealed to Dulness for 'one dim ray of light' so that he might celebrate her restored mysteries. He had described Dulness mounting her throne with all her allegorical captives beneath her. Now, at the end of the book, Dulness, having suspended her 'Force inertly strong' for long enough, gives a last blessing to her children and begins the mighty yawn that envelops the entire civilized world, as all light is finally extinguished.

CRITICISM   The most striking thing to notice about the first paragraph is the way Pope's syntax enacts the extent of Dulness's yawn. The first couplet offers a brief introductory statement of her yawn, followed by a rhetorical question that establishes its epic scale, but the next six couplets are all part of one long sentence that creates the vast scope of the yawn as the sentence itself spreads to its drawn out close. Just as the clauses pile on top of each other through twelve lines that constitute one meandering sentence, so Dulness's yawn drifts through first London and Westminster, then the whole nation, and finally to armies abroad and navies at sea.

At the same time as Dulness is putting everyone to sleep, however, Pope's wit is keeping his readers awake. Thus the images of 'All Nature' (605), and 'Ev'n Palinurus' (i.e. Walpole, 614) nodding possess a double force since they suggest not only that they are nodding off to sleep, but also nodding in agreement with such a state of affairs. Then again, the image of the yawn as a 'Vapour mild' carries a set of associations with it that are far more ominous. Vapours were directly associated with madness in Pope's day (cf. Swift's 'Digression on Madness' in *A Tale of a Tub*, or even Pope's own description of them as the source of madness in the Cave of Spleen in *The Rape of the Lock*).

The four couplets that constitute the next paragraph are bound together by a basic pattern of structural parallelism ('relate', 619, and 'relate', 621; 'who first' and 'who last', 621; 'whose . . . whose . . .', 622; 'what . . . what . . .', 623; and the chiasmus of 624) that sweeps Dulness's various followers (the Wits and the Dunces, 620; the partly and the completely blest, 622; the factious and the ambitious, 623; and the Venal and the Dull, 624) toward the conclusiveness of the last couplet. The paragraph mounts, through the relative pronoun clauses, to the climactic clause introduced by ''Till', and clinched with the packing of four nouns of immense moral force into one line. The fundamental moral opposition of Sense and Shame, and Right and Wrong, is subservient to the all-conquering force of Dulness. Moral distinction has become as irrelevant as the distinction, in line 621, between those who were first and last to succumb to Dulness. All are included in the one yawn just as all moral standards are crammed together in one line.

In the final paragraph of the poem the Muse herself has yielded to Dulness's power, and the poet alone now stands between the reader and Universal Darkness. The poet's voice assumes an urgency made poignant by the inevitability of the approaching cataclysm:

In vain, in vain, – the all-composing Hour
Resistless falls: The Muse obeys the Pow'r.
She comes! she comes! the sable Throne behold
Of *Night* Primaeval, and of *Chaos* old!

Where the poet had seemed through the preceding part of the poem to speak like an observer describing with minute detail the Court of Dulness in eighteenth-century London, he speaks now like an omniscient commentator recording the final work of Dulness in the world. At the same time as the speaker's tone has shifted from that of ironic observer to that of prophetic commentator, so the scene has changed from local to universal. The particularities of the main body of Book IV have given way to the generalities of the close. The Busbys and Bentleys of this world are subsumed within the mountains of casuistry that are heaped over Truth's head, although their example, gives force and validity to that picture.

This last paragraph, which envisages the end of civilization, is built upon a terrible inversion of two of its great beginnings. The account of the Creation at the beginning of the Old Testament, and of the birth of Christ at the beginning of the New, lies just beneath the surface adding a sacrilegious dimension to the restoration of Dulness's empire. In Genesis darkness dies before God's creating command, 'Let there be light', and in the Gospel according to St John Christ's divinity is similarly described as a light that 'shineth in darkness'. But in *The Dunciad* light dies before Dulness's 'uncreating word', until 'art after Art goes out, and all is Night'. Dulness's victory has a profoundly evil, even Satanic force. She is the 'great Anarch' just as Satan in *Paradise Lost*, which was never very far from Pope's mind, is the 'great Adversary'.

Dulness has been associated with various images of obscurity – fogs, mists and clouds – throughout *The Dunciad*, but now she is associated with total blackness. Her throne is sable, and the restoration of her reign completely destroys everything connected with the sun. The various rainbow colours of the imagination die away, and the momentary meteoric fires of wit expire. Her destructiveness is heightened through comparison to two great destroyers of classical mythology. Medea, who was celebrated for her sorcery, murdered her own children, and Hermes slaughtered Argus, the hundred-eyed giant. Argus normally slept with only two eyes closed, but Hermes, by playing sweet music on his flute, put them all to sleep and then cut off Argus's head. In such darkness Dulness's approach can only be 'felt' and not seen, while her power, like Medea's possesses a magical and 'secret' might.

The closing couplets are gathered together through the grave imperatives ('See . . .', 641; 'See . . .', 647; and 'Lo! . . .', 653) that command our attention and give an epic strain to the finale. Pope's own moral positives make a last tragic appearance in a scene suggestive of the medieval *danse macabre*. Truth, which should be open, has been forced to sneak off, 'skulking', to her old cavern. Philosophy 'shrinks', like aging flesh, until she 'is no more'. Physic and Metaphysic call out for help. Mystery 'flies' in a frenzy to Mathematics. Religion, 'blushing' at such grotesque happenings, 'veils her sacred fires', and Morality, who has been unconscious since the beginning of Book IV (see lines 27–30) and waiting only for Dulness to give her Page the word, finally expires. The whole episode is vividly summed up in the single line: 'In vain! they gaze, turn giddy, rave, and die'. Pope skilfully uses the repeating caesura to create the frantic stepping movement of the Dance of Death. The participants are first dumbfounded as they realize that the Queen of Dulness is Death in disguise, then as the shock of recognition wears off they join dizzily in the dance until, mentally bewildered, they drop dead from madness and exhaustion.

In the last lines the image of the dance merges with that of the theatre. In the same way as all the lights are first dimmed and then extinguished at the end of a play, so the smallest 'Flame' or 'Spark' is snuffed out before Dulness's dread empire is fully restored at the end of the world. The tragedy of the fall of civilization and decay of all moral standards is then brought to its recognized dramatic close:

> Thy hand, great Anarch! lets the curtain fall;
> And Universal Darkness buries All.

And yet the final ironic paradox is that the terrible cataclysm of this darkness is only apparent to us because of the clarity of Pope's poetry. The brilliance of the poetic creation refutes the very darkness it records. Universal Darkness does not, and cannot, bury all when poetry of such intellectual splendour survives.

Notes

The closed heroic couplet

1. Samuel Johnson, 'Dryden', in *Lives of the English Poets* (1779–81); ed. G. B. Hill (Clarendon Press, Oxford, 1905), Vol. I, p. 419.
2. Ibid., p. 469.

An Essay on criticism

1. Bouhours, *Les Entretiens d'Ariste et D'Eugène* (1671), Boileau, *Art Poétique* (1674); Rapin, *Réflexions sur la Poétique* (1674); Le Bossu, *Traité du Poème épique* (1675); Dacier, translation of Aristotle's *Poetics* (1692).
2. Pope specifically refers to both these works between lines 723 and 728.
3. See Samuel Holt Monk, *The Sublime* (1935; University of Michigan Press, Ann Arbor, 1960).
4. Johnson, 'Pope', op.cit., Vol. III, p. 217.

Windsor-Forest

1. We know this from the footnote Pope added to the 1736 edition of his *Works*.
2. *Pastoral Poetry and An Essay On Criticism*, ed. E. Audra and Aubrey Williams, the Twickenham Edition of *The Poems of Alexander Pope*, Vol. I (Methuen, London, 1961), p. 131.
3. Johnson, 'Denham', op.cit., Vol. I, p. 77.
4. For a detailed discussion of the development of this idea in *Coopers Hill* and *Windsor-Forest* see Earl Wasserman, *The Subtler Language*, (Johns Hopkins University Press, Baltimore, 1959).
5. For a more detailed discussion of these lines see chapter 3, p. 83.
6. See John Chalker, *The English Georgic* (Routledge and Kegan Paul, London, 1969).

The Rape of the Lock

1. Johnson, 'Pope', op.cit., Vol. III, p. 101.
2. See Felicity A. Nussbaum, *The Brink of All We Hate* (University Press of Kentucky, Lexington, 1984); Ellen Pollak, *The Poetics of Sexual Myth; Gender and Ideology in the Verse of Swift and Pope*, (University of Chicago Press, Chicago, 1985); Penelope Wilson, 'Engendering the reader: "Wit and Poetry and Pope" once more', *The Enduring Legacy*, ed. G. S. Rousseau and Pat Rogers (Cambridge University Press, Cambridge, 1988); Carolyn D. Williams, 'Breaking Decorums: Belinda, Bays and epic effeminacy', *Pope: New Contexts*, ed. David Fairer (Harvester Wheatsheaf, Brighton, 1990).
3. Spence, Anecdote 194.
4. See, for example, the range of essays collected in *The Rape of the Lock: A Casebook*, ed. J. D. Hunt (Macmillan, London, 1968).

Eloisa to Abelard

1. Joseph McCabe, *Peter Abelard* (Duckworth, London, 1901), p. 226.
2. *The Letters of Abelard and Héloise*, translated by C. K. Scott Moncrieff (London, 1925), p. 10.
3. Gillian Beer, '"Our Unnatural No-voice": The Heroic Epistle, Pope, and Women's Gothic', *The Yearbook of English Studies*, Vol. 12, 1982, p. 243.
4. Heloise and Abelard were buried alongside one another at the *Paraclete*. Their remains were re-interred in the cemetery of Pére-Lachaise in Paris in the nineteenth century.
5. 'According to Lady Mary's granddaughter, Lady Louisa Stuart, at some ill-chosen time, when she [Lady Mary] least expected what romances call a *declaration*, he [Pope] made such passionate love to her, as, in spite of her utmost endeavours to be angry and look grave, provoked an immoderate fit of laughter; from which moment he became her implacable enemy' 'Biographical Anecdotes of Lady M. W. Montagu', *Lady M. W. Montagu: Essays and Poems*, eds. R. Halsband and I. Grundy (Clarendon, Oxford, 1977), p. 37.

Epistle to Burlington

1. See George Sherburn, '"Timon's Villa" and Cannons', *Huntington Library Bulletin*, October 1935; *Alexander Pope: Epistles to Several Persons*, ed. F. W. Bateson, The Twickenham Edition, Vol. III, ii, (Methuen, London, 1951), pp. xxvii – xxxii and 164–8; Kathleen Mahaffey, 'Timon's Villa: Walpole's Houghton', *Texas Studies in Literature and Language*, IX (1967), pp. 193–222; and Maynard Mack, *The Garden and the City* (University of Toronto Press, Toronto, 1969), Appendix F, pp. 272–8.
2. Jane Austen, *Pride and Prejudice* (1813), ed. Tony Tanner (Penguin Books, Harmondsworth, 1972), p. 267. Tanner draws attention, in a footnote, to the contrast between Pemberley House and Timon's Villa.

An Essay on Man

1. For a full account of the developing stages of Pope's *opus magnum* see Miriam Leranbaum, *Alexander Pope's 'Opus Magnum', 1729–1744* (Clarendon Press, Oxford, 1977).
2. For a development of this see Bernhard Fabian, 'On the Literary Background of the "Essay On Man": A Note On Pope and Lucretius', *Pope: Recent Essays by Several Hands*, ed. Maynard Mack and James A. Winn (The Harvester Press, Brighton, 1980), pp. 417–27.
3. See Alexander Pope, *An Essay on Man: Reproductions of the Manuscripts in the Pierpont Morgan Library and the Houghton Library with the Printed Text of the Original Edition*. Introduction by Maynard Mack (Roxburghe Club, Oxford, 1962).
4. Maynard Mack, *Alexander Pope: A Life* (Yale University Press, New Haven, 1985), p. 540.

An Epistle to Dr Arbuthnot

1. For a full account of the poem's complex genesis and for a facsimile edition of the manuscript verses to Cleland see Maynard Mack, *The Last*

and Greatest Art: Some Unpublished Poetical Manuscripts of Alexander Pope (University of Delaware Press, Newark, 1984), pp. 419–54.

2. Bavius was a poetaster ridiculed by Horace, and Codrus one ridiculed by Juvenal.

3. Hervey had been put on a strict milk and vegetarian diet by Dr Cheyne, a famous food reformer, and became a strong advocate of such a regime.

4. The full passage from the *Memoirs*, in which Hervey writes about himself in the third person, reads:

> This summer [1733] Lord Hervey had more frequent opportunities than any other person about the Court of learning the Queen's sentiments on these affairs, and conveying to her his own. Wednesdays and Saturdays, which were the King's days for hunting, he had her to himself for four or five hours, Her Majesty always hunting in a chaise, and as she neither saw nor cared to see much of the chase, she had undertaken to mount Lord Hervey the whole summer (who loved hunting as little as she did), so that he might ride constantly by the side of her chaise, and entertain her whilst other people were entertaining themselves with hearing dogs bark and seeing crowds gallop.

> *Lord Hervey's Memoirs*, ed. Romney Sedgwick (William Kimber, London, 1952), p. 65.

Epilogue to the Satires

1. *The Correspondence of Jonathan Swift*, ed. Sir H. Williams, 5 Vols (Clarendon, Oxford, 1963), Vol. V, pp. 119–20.

2. Maynard Mack, '"Wit and Poetry and Pope": Some Observations on His Imagery', *Pope and His Contemporaries*, ed. J. L. Clifford and L. A. Landa (Clarendon, Oxford, 1949), p. 28.

3. The Licensing Act of 1737 provided that no play could be publicly acted without the approval of the Lord Chamberlain, and the Opposition believed that similar prohibitions were about to be imposed on the press.

The Dunciad

1. Aubrey L. Williams, *Pope's Dunciad: A Study of its Meaning* (Methuen, London, 1955), p. 105.

2. Ibid., p. 109.

3. John Dennis, 'Remarks Upon Mr. Pope's Dunciad', 1729, selections reprinted in J. V. Guerinot, *Pamphlet Attacks on Alexander Pope*, 1711–44 (Methuen, London, 1969), p. 174.

Part Three
Reference Section

> *You* then whose Judgment the right Course wou'd steer,
> Know well each ANCIENT's proper *Character*,
> His *Fable*, *Subject*, *Scope* in ev'ry Page,
> *Religion*, *Country*, *Genius* of his *Age*:
> Without all these at once before your Eyes,
> *Cavil* you may, but never *Criticize*.
>
> (*An Essay on Criticism,* 118–23)

Glossary of technical terms used
in discussing Pope's poetry

ADVERSARIUS   The adversary, or opponent, used as a foil for the persona of the satirist in formal verse satire. Horace introduced an adversarius into many of his satires and Pope follows his examples as with the use of the 'Friend' in the *Epilogue to the Satires*.

ALEXANDRINE   A six-foot iambic line, used more often by Dryden than Pope in order to introduce variety of movement. Pope makes his attitude to the Alexandrine clear in *An Essay on Criticism* when he says that for too many poets

> A needless Alexandrine ends the Song,
> That like / a wound/ed Snake, / drags its / slow length /
>   along.   (356–7)

ALLITERATION   The repetition of sounds, usually consonants, at the beginning of closely placed words. Pope uses the technique particularly to add resonance to lists as, for example, in his description of Caius Gabriel Cibber's statues of raving and melancholic madness over the gates of Bedlam in *The Dunciad*:

> 'Where o'er the gates, by his fam'd father's hand
> Great Cibber's brazen, brainless brothers stand;
>
>   (I, 31–2)

ANTITHESIS   Two phrases or clauses having an opposite or conflicting meaning brought together in a parallel structure as in the following lines from *An Epistle to Dr Arbuthnot*:

> Did some more sober Critic come abroad?
> If wrong, I smil'd; if right, I kiss'd the rod.
> Pains, reading, study, are their just pretence,
> And all they want is spirit, taste, and sense.   (157–60)

Antithesis can work within the individual line, as in line 2 above, or within the couplet, as in lines 3 and 4. It is perhaps the most important single technique for the skilful master of the closed couplet for it enables him to bring together words, phrases and clauses that would otherwise have a diversity of meaning. It therefore functions as a kind of imagery forcing the reader to make connections between surprising or unalike things.

237

APOSTROPHE   An exclamatory address to an absent person, concept or thing. It often has the effect of raising the emotional or rhetorical level. Eloisa apostrophizes Abelard throughout much of her heroic epistle, and Pope frequently uses the technique in his satire to raise the tone to a more formal level, as when he addresses his friend Swift at the beginning of *The Dunciad*:

> O Thou! Whatever title please thine ear,
> Dean, Drapier, Bickerstaff, or Gulliver!   (I, 19–20)

ASSONANCE   The repetition of vowel sounds within a sequence of closely placed words. Pope uses the technique at many points in his poetry, but perhaps nowhere more effectively than in the repeated short 'u' and 'i' sounds in the following lines from *The Rape of the Lock*:

> Gums and Pomatums shall his Flight restrain,
> While clog'd he beats his silken Wings in vain;
> Or Alom-Styptics with contracting Power
> Shrink his thin Essence like a rivell'd Flower.   (II, 129–32)

AUBADE   A French term (from *aube*, the dawn) used to describe a piece of music played or sung in the early morning. Originally the dawn song of the Provençal troubadours, an aubade saluted the dawn and announced the sun's imminent arrival. Since the aubade was also associated with requests to the beloved to wake up, its relationship to the morning can be contrasted with that of the serenade to the evening.

BATHOS   Unintentional anti-climax when striving for effect: a ludicrous descent from the elevated to the banal. Pope introduced the word into English in his parody of Longinus's treatise, *Peri Hupsous* (*On the Sublime*). 'Bathos' is Greek for 'depth' and Pope's essay, *Peri Bathous: Of the Art of Sinking in Poetry*, 1727, is a mock solemn treatment of 'profundity', or descents from the sublime, in the 'Modern' poetry of his day.

BURLESQUE   An incongruous imitation of a piece of writing that excites laughter through disparity in form or subject matter. There are many different kinds of burlesque, such as parody and travesty, and they can be used for satiric or comic purposes. Mock-epic is a form of high burlesque which applies an elevated epic style to a trivial subject matter.

CAESURA   A pause within a line of poetry. In the normal closed couplet this pause usually falls after the second or third foot, but in

Pope's poetry, especially the later poetry, it falls in a great variety of places depending on the meaning of the line. Sometimes he will use the caesura three or even four times in one line, and sometimes he will not use it at all. The variation of the place of the caesura is Pope's chief method of varying the movement of the couplet. Consider, for example, the staccato movement of the first line, and the contrasting release of the second, in the following couplet from *Epilogue to the Satires: Dialogue II*:

> Ye Rev'rent Atheists! // – (*F.*) Scandal! // name them, //
> Who?
> (*P.*) Why that's the thing you bid me not to do.   (18–19)

CHIASMUS   Two phrases of parallel syntactical structure but reversed word order. Pope's description of old women in the *Epistle to a Lady* reinforces chiasmus with alliteration: 'A Fop their Passion, but their Prize a Sot' (247). The reversed order of the elements that make up the second phrase awakes the reader from any temptation to gloss over them mechanically, and forces one to re-examine the relation in meaning between them.

CONSONANCE   The repetition of consonants within a sequence of closely placed words but with variation in the intervening vowels, as in Pope's description of Dennis in *The Dunciad*:

> Dennis and Dissonance, and captious Art,
> And snip-snap short, and Interruption smart,   (II, 239–40)

Sometimes consonance is used simply to describe the repetition of consonants.

DECORUM   The concept of literary propriety. Proper words in proper places. The idea that the form should be appropriate to the subject matter. The level of style should match the content; as Pope says in *An Essay on Criticism*:

> For diff'rent *Styles* with diff'rent *Subjects* sort,
> As several Garbs with Country, Town, and Court.   (322–3)

DEUS EX MACHINA   Latin for 'a god from a machine'. In Greek drama the gods descended to the stage, via a mechanical structure, and solved human problems, thus allowing the play to end. The phrase is used for an unexpected and improbable device used to resolve the plot. In *The Rape of the Lock* Pope refers to the Rosicrucian spirits as the 'Machinery'.

ENJAMBEMENT   A run-on line in which the meaning flows directly on to the first word of the next line with no pause at the end of the first line, as in the following couplet from *An Epistle to Dr Arbuthnot*:

> All fly to Twit'nam, and in humble strain
> Apply to me, to keep them mad or vain.   (21–2)

This is much more frequent in Dryden than Pope. It is used as a further way (cf. caesura) of gaining variety of movement.

EPIC SIMILE   An extended comparison where a subject is compared to something at such length that the subject is briefly lost sight of. It is a way of building up the ceremonial quality of the epic style. Pope puts it to burlesque use in his description of Lintot in his race with Curll in *The Dunciad*:

> As when a dab-chick waddles through the copse
> On feet and wings, and flies, and wades, and hops;
> So lab'ring on, with shoulders, hands and head,
> Wide as a wind-mill all his figures spread,
> With arms expanded Bernard rows his state   (II, 63–7)

EPITHET   An adjective, or adjectival phrase, expressing a characteristic of someone or something.

HYPERBOLE   A figure of speech consisting in exaggeration that is not intended to be taken literally. Pope uses the technique especially for lighthearted and comic effects, as when he says of the sun waking Belinda, in *The Rape of the Lock*, that it 'op'd those Eyes that must eclipse the Day' (I, 14).

INVERSION   The changing of the normal English word order. Inversion is a technique that allows the poet to place emphasis on certain key words, particularly those falling at the beginning and end of a line. It undoubtedly owes much to Latin, where the verb comes at the end of the sentence. Two very obvious examples are the opening lines of *The Rape of the Lock* and *The Dunciad*.

INVOCATION   An address to a deity seeking his or her inspiration and aid, usually at the beginning of a poem. Pope invokes the Muses' aid at the beginning of *Windsor-Forest* as follows:

> *Granville* commands: Your Aid O Muses bring!
> What Muse for *Granville* can refuse to sing?   (5–6)

LAMPOON   A savage, or scurrilous satire on an individual. A lampoon can either be a complete poem in itself, usually fairly short, as Dryden's assault on Shadwell in *MacFlecknoe*, or it can be a short passage within a longer poem, as Pope's attack on Lord Hervey, as 'Sporus', in *An Epistle to Dr Arbuthnot*.

METONYMY   A figure of speech in which the name of an attribute or adjunct is substituted for that of the thing meant, as when Pope refers to George II as 'the Crown'.

ONOMATOPOEIA   The use of words whose sounds suggest their meaning. Pope frequently uses the technique to reinforce his satiric thrusts, but perhaps nowhere so skilfully as in *The Rape of the Lock*. Consider, for example, Ariel's description of the torture awaiting those sylphs who neglect their posts:

> Or Alom-Stypticks with contracting Power
> Shrink his thin Essence like a rivell'd Flower.   (II, 131–2)

OXYMORON,   The bringing together of two terms that are usually considered to be contradictory, and whose juxtaposition is therefore especially arresting. In the battle of the sexes at the end of *The Rape of the Lock* Dapperwit cries out: 'O cruel Nymph! a living Death I bear' (V, 61). It is a highly compressed form of antithesis.

PARALLELISM   The repetition of like elements of syntax. It is a technique that allows the poet to exploit the equal metrical segments of the couplet form, and is far too frequent a technique in Pope's poetry to need illustration.

PARODY   A form of burlesque (*q.v.*) in which the form or style of a particular work, or writer, is mimicked, but applied to inappropriate or risible subject matter. Pope parodies many writers in his work, sometimes affectionately, sometimes satirically.

PASTORAL   A *kind* of literature in which shepherds and shepherd-esses speak in an idealized way about life in the country. It originated in the idylls of the Greek poet Threocritus, who described the rustic activities of Sicilian shepherds in the third century B.C. Later poets, especially Virgil, transformed a realistic kind of writing into a convention based on an image of life in the Golden Age. The convention reached its acme in English literature during the Renaissance particularly in the work of Spenser, Sidney, Shakespeare and Milton.

PERIPHRASIS   A roundabout way of saying something. Sometimes referred to as circumlocution; in the hands of a good poet, however, periphrasis is never a matter of mere wordiness. When Pope refers to the scissors in *The Rape of the Lock* as 'A two-edged Weapon', or 'The little Engine', or 'the glitt'ring Forfex', he is deliberately investing them with an epic inflation that is ludicrously disproportionate to their trivial significance.

PERSONA   The Latin for the mask used by actors in the theatre, hence the phrase 'dramatis personae'. The term 'persona' is used to describe the voice of the speaker in a poem, as opposed to that of the author. Pope creates a number of different personae in his satires which are based partly on his autobiographical self, partly on his idealized self, and partly on previous satiric personae, particularly those of Horace and Juvenal.

PERSONIFICATION   A figure of speech in which an abstract concept or inanimate object is conceived of as a human being. Pope makes frequent use of personification as in the following description of Melancholy from *Eloisa to Abelard*:

> Black Melancholy sits, and round her throws
> A death-like silence, and a dread repose: (165–6)

POETIC DICTION   The distinctive language and syntax used by poets and particularly the special procedures used by eighteenth-century poets. The procedures include the use of archaism, inversion of the normal work order, personification, repeated epithets, and periphrasis. In his Preface of 1800 to the *Lyrical Ballads* Wordsworth launched a strong attack on these procedures calling them 'artificial' and 'unnatural'. He argued that poetry should be written in the real language of real men.

RHETORICAL QUESTION   A question inviting the reader, or listener, to supply the answer; a question with the answer built in for rhetorical effect. When Thalestris asks Belinda the following rhetorical question in *The Rape of the Lock* she knows very well what answer must be supplied:

> And shall this Prize, th' inestimable Prize,
> Expos'd thro' Crystal to the gazing Eyes,
> And heighten'd by the Diamond's circling Rays,
> On that Rapacious Hand for ever blaze?
>
> (IV, 113–16)

SYLLEPSIS   The binding together of two words or phrases of different meaning through a common word that operates in a different way with each. Consider Belinda who might '*stain* her

Honour, or her new Brocade' (*Rape of the Lock*, II, 107), or Sir Balaam's daughter who '*bears* a Coronet and Pox for life' (*Epistle to Bathurst*, 392). In these two examples the italicized word equates Belinda's moral esteem with an item of clothing in the first instance, and Sir Balaam's daughter's status with the cost of it in the second. In both examples the grammatical structure is correct. Compare 'zeugma' where it is incorrect.

TRIPLET   The use of three, instead of two, rhyming lines. This is another technique, introduced for variation, that is far more frequent in Dryden than Pope (cf. alexandrine and enjambement). Triplets are usually marked off with brackets down the side of the page.

ZEUGMA   A figure of speech frequently confused with syllepsis. Like syllepsis it involves the binding together of two words or phrases of different meaning through a common word that operates in a different way with each. Consider *Windsor-Forest* where Pope invites us to 'See Pan with Flocks, with Fruits Pomona *crown'd*' (37). As with syllepsis the italicized word governs two separate phrases: the difference is that here it is not grammatically correct and the reader has to supply the appropriate word. Pan is clearly imagined 'surrounded' with Flocks, not 'crowned' with them.

Gazetteer of place names in eighteenth-century London relevant to Pope's poetry

ALDGATE   One of the eight main gates or entrances to London, situated at the eastern end of the city.

BANK OF ENGLAND   Founded in 1694, the business of the Bank was transacted in the Grocer's Hall until 1732 when it moved into a new building situated at the west end of Threadneedle Street and behind the Royal Exchange. Both buildings were literally and metaphorically in the heart of the City.

BEDLAM, or BETHLEHEM, HOSPITAL   The hospital for lunatics built in 1675 on the south side of the lower quarters of Moorfields, and adjacent to the north wall of the City. The two figures on the grand entrance, one representing raving and the other melancholy madness, were carved by Caius Cibber, the father of Colley (see *The Dunciad*, I, 29–32). The hospital was connected with the house of correction at Bridewell having the same President, Governors, Physician, Surgeon and Apothecary. There were 200 rooms or cells at Bedlam 'furnished with beds when the patient is found capable of using one, or with clean straw every day when the patient is mischievous'. (See *The Dunciad*, III, 7, and Hogarth's *The Rake's Progress*, Plate 8, opposite).

BILLINGSGATE   The largest watergate on the river Thames in the early eighteenth century, and the site of a great fish market in Thames Street, notorious for the 'shameless' language of its fishwives. (See *The Dunciad*, I, 307 and IV, 26.) The actual dock was just to the east of London Bridge.

BOW   The church of St Mary-le-Bow, in Cheapside, just south of the Guildhall, was originally built in the reign of William the Conqueror. It obtained its name from its stone arches. The church was burned down in the fire of 1666, and a new church, with a particularly lovely steeple, was erected in 1673, after plans by Sir Christopher Wren. The church is in the heart of the city, the last place where 'Wits take Lodgings' (*The Rape of the Lock*, IV, 118).

244

Bedlam, The Rake's Progress, Plate VIII, by William Hogarth, 1735

BRIDEWELL   The house of correction, euphemistically called a hospital, situated on the west side of Fleet Ditch and meant for 'all strumpets, nightwalkers, pick-pockets, vagrants, and incorrigible and disobedient servants . . .' The Inmates were obliged to beat hemp (see Hogarth's *A Harlot's Progress*, Plate 4), and if the nature of their offence required it, to undergo the correction of whipping. (See *The Dunciad*, II, 269–70.)

CHANCERY LANE   The place where the courts of Chancery were kept. The long detention of clients in those courts and the difficulty of getting out of them is humorously allegorized in the description of Sir Richard Blackmore's reading from one of his epic poems in Book II of *The Dunciad*:

> Long Chanc'ry-Lane retentive rolls the sound,
> And courts to courts return it round and round: (263–4)

COVENT GARDEN   Originally a residential square in Westminster built by the Earl of Bedford in 1631 with Inigo Jones as his architect. The area had become somewhat run down in Pope's time and was best-known for its houses of ill fame. The market for fruit, flowers and vegetables was to the south of the square.

CRIPPLEGATE WARD   A large ward lying partly within and partly without the City wall. The gate itself, in the north-west corner of the City between Newgate and Moorgate was named after the cripples who begged there. The ward was a depressed area in the early eighteenth century and was the main residential area for the hack writers, or Dunces, who attacked Pope throughout his life. Grub Street itself (*q.v.*) lay within the ward.

DRURY LANE   A street in the parish of St Giles-in-the-Fields in the suburbs between London and Westminster. It connected High Holborn in the north with the Strand in the south. It was well known for its theatre, but was perhaps even more notorious as a centre for prostitution. (See Pope's *Versification of the Second Satire of Dr John Donne*, 64.)

FLEET DITCH   The town ditch which flowed from Clerkenwell in the north, down along the western limit of the City, and out into the Thames at Blackfriars Stairs. It was a common sewer for human excrement (see *The Dunciad*, II, 271–4) and animal offal, especially from the slaughterhouses at Smithfield. (See Swift's *A Description of a City Shower*.)

GRUB STREET   A street running north and south in the parish of St Giles, Cripplegate (outside the City walls), and lying just to the west of Moorfields. The street offered cheap lodgings to poor and out of work writers so that the name came to be used figuratively to refer to such a body of persons. (See chapter 2, pp. 48–57 and especially Pope's *An Epistle to Dr Arbuthnot* and *The Dunciad*.)

GUILDHALL   The hall for transacting City business, situated at the north end of King Street, Cheapside. It was badly damaged by the Fire of London and rebuilt two years later.

HAMPTON COURT   This royal palace at Richmond, fifteen miles upstream on the Thames from the City of London, was first built by Cardinal Wolsey, in ostentation of his great wealth, and then given by him to Henry VIII. It was enlarged, in Pope's time, by William III. Queen Anne only went there occasionally:

> Here Thou, great *Anna*! whom three Realms obey,
> Dost sometimes Counsel take – and sometimes *Tea*,

Hampton Court is where the 'rape' takes place in *The Rape of the Lock*.

HOCKLEY IN THE HOLE   A bear-garden near Clerkenwell north of Smithfield (see *The Dunciad*, I, 222 and 326) where, in 1715, 'the sum of 2s. 6d. gave access to a combined performance of bull and bear-baiting, or to a contest between battling women, or between a dog and a man' (Rudé, *Hanoverian London*, p. 75).

HUNGERFORD   Hungerford market was built in 1680 on the site of the modern Charing Cross Station. It obtained its name from being built on land owned by Sir Edward Hungerford. Blackmore's monotonous reading of his epic poetry echoes round the market, like the stall-holders cries, in *The Dunciad*, Book II:

> And Hungerford re-echoes, bawl for bawl.   (II, 266)

HYDE PARK CIRCUS   A circular drive, also called 'the Ring', where fashionable persons drove round and round in their coaches to see and be seen. The circus occupied the north-eastern part of Hyde Park, or what is now the Serpentine.

KEW   The royal estate at Richmond, now famous for its Botanical Gardens. During the reign of George II the Prince of Wales lived there. Pope wrote a memorably witty epigram to be engraved on the collar of a dog he gave the Prince:

> I am his Highness' Dog at *Kew*;
> Pray tell me Sir, whose Dog are you?

LINCOLN'S INN FIELDS   A large square, partly designed by Inigo Jones, in the ward of Farringdon Without, between London and Westminster. The theatre there was one of the two patent theatres in eighteenth-century London (Drury Lane was the other) until its rights passed to Covent Garden in 1732. (See *The Dunciad*, III, 270.)

LOMBARD STREET   A street in the centre of the City of London that extended from the Lord Mayor's Mansion House to Gracechurch Street. It was originally inhabited by Italian bankers from Lombardy and was still the home of banking in the eighteenth century. Pope was born and lived the first few years of his life there.

LONDON BRIDGE   The only bridge over the Thames until Westminster Bridge was opened in 1750. Rebuilt after the Great Fire with houses four storeys high and a street twenty feet broad. These houses were removed in the mid-eighteenth century.

LUDGATE   The gate in the west of the City leading from St Paul's to Fleet Street. A gate is supposed to have been first built there by King Lud, who began his reign about 69 B.C., but it is more likely that the name of the gate derives from its situation near the rivulet Flood, Flud, Fleote or Fleet. The dunces pour through this gate in *The Dunciad*, Book II:

> Thro' Lud's famed gates, along the well-known Fleet
> Rolls the black troop, and overshades the street.   (359–60)

MALL, THE   An enclosed walk running parallel to the front of St James's Palace. It rivalled the Ring, in Hyde Park (*q.v.*), as a fashionable resort in the early eighteenth century. It is from here that the beau-monde is imagined surveying Belinda's lock of hair, transformed into a star, at the end of *The Rape of the Lock*.

MINT, THE   A neighbourhood in Southwark, so called because Henry VIII erected a mint there. For many years it was an asylum for debtors. (See *An Epistle to Dr Arbuthnot*, 13 and 156, and *Imitation of Horace, Satire II, i,* 99.) Thus *An Epistle to Dr Arbuthnot*, 156, means 'I waged no war with the mad or the insolvent'.

MONUMENT, THE   A column erected on the east side of Fish Street hill in commemoration of the Fire of London. The west side of the pedestal was carved by Caius Cibber (cf. Bedlam entrance). The following inscription was carved on the Monument:

This Pillar was set up in perpetual Remembrance of the most dreadful Burning of this Protestant City, begun and carried on by the Treachery and Malice of the Popish faction, in the beginning of September, 1666, in order to the effecting their horrid Plot for the extirpating the Protestant Religion and English Liberties and to introduce Popery and Slavery.

This inscription was erased on James II's accession, but restored soon after the Revolution. It is not hard to see why Pope, a Catholic, says in the *Epistle to Bathurst* (340) that London's column 'like a tall bully, lifts the head, and lyes'.

NEWGATE   The gate to the south-west part of the City between Ludgate to the south and Aldersgate to the north. It also served as a chief city prison for criminals and debtors, and was notoriously full of infection. There were however commodious and airy apartments for the use of those who were able to pay for them. (See John Gay's 'Newgate Pastoral', *The Beggar's Opera*, where Macheath buys a light set of chains.)

RING, THE   See Hyde Park Circus. The Rosicrucian spirits of *The Rape of the Lock* 'hover round the *Ring*' (I, 44).

ROSAMONDA'S LAKE   An oblong pond at the south-western end of St James's Park.

ROYAL EXCHANGE   The place for merchants to meet and transact business, situated between Cornhill and Threadneedle Street in the very centre of the City. The original sixteenth-century building was destroyed by the Great Fire but was magnificently rebuilt at a cost of £80,000 and reopened in 1669. In *The Rape of the Lock* (Canto III, 23–4) Pope ironically compares the merchant's return from the Exchange with Belinda's completion of her toilet.

ST GILES-IN-THE-FIELDS   So named to distinguish it from St Giles, Cripplegate. The parish was truly an urban suburb by Pope's time, being contiguous to the two cities of London and Westminster. It was another depressed area 'filled with abundance of Poor' (Strype), particularly in the side streets, alleys and courts around St Giles' church itself and off Drury Lane, the main north-south thoroughfare in the parish.

ST JAMES'S PALACE   The chief residence of the Court (particularly that of George I and George II), in London after Whitehall was burned down in 1697. Originally founded in the twelfth century as a hospital for leprous maidens, it was acquired for the Crown by

Henry VIII, who also rebuilt it. The palace gave rise to a highly fashionable area around it generally known as St James's. (See *Epistle to Bathurst*, 388; *Epistle to Bolingbroke*, 82 and 110; and *The Dunciad*, IV, 280 and 608.)

ST PAUL'S CATHEDRAL   The cathedral in the west end of the City of London magnificently rebuilt after the Great Fire according to designs by Sir Christopher Wren.

ST STEPHEN'S CHAPEL   The meeting-place for the House of Commons (see *Epistle to Bathurst*, 394). The chapel was situated at the south-east corner of Westminster Hall which had been added to Westminster Palace by Edward III in 1347.

SMITHFIELD   The great cattle market just north-west of the City walls. An area of filth and nastiness. It was also, as Martinus Scriblerus reminds us in the notes to the *The Dunciad* I, 2,

> the place where Bartholomew Fair was kept, whose Shews, Machines, and Dramatical Entertainment, formerly agreeable only to the Taste of the Rabble, were by the Hero of this Poem and others of equal Genius, brought to the Theatres of Covent-Garden, Lincoln-inn-Fields, and the Hay-market, to be the reigning Pleasures of the Court and Town.

The 'Smithfield Muses' are associated with brutality and vulgarity.

STEWS   A number of brothels situated on the Bank side of Southwark and licensed by Act of Parliament in the reign of Henry II. There were originally eighteen of these houses, which stood in a row and had signs on their fronts towards the Thames, such as the Boar's Head, the Cross Keys, the Cardinal's Hat etc. These houses were subject to strict regulations concerning sanitation, including weekly searches by constables and bailiffs. Henry VIII put them down by public proclamation in 1546, but the allusion remained a common one in the eighteenth century. (See *Epistle to Bolingbroke*, 129, and *Epistle to Murray*, 119.)

TEMPLE BAR   A gate, at the point where Fleet Street joined the Strand, marking the end of the 'liberties' of the City of London. The heads of those executed for high treason were placed on the gate. (See *Versification of the Fourth Satire of Dr John Donne*, 277.)

TOWER OF LONDON   On the eastern boundary of the City, next to the Thames. Tradition claimed that Julius Caesar was the founder. The series of buildings known as the Tower of London included the church, the White Tower, the Offices of Ordnance, the Mint, the

Jewel House and the Horse Armoury, so that the Tower seemed to the eighteenth century more 'like a town than a fortress'. Prisoners (e.g. Bishop Atterbury) were confined in the dungeons and chambers of the various buildings.

TYBURN   Known in the eighteenth century for the gallows erected where anciently a village used to stand. Tyburn was to the north-west of the city and condemned persons were taken there from Newgate, passing along a route that went through High Holborn and out on the road to Oxford (Oxford Street today). There were eight hanging days in the year and it was considered great sport to toast criminals on their way to execution. (See *The Dunciad*, I, 41.) Journeymen were given a public holiday on the hanging days.

WESTMINSTER SCHOOL   A celebrated school lying east of the Abbey. It was famous in the seventeenth century for its headmaster Dr Richard Busby, whose name became proverbial as a type of the severe schoolmaster. Busby was headmaster from 1640 until his death in 1695 and he ruled the school 'with a rod of iron, or rather a birch' (*Dictionary of National Biography*). Dryden, Locke and Atterbury were among his many distinguished pupils. (See *The Dunciad*, IV, 135–74.)

WHITE'S   A chocolate-house in St James's Street with a special appeal to fashionable society. It was notorious for the gambling that went on and was converted to a club about 1730 to exclude the professional sharpers. (See *Epistle to Bathurst*, 55–64 and *The Dunciad*, I, 203–4, 222, and 321; also Hogarth's parody of the gambling in *The Rake's Progress*, Plate 4.)

WHITEHALL PALACE   Purchased by Henry VIII from Cardinal Wolsey in 1530. From this time onwards Whitehall was the chief royal residence of English sovereigns near London until it was destroyed by fire in 1697. There were many plans to rebuild it but they were never carried out. Pope frequently alludes to these plans (see *Windsor-Forest*, 380; *Imitation of Horace, Satire II*, ii, 120; *The Dunciad*, III, 327–8 and Pope's note). It was in the reign of George I that Whitehall became officially connected with the Government when Robert Walpole became the first prime minister to occupy 10 Downing Street. He lived there from 1735 to 1742.

251

Short biographies

ADDISON, JOSEPH, 1672–1719   Whig statesman (rising to Secretary of State, 1717–18); poet (*The Campaign* was written for the Whig Government in 1705 to celebrate the victory at Blenheim); playwright (*Cato. A Tragedy* appeared in 1713); and essayist (best-known for his contributions to the *Tatler* and *Spectator*). He was the centre of the Whig circle of writers who met at Buttons' coffee-house, and who Pope satirized as 'his little Senate'. Pope fell out with Addison early in his life when Addison praised Philips's *Pastorals* above Pope's (see p. 13). Addison later backed Tickell's translation of the *Iliad* over Pope's, and it was in reply to this affront that Pope wrote his famous character sketch of Addison in the summer of 1715. Pope sent the lines to Addison who, as Pope later told Spence, 'used me very civilly ever after'. The lines were printed piratically in several journals of the time, but were not acknowledged by Pope until 1727. In 1734 they were worked into *An Epistle to Dr Arbuthnot* with the pseudonym Atticus substituted for Addison who had been dead for fifteen years by then.

ALLEN, RALPH, 1694–1764   As Postmaster at Bath he became famous for devising a system of cross-posts that greatly improved the efficiency of the Post Office. He was a well-known philanthropist whom Pope described in the *Epilogue to the Satires: Dialogue I* as doing good by stealth and blushing to find it fame. Fielding is reputed to have based Squire Allworthy in *Tom Jones* on Allen. He befriended Pope after the publication of the 'pirated' edition of his letters in 1735, and helped to finance the 'authentic' edition of his letters in 1737 (see pp. 24–26). The two men became close friends and Pope spent a considerable amount of time during his later years visiting Allen at his Prior Park estate near Bath.

ANNE, 1665–1714   Queen of Great Britain. Second daughter of James II. Married Prince George of Denmark in 1683. Between 1684 and 1700 she gave birth to seventeen children none of whom survived her. She ascended the throne in 1702 and declaration of war with France soon followed. The Duke of Marlborough prospered enormously under her, especially on account of his wife Sarah Jennings, who was for many years her favourite until Mrs Masham superseded her in 1711. Whig and Tory strife was very strong during her reign with the Whigs holding power for the first eight years, and the Tories for the last four. Pope celebrated her rule in *Windsor-Forest*.

ARBUTHNOT, JOHN, 1667–1735   Physician to Queen Anne. He created the nickname, John Bull, for the patriotic Englishman, and in *The History of John Bull*, 1712, wittily attacked the war policy of the Whigs. He was a member of the Scriblerus Club (see p. 15) and one of the chief contributors to the *Memoirs of Martinus Scriblerus*, first published in 1741. He took part with Pope and Gay in writing *Three Hours After Marriage*, a farce satirizing the antiquarian Woodward, produced in 1717. He also contributed to the notes to *The Dunciad Variorum*. Pope addressed his finest epistle to him and thanked him for preserving his life:

> Friend to my Life, (which did not you prolong,
> The World had wanted many an idle Song)   (27–8)

An Epistle to Dr Arbuthnot was published on 2 January 1735, two months before Arbuthnot's death on 27 February.

ATTERBURY, FRANCIS, 1662–1732   Bishop of Rochester and one of the leaders of the High Church party. He was involved in the Jacobite cause for which he was tried and exiled in 1723. He was a close friend of Pope's, who gave evidence in his favour at his trial. In the *Epilogue to the Satires: Dialogue II* Pope paid tribute to his courage in adversity:

> How pleasing ATTERBURY's softer hour!
> How shin'd the Soul, unconquer'd in the Tow'r!   (82–3)

BATHURST, ALLEN, EARL BATHURST, 1684–1775   M.P. for Cirencester from 1705 to 1711 when he was made a baron, being one of the twelve men who were raised to the peerage at the same time in order to secure a majority for the Tories. He was a close friend of Pope and Swift, and shared the former's interest in gardening. Pope often visited him at his country seat near Cirencester and addressed his third *Moral Essay, Of the Use of Riches*, 1733, to him.

BENTLEY, RICHARD, 1662–1742   A famous classical scholar who was Master of Trinity College, Cambridge, 1700–42. Throughout this period he constantly feuded with the fellows, treating them with arrogance and disdain. As keeper of the royal libraries at St James's Palace he offended Charles Boyle (later Earl of Orrery) in 1693 and consequently found himself immortalized by Swift in *The Battle of the Books*, 1704, as an arch 'Modern'. He became, for Swift and Pope, the typical modern textual pedant, and his editions of Horace, 1711, and Milton, 1732, which went in heavily for verbal emendations, confirmed this reputation. Pope attacked him in *The Dunciad*, 1728–43, *An Epistle to Dr Arbuthnot*, 1735, and *Imitation of Horace, Epistle II, i*, 1737.

BETHEL, HUGH, 1689–1748   M.P. for Pontefract and one of Pope's most intimate and esteemed friends. Pope called him 'blameless Bethel' in *An Essay on Man*, 1734, and cast him as Ofellus, a sturdy peasant farmer, in his *Imitation of Horace, Satire II, ii*, 1734.

BLOUNT, MARTHA, 'PATTY', 1690–1763; and TERESA, 1688–1759   The two sisters came from a family that had long been of the highest position among Roman Catholic gentry. The family seat was at Mapledurham near Reading. Their grandfather, Anthony Englefield, lived near the Pope family at Binfield, and Pope first met them at his home, Whiteknights. Another indication of the closeness of the Catholic families to each other is that Pope's friend, John Caryll, was Martha's god-father. Pope became especially friendly with them from 1711 onwards. Martha, or 'Patty', was his favourite and his friendship with her was perhaps the strongest and most lasting of his life. There was much gossip that she was his mistress, and even that he had secretly married her. But there is nothing to validate such speculation, which is far more likely to be malicious scandal spread by his enemies. Pope addressed his second *Moral Essay, To a Lady*, to Martha Blount, and handsomely complimented her at the end of the poem. His devotion to her remained unbroken throughout his life, and in his will he left her £1,000, all his goods and chattels and a life interest in the rest of his estate.

BOLINGBROKE, VISCOUNT: *see* ST JOHN, HENRY

BOYLE, RICHARD, THIRD EARL OF BURLINGTON, 1695–1753   Celebrated for his architectural interests and his friendship with artists and men of letters. He introduced the ideas of the Italian architect, Andrea Palladio (1508–80), to England, and championed the designs of the English architect, Inigo Jones (1573–1652). He reconstructed Burlington House, Piccadilly, about 1716, according to Palladian principles, and was the chief patron of a group that included Colen Campbell (architect), William Kent (painter, architect and landscape gardener) and Pope, who was deeply interested in both architecture and landscape gardening. This group wanted to see a return to the simpler, more formal lines of Palladio and Jones. They saw the ideal country house as a villa rather than as a palace. Pope was friendly with Burlington from about 1716 or earlier, and addressed his fourth *Moral Essay, On False Taste*, 1731, to him.

BURLINGTON, EARL OF: *see* BOYLE, RICHARD

CAROLINE, 1683–1737   Queen of Great Britain. In 1705 she married George Augustus, electoral prince of Hanover, who later became

George II. In 1719 her husband, then Prince of Wales, bought Richmond Lodge, and it was here that Queen Caroline eventually had the famous Merlin's Cave constructed. Pope satirized this in his *Imitation of Horace, Epistle II, i,* 355. She was a gifted woman who maintained a strong control over her husband. Walpole realized this and one of the secrets of his success was his intimacy with Queen Caroline, to which Pope refers in *An Epistle to Dr Arbuthnot* (69–82). Her most devoted admirer was Lord Hervey. Pope's image of Sporus as a familiar toad 'at the ear of Eve', in the same poem, alludes to this relationship. She detested both her father-in-law, George I, and her son, Frederick, Prince of Wales, who became the focal point for the Patriot opposition in the 1730s. Pope seems to have especially disliked Queen Caroline and wrote a cruel epigram on her death.

CARYLL, JOHN, 1666–1736   Came from an old Roman Catholic family who lived at Ladyholt House at West Harting in Sussex where Pope paid him frequent visits. Like the Blounts he was related to the Englefields of Whiteknights and first met Pope there. It was Caryll who suggested that Pope write *The Rape of the Lock* about his relative, Lord Petre: 'This Verse to Caryll, Muse! is due'. Caryll was one of Pope's oldest and closest friends and one of his chief correspondents. Pope's letters to him show the poet at his most relaxed. He later published these letters in his 'Authentic' edition, 1737, but frequently changed Caryll's name, which was little known, to that of Addison or Wycherley, which were much better known (see pp. 24–26).

CHARTRES or CHARTERIS, FRANCIS, 1675–1732   A notorious debauchee. Pope's own note to his third *Moral Essay, To Lord Bathurst,* 1733, line 20, gives a graphic portrait of this man, who was twice drummed out of the army for cheating. Part of Pope's note reads:

> His house was a perpetual bawdy-house. He was twice condemn'd for rapes, and pardoned: but the last time not without imprisonment in Newgate, and large confiscations. . . . The populace at his funeral rais'd a great riot, almost tore the body out of the coffin, and cast dead dogs, etc. into the grave along with it.

Pope then quotes Dr Arbuthnot's Epitaph for Chartres, which begins as follows:

HERE continueth to rot

The Body of FRANCIS CHARTRES,

Who with an INFLEXIBLE CONSTANCY,

and INIMITABLE UNIFORMITY of Life,

PERSISTED,

In spite of AGE and INFIRMITIES
In the Practice of EVERY HUMAN VICE;
Excepting PRODIGALITY and HYPOCRISY:
His insatiable AVARICE exempted him from the
first,
His matchless IMPUDENCE from the second.

Chartres, who accumulated a considerable fortune by lending money, was a frequent subject of Pope's satire. He is also satirized in Plate I of Hogarth's *The Harlot's Progress*, 1732, where he is the lecher leering from Mother Needham's door.

CIBBER, COLLEY, 1671–1757   A highly successful comic actor, dramatist, theatre manager and autobiographer. A very bad poet, he was rewarded by being made Poet Laureate in 1730. Cibber was a vain man and enjoyed playing the coxcomb, both on and off the stage. His most famous comic role was as Lord Foppington in Vanbrugh's *The Relapse*, 1697. Pope made frequent fun of him in his satires before their feud came to a climax with Cibber's elevation in *The New Dunciad*, 1742. Pope's antagonism to Cibber seems to have sprung from jocular references to Pope and Gay's *Three Hours After Marriage*, which Cibber had made in a revival of Buckingham's *Rehearsal*, 1717.

COBHAM, VISCOUNT: *see* TEMPLE, SIR RICHARD

CURLL, EDMUND, 1675–1747   An infamous bookseller whom George Sherburn describes in *The Early Career of Alexander Pope* as a 'foul bird acting as scavenger for a literary battle-field'. He specialized in scandalous biographies which, according to Arbuthnot, 'added a new terror to death', and in seditious and pornographic pamphlets, which more than once put him in the pillory. He kept a garret full of impoverished authors who wrote to his command. Pope's first major encounter with him came in 1716 when Curll piratically published some poems by Lady Mary Wortley Montagu satirizing the Court. Pope avenged Lady Mary by first administering an emetic to Curll and then publishing *A Full and True Account of a Horrid and Barbarous Revenge by Poison on the Body of Mr Edmund Curll*. This is perhaps the most unsavoury incident in Pope's life and it perpetuated the hostility between the two men. Curll later published numerous attacks on Pope, while Pope satirized Curll in *An Epistle to Dr Arbuthnot* and in *The Dunciad*, Book II. In 1733 Pope manoeuvred Curll into publishing a pirated edition of his *Letters* (eventually published in 1735), so that he, Pope, would have an excuse to publish the 'Authentic' edition of 1737.

DENNIS, JOHN, 1657–1734   Critic and playwright. He was well known for his quick temper and for his constant use of the adjective 'tremendous'. Pope made light fun of both in *An Essay on Criticism* (see pp. 14–15) and Dennis replied with a savage attack on Pope's character. The hostility of the two men lasted, on and off, through both their lifetimes. Pope attacked Dennis in *The Narrative of Dr Robert Norris* (1713), *Three Hours After Marriage* (1717, where Dennis appears as Sir Tremendous), *The Dunciad, An Epistle to Dr Arbuthnot* and the *Epilogue to the Satires*.

DRYDEN, JOHN, 1631–1700   Poet, dramatist and critic. He dominated the last quarter of the seventeenth century much as Pope did the second quarter of the eighteenth. Pope saw Dryden at Will's Coffee House in 1700, and retained immense respect for him throughout his life. He told Spence that he 'learned versification wholly from Dryden's works', and praised him in many of his poems.

FORTESCUE, WILLIAM, 1687–1749   A lawyer and judge who rose to be Master of the Rolls. He probably met Pope through Gay with whom he went to school in Barnstaple. Unlike most of Pope's friends he remained a staunch Whig throughout his life and was Robert Walpole's private secretary in 1715. Pope addressed his *Imitation of Horace, Satire II, i*, 1733, to him.

FREDERICK, LOUIS, PRINCE OF WALES, 1705–51   Eldest son of George II and Queen Caroline, and father of George III. He was at loggerheads with his father ever since coming to England in 1728. He became a figurehead for the Patriot Opposition to Walpole after his father had expelled him from St James's Palace in 1737. Pope refers to his friendship with Frederick in the *Epilogue to the Satires*. In 1737 Pope wrote an epigram which he had engraved on the collar of a dog which he gave to his Royal Highness:

> I am his Highness' Dog at *Kew*;
> Pray tell me Sir, whose Dog are you?

GARTH, SIR SAMUEL, 1661–1719   Physician and poet. In 1699 he published *The Dispensary*, a mock-epic poem which ridiculed the apothecaries of the day. It was a forerunner of *The Rape of the Lock* in form. Garth was an early friend whom Pope described as 'one of the best-natured men in the world', and dedicated the second of his *Pastorals* to him.

GAY, JOHN, 1685–1732   Poet and dramatist. Pope met him sometime in 1711. His *Rural Sports*, 1713, was dedicated to Pope, and his

Shepherd's Week, 1714, supported Pope in his battle with Ambrose Philips (see p. 13). He was a member of the Scriblerus Club in 1714, and in 1717 collaborated with Pope and Arbuthnot to write *Three Hours After Marriage*, which ran feebly for seven nights before failing. The Duke and Duchess of Queensberry became his patrons in 1720 and he lived with them for the rest of his life. His most famous work was *The Beggar's Opera*, originally suggested at meetings of the Scriblerus Club and first produced on 29 January 1728. This forerunner of the modern 'musical' had an opening run of sixty-three performances and was produced every year during the eighteenth century. Pope, Swift and Arbuthnot were extremely attached to Gay, and each wrote about him with great affection (see, for example, *An Epistle to Dr Arbuthnot*, 255–6). Pope was deeply moved by Gay's death in 1732 (see p. 22).

GEORGE II, 1683–1760   George II came to the throne in 1727. He was content to let his wife, Queen Caroline, and his First Minister, Robert Walpole, who had a good understanding with one another, decide affairs of state, while he spent much of his time abroad in the arms of his German mistress, Madame Walmoden. After Queen Caroline's death in 1737, George brought Madame Walmoden to England where she was accommodated in the Palace and in 1739 made Countess of Yarmouth. There are numerous satiric allusions to George II's neglect of the arts in Pope's poetry. Nowhere are they more damning than in the *Imitation of Horace, Epistle II, i: To Augustus*, 1737, where Pope makes ironic play of the fact that George II was christened George Augustus. George II's opinion of Pope was hardly more flattering: 'Who is this Pope that I hear so much about? I cannot discover what is his merit. Why will not my subjects write in prose?'

GRANVILLE, GEORGE, BARON LANSDOWNE, 1667–1735   Poet, dramatist and statesman, rising to Treasurer of the Household in 1713. One of the twelve gentlemen elevated to the peerage in 1711, in order to create a Tory majority in the Lords (cf. Bathurst). At the accession of George I he fell from favour. Confined to the Tower from 1715 to 1717 under suspicion of helping the Pretender. Spent most of his life abroad after his release. He was an early patron of Pope, who dedicated *Windsor-Forest* to him.

HARLEY, ROBERT, FIRST EARL OF OXFORD, 1661–1724   Politician who eventually became Prime Minister, in all but name, of the Tory Ministry that held office from 1710 to 1714. He employed both Defoe (in the *Review*), and Swift (in the *Examiner*) to write for him and secure public approval of his peace policy. He could not get on with St John (*q.v.*), and their disagreement finally brought about the collapse of the Tory Ministry. After the death of Anne, he was impeached by the Whigs and put in the Tower from 1715 to 1717. He was a member of the Scriblerus Club and a particular friend of Swift, who described him as 'the most virtuous minister, and the most able, that ever I remember to have read of'. Pope addressed an epistle to him in 1721 in which he referred to him as 'One truly Great'.

HEATHCOTE, SIR GILBERT, 1652–1733   A founder of the Bank of England, of which he was appointed Governor in 1709. Lord Mayor of London 1710–11. A staunch Whig who was five times elected to Parliament. He was a very wealthy man and was reputed to be the richest commoner in England. He was notorious for his parsimony, which Pope attacks in his *Epistle to Bathurst*, 1733:

> The grave Sir Gilbert holds it for a rule,
> That 'every man in Want is knave or fool'.   (103–4)

HERVEY, JOHN, LORD HERVEY OF ICKWORTH, 1696–1743   The 'Sporus' of Pope's *An Epistle to Dr Arbuthnot* and one of Pope's major enemies in the 1730s. He was a friend of George II when he was Prince of Wales and in 1720 married Mary Lepell, one of his Maids of Honour and a friend of Pope. When George II came to the throne in 1726 Lord Hervey became an important liaison between Walpole's Ministry (he had been elected M.P. for Bury St Edmunds in 1725) and the Court, where he was an intimate friend of Queen Caroline. His *Memoirs of the Reign of King George II*, not published till 1848, are an invaluable historical record of the first ten years of George II's reign. His enmity with Pope did not come into the open till 1732, when Pope attacked him in a short lampoon. The origin of the disagreement is not known. In 1733 Lord Hervey and Lady Mary Wortley Montagu (*q.v.*) collaborated to abuse Pope's shape, amongst other things, in *Verses Addressed to the Imitator of Horace*. Pope's *Epistle to Dr Arbuthnot* was published the following year.

HOGARTH, WILLIAM, 1697–1764   Painter and engraver. After an early apprenticeship as a silversmith he achieved independence in 1720 when he opened his own shop and sold engravings. His great original contribution to art was the narrative cycle. By making engravings of his paintings he was able to reach a wider audience with his satiric portrayal of eighteenth-century society than most artists. He sold over 2,000 sets of the prints of *The Harlot's Progress*, 1732, at a guinea a set. *The Rake's Progress*, 1735, and *Marriage à la Mode*, 1745, continued to boost his reputation and fortune. In order to reach a more popular audience he sold the twelve prints of *Industry and Idleness*, 1747, for a shilling each. His paintings and prints bring eighteenth-century London vividly to life and offer a pictorial complement to much of Pope's satiric poetry.

JERVAS, CHARLES, 1675?–1739   Portrait painter. An Irishman who became a student of Sir Godfrey Kneller when he first came to England. He succeeded Kneller as principal painter to George I and was continued in that post by George II. Pope took lessons from Jervas in 1713, receiving daily instruction for much of the time. The two men became close friends and for a number of years Jervas's house in Cleveland Court became Pope's regular home when he was in town. Pope addressed an epistle to him in 1716, which was prefixed to the publication of Dryden's translation of *Fresnoy's Art of Painting*, and which expands some of Pope's ideas about the sister arts (see chapter 3). Jervas painted Pope several times. He also painted Swift and Arbuthnot.

JONES, INIGO, 1573–1652   Architect. One of his finest works was the banqueting house at Whitehall, which he designed as part of the plan to rebuild the palace. He also designed Covent Garden and the piazza for the Earl of Bedford. Pope admired his work and praised his taste in the *Epistle to Burlington*.

KYRLE, JOHN, 1637–1724   The Man of Ross (*Epistle to Bathurst*, 1733, 249–90). Lived a life of extreme simplicity at Ross in Hereford-shire, devoting the surplus income from his small estate of £600 a year to charity and the improvement of the town and countryside. He was an enthusiastic amateur architect, builder and landscape gardener. Pope did not know him. The details of the character sketch, which is based on fact, were supplied by Jacob Tonson (*q.v.*).

LINTOT, BARNABY BERNARD, 1675–1736   Publisher of many of Pope's poems including the lucrative *Iliad*, in six volumes, 1715–20, and *Odyssey*, in five volumes, 1725–26. They fell out after this over the number of free subscription copies to be provided, and Pope introduced him into *The Dunciad*, Book II, in which he races against his fellow bookseller, Edmund Curll.

LYTTLETON, GEORGE, FIRST BARON LYTTLETON, 1709–73   Author and politician. Equerry and later Secretary to the Prince of Wales during the 1730s. He was elected M.P. for Okehampton, Devon, in 1735, and soon became one of the leaders of the Whig Opposition to Walpole. He was a patron of Thomson, who described Lyttleton's home in *The Seasons*, and Fielding, who dedicated *Tom Jones* to him. Pope knew him as one of the group of young politicians with whom he became friendly towards the end of his life. He praised him in the *Imitation of Horace, Epistle I, i: To Bolingbroke*, 1737 and in the *Epilogue to the Satires: Dialogues I* and *II*.

MONTAGU, LADY MARY WORTLEY, 1689–1762   Poet and lady of letters. Married Edward Wortley Montagu in 1712. In the next few years she spent much time at Court where she became well known for her wit. Pope met her in 1715 and formed an infatuation for her that spurred him to revenge Curll's surreptitious publication of her *Court Poems* in 1716 by the infamous administration of an emetic. Later in the same year she accompanied her husband to Constantinople when he was appointed ambassador. While there she wrote the *Letters* (first published 1763) for which she is best-known. Pope meanwhile was writing her letters of passionate gallantry. On their return to England in 1718 the Montagus became close neighbours of Pope at Twickenham. Lady Mary's reputation increased during this time when she introduced the practice of inoculation against smallpox. Sometime before 1727 Pope's admiration for her turned sour and for the rest of their lives the two former friends were ardent enemies. Lady Mary became especially friendly with Lord Hervey (*q.v.*), and collaborated with him in attacking Pope, who, in his turn, frequently attacked her, under the pseudonym of Sappho, in his satires of the 1730s.

MORDAUNT, CHARLES, THIRD EARL OF PETERBOROUGH, 1658–1735 Admiral, general and politician. He had an erratic and wild career, and was already an old man by the time Pope became acquainted with him about 1723. The two men became close friends and Pope frequently visited his home at Bevis Mount, Southampton. They shared an interest in landscape gardening, and it is in this regard that Pope praises him in him *Imitation of Horace, Satire II, i:*

> And He, whose Lightning pierc'd th'*Iberian* Lines,
> Now, forms my Quincunx, and now ranks my Vines. (129–30)

NEWTON, ISAAC, 1642–1727   Physical scientist and mathematician. Discovered the laws of gravitation and published his account of them in *Principia*, 1687. He also invented the reflecting telescope which enabled him to discover the composition of white light and the nature of colours. He published these theories in *Opticks*, 1704.

OXFORD, EARL OF: *see* HARLEY, ROBERT.

PARNELL, THOMAS, 1679–1718   Poet. Of Irish birth, he was ordained in 1703, and was archdeacon of Clogher, 1706–16. He was a particular friend of Swift's and a member of the Scriblerus Club, for which he wrote the 'Essay concerning the Origin of the Sciences'. He contributed an introductory 'Essay on the life of Homer' to Pope's *Iliad*, Vol. I, 1715. After the death of Queen Anne he returned to Ireland. Pope prepared a posthumous edition of his *Poems* which was published in 1721.

PETERBOROUGH, THIRD EARL OF: *see* MORDAUNT, CHARLES.

POPE, ALEXANDER, 1646–1717   The poet's father. A Catholic linen merchant who traded from London. His first wife, Magdalen, died in 1678. He married the poet's mother, Editha, sometime during the next ten years. Their only child, Alexander, was born in the same year that Alexander senior retired from business. He had been a successful merchant, worth at least £10,000 at the time of his early retirement owing to anti-Catholic laws passed on the arrival of William III. For the remaining twenty-nine years of his life he seems to have interested himself mainly in gardening and the upbringing of his son. About 1700 he moved the family to Binfield, in Windsor Forest, where they remained till shortly before his death. For his son's moving remembrance of him see the close of *An Epistle to Dr Arbuthnot*.

POPE, EDITHA, (née Turner), 1642–1733   The poet's mother. Born to a Yorkshire family of some means. Since she was a Catholic no records were kept of her marriage to the poet's father, and hence we do not know the date. Alexander was her only son and she was already forty-six when he was born. He was devoted to her throughout his life, and on her death at the age of ninety-one, he constructed an obelisk to her memory in a prominent position in his garden at Twickenham. His correspondence is full of references to his love for her. Further testimony to it is to be found at the end of *An Epistle to Dr Arbuthnot*.

RYMER, THOMAS, 1641–1713   A literary critic who believed that neglect of the rules had seriously injured English drama. Published *A Short View of Tragedy*, 1692, in which he attacked Shakespeare's *Othello* as 'a bloody farce without salt or savour'. He represents an extreme neoclassical position at the end of the seventeenth century.

ST JOHN, HENRY, VISCOUNT BOLINGBROKE, 1678–1751   Tory statesman, philosopher and man of letters. Held office in Harley's ministry 1710–14. His disagreement with Harley brought about the fall of the ministry. He then fled to the Pretender's Court in France while his lands and titles were seized by Act of Attainder in 1715. He returned to England after a pardon in 1723, and settled near Pope at Dawlay Farm, Uxbridge, in 1725. He became the leader of the Tory Opposition to Walpole from 1726 to 1735 when he retired to France again. In 1726 he began the Opposition newspaper *The Craftsman*. He was a particularly intimate friend of Pope's, living with him at Twickenham for nine months when he returned to England to sell Dawlay in 1738. He was never a member of the Scriblerus Club but was closely associated with it. Pope admired Bolingbroke enormously and told Spence that he was 'something superior to anything I have seen in human nature'. He dedicated *An Essay on Man*, 1733–34, to him and worked some of Bolingbroke's ideas into it. The *Imitations of Horace* were started at Bolingbroke's suggestion, and the *Imitation of Horace, Epistle I, i* was addressed to him. At the close of this poem Pope picks up and restates the tribute he had paid Bolingbroke at the end of *An Essay on Man* (373–98) where he calls him his 'guide, philosopher, and friend'.

'SCRIBLERUS, MARTINUS'   The name of the imaginary hero created by the five members of the Scriblerus Club (Swift, Parnell, Arbuthnot, Pope and Gay) which met during 1714. The members of the club set about writing a biography of their hero, in the form of Memoirs, which would ridicule abuses in learning. The club only met for a few months before the death of Queen Anne on 1 August 1714 scattered its members. The true harvest was reaped much later with the publication of Swift's *Gulliver's Travels* in 1726, Gay's *Beggar's Opera* and Pope's *Dunciad* in 1728, and finally the belated appearance of the *Memoirs of Martinus Scriblerus* in 1741.

SERLE, JOHN   Pope's gardener at Twickenham. He drew up a plan of the garden at Pope's death which was published in 1745 (see p. 76). Pope addresses him in the opening lines of *An Epistle to Dr Arbuthnot*.

SETTLE, ELKANAH, 1648–1724   Dramatist and poet. He was appointed City poet in 1691, his office being to write pageants for lord-mayor's day. As City poet he celebrated with equal readiness the Tory peace of 1713 (*Irene Triumphans*, 1713) and the Whig triumph two years later (*Rebellion Display'd*, 1715). Pope satirizes him in *The Dunciad*, Book III, where his ghost appears and prophesies the future to Cibber, who is described as his son.

SPENCE, JOSEPH, 1699–1768   Anecdotist and friend of Pope. He first met Pope in 1726, and in 1728 Pope helped to get him elected Professor of Poetry at Oxford. From 1728 onwards Spence recorded

Pope's conversations. These anecdotes, which are invaluable for any biographer of Pope, were not published till 1820, although Warburton, Warton and Johnson had each consulted them in manuscript.

SWIFT, JONATHAN, 1667–1745   Tory satirist and Anglican priest. Pope first met Swift in 1712. The two men were both members of the Scriblerus Club in 1714. After the death of Queen Anne Swift returned to the Deanery of St Patrick's, Dublin. He only visited England twice again, first in 1726 to arrange for the publication of *Gulliver's Travels*, and second in 1727. During both visits he spent much of his time with Pope. A moving record of the intimate friendship between the two satirists is to be found in their correspondence, first published in 1737. Pope's most notable public praise of Swift occurs in *The Dunciad*, Book I, 19–28.

TEMPLE, SIR RICHARD, VISCOUNT COBHAM, 1675–1749   Soldier and Whig politician. Supported Walpole until the Excise Bill of 1733, after which he formed an independent Whig section known as the Boy Patriots. He rebuilt the house at Stowe and laid out the famous gardens. Bridgeman, Kent and 'Capability' Brown all worked there at some stage. Pope frequently visited Stowe, and addressed his first *Moral Essay, Epistle to Cobham*, 1734, to him.

THEOBALD, LEWIS, 1688–1744   Editor, scholar, dramatist and poet. His *Shakespeare Restored*, 1726, found fault with Pope's edition of Shakespeare which had been published the previous year. Pope revenged himself by making Theobald, whom he considered a verbal pedant, the hero of *The Dunciad*, 1728.

TONSON, JACOB, 1656?–1736   The leading publisher of his day. He was closely associated with Dryden, and was later publisher of the *Tatler* and the *Spectator*. He was Pope's first publisher, printing the *Pastorals* in his *Miscellany* for 1709.

TRUMBULL, SIR WILLIAM, 1639–1716   Statesman, who was appointed Secretary of State in 1695, but then withdrew from active life in 1698 and settled at Easthampstead Park. Pope met him about 1705. The two men used to go riding together and talk about poetry. Pope dedicated the 'Spring' pastoral to him and celebrated him as a model for the ideal Happy Man in *Windsor-Forest* (235–58).

WALMODEN, AMELIE SOPHIE MARIANNE, COUNTESS OF YARMOUTH, 1704–65   Married to Gottlieb von Walmoden, she became the mistress of George II, and moved permanently to St James's Palace on the death of Queen Caroline in 1737. In 1739 she was divorced from her husband and created Countess of Yarmouth. It is she to whom Pope punningly alludes in *Imitation of Horace, Epistle II, i,* when he ironically addresses George II: 'Your Country, chief, in Arms abroad defend'(3).

WALPOLE, SIR ROBERT, FIRST EARL OF ORFORD, 1676–1745   Whig First Lord of the Treasury 1715–17 and 1721–42. He was a skilful manager of men, somewhat harshly characterized by the saying attributed to him that 'every man has his price'. He was supported in power by the merchant classes and the new moneyed men. He had a close understanding with Queen Caroline and relied on her influence with the King. He was as unfaithful to Lady Walpole as she was to him, and kept a mistress, Molly Skerrett, from 1728 onwards, marrying her shortly before her death in 1738. He built a palatial mansion on his country estate at Houghton in Norfolk. Pope's portrait of Timon's Villa is to some extent a satire on it. Walpole visited Pope at Twickenham in 1725 but the two men were never close friends and increasingly found themselves representative of opposite ways of life. For a development of this idea see Maynard Mack, *The Garden and the City.* Nicknamed the 'Great Man' (he was extremely corpulent), it is probably true to say that Walpole was more violently attacked by a greater number of literary luminaries than any English politician before or since. Gay, Swift, Pope, Arbuthnot, Thomson, Fielding and Dr Johnson each entered the fray at various stages. Allusions to Walpole and his Ministry are too frequent in Pope's poetry to list here.

WALSH, WILLIAM, 1663–1708   Critic and poet. Lived at Abberley in Worcestershire. Dryden had called him 'the best critic of our nation'. Walsh commended Pope's *Pastorals* before they were published and generally encouraged Pope as a young poet. Pope praised Walsh in *An Essay on Criticism* for having 'the *clearest Head* and the *sincerest Heart*'. He also paid tribute to him in *An Epistle to Dr Arbuthnot.*

WALTER, PETER, 1664?–1746   A money-lender. He made a considerable fortune by lending money to the aristocracy at exorbitant rates of interest, and was said to be worth £300,000 on his death. The original of Peter Pounce in Fielding's *Joseph Andrews,* 1742. Pope attacked him again and again in the 1730s, seeing him as the outstanding representative of the new moneyed interest he so much abhorred.

WARBURTON, WILLIAM, 1698–1779   Bishop of Gloucester. First became associated with Pope late in the poet's life when he defended Pope's *Essay on Man* against the attacks of the Swiss theologian

Jean-Pierre de Crousaz, in his *Vindication of the Essay on Man*, 1739. In 1740 he met Pope and during the last four years of his life became his general editor. Pope introduced him to Ralph Allen whose niece Warburton eventually married. In 1741 Pope refused to accept an honorary doctorate from Oxford because they would not give Warburton one too. Warburton brought out a general edition of Pope's *Works* in 1751.

WILD, JONATHAN, 1682–1725   Receiver of stolen goods and informer. He became head of a large corporation of thieves and made money selling 'lost property' back to its original owners. In public he appeared not just as an honest citizen, but as an actual instrument of justice. He was ultimately apprehended, tried and hanged at Tyburn. He was mythologized by political satirists who used him as a pseudonym for attacking Robert Walpole. Gay took him as the model for Peachum in *A Beggar's Opera*, Pope referred to him in the *Epilogue to the Satires: Dialogue II*, and Fielding used the analogy in *The Life of Jonathan Wild, The Great*.

WREN, CHRISTOPHER, 1632–1723   Architect and astronomer who became President of the Royal Society in 1680. He is best-known for his architecture, especially his rebuilding of St Paul's Cathedral and fifty-two churches in London after the Great Fire of 1666.

WYCHERLEY, WILLIAM, 1640?–1716   Dramatist and poet. A wit at the Court of Charles II and a famous writer of Restoration comedies. Pope was a young man of sixteen when he first met Wycherley, aged sixty-four, who introduced him to literary society. When Wycherley asked Pope to correct his poems, Pope suggested that he transpose them into maxims like those of Rochefoucauld. This caused some ill feeling on Wycherley's part but no permanent break in their friendship, which lasted to Wycherley's death. Pope published a posthumous volume of Wycherley's *Poems* in 1729.

Bibliography

Primary texts

Poetry

The definitive edition is the Twickenham Edition of *The Poems of Alexander Pope*, general editor John Butt *et al.*, 11 vols (Methuen, London, 1938–68):

I	*Pastoral Poetry and An Essay on Criticism*, ed. E. Audra and A. Williams (1961).
II	*The Rape of the Lock and Other Poems*, ed. G. Tillotson (1940; revised 1962).
III, i	*An Essay on Man*, ed. M. Mack (1950).
III, ii	*Epistles to Several Persons*, ed. F. W. Bateson (1951; revised 1961).
IV	*Imitations of Horace*, ed. J. Butt (1939; revised 1953).
V	*The Dunciad*, ed. J. Sutherland (1943; revised 1963).
VI	*Minor Poems*, ed. N. Ault and J. Butt (1954).
VII–X	*Iliad and Odyssey*, ed. M. Mack, N. Callan, R. Fagles, W. Frost and D. Knight (1967).
XI	*Index*, ed. M. Mack (1969).

These texts have been conveniently condensed into one volume (minus the Homer translation) in *The Poems of Alexander Pope*, ed. J. Butt (Methuen, London, 1963). This is available in paperback.

Prose

The prose has been collected in two volumes, *The Prose Works of Alexander Pope*, eds N. Ault and R. Cowler, 2 vols (Blackwell, Oxford, 1936–86):

| I | *The Earlier Works, 1711–1720*, ed. N. Ault (1936). |
| II | *The Major Works, 1725–1744*, ed. R. Cowler (1986). |

The standard edition of the letters is *The Correspondence of Alexander Pope*, ed. G. Sherburn, 5 vols (Clarendon Press, Oxford, 1956).

Pope's reminiscences about his life were recorded by Joseph Spence and are available in *Observations, Anecdotes and Characters of Books and Men, collected from the conversation of Mr. Pope and other eminent persons of his time*, ed. J. M. Osborn, 2 vols (Clarendon Press, Oxford, 1966).

267

Biographical studies

Dobrée, B., *Alexander Pope* (Sylvan Press, London, 1951).

Erskine-Hill, H., *The Social Milieu of Alexander Pope* (Yale University Press, New Haven, 1975).

Guerinot, J. V., (ed.) *Pamphlet Attacks on Alexander Pope, 1711–1744: A Descriptive Bibliography* (Methuen, London, 1969).

Hammond, B. S., *Pope and Bolingbroke: A Study of Friendship and Influence* (University of Missouri Press, Columbia, 1984).

Johnson, S., 'Pope', *Lives of the English Poets* (*1779–81*); ed. G. B. Hill, 3 vols (Clarendon Press, Oxford, 1905), Vol. III.

Mack, M., *Alexander Pope: A Life* (Yale University Press, New Haven, 1985).

Nicolson, M. H. and Rousseau, G. S., *This Long Disease, My Life* (Princeton University Press, Princeton, 1968).

Rosslyn, F., *Alexander Pope: A Literary Life*, Macmillan Literary Lives (Macmillan, London, 1990).

Rumbold, V., *Women's Place in Pope's World* (Cambridge University Press, Cambridge, 1989).

Sherburn, G., *The Early Career of Alexander Pope* (Clarendon Press, Oxford, 1934).

Wimsatt, W. K., *The Portraits of Alexander Pope* (Yale University Press, New Haven, 1965).

Criticism

Collections

Barnard, J., (ed.) *Pope: The Critical Heritage* (Routledge and Kegan Paul, London, 1973).

Bateson, F. W. and Joukovsky, N. A., (eds) *Alexander Pope: A Critical Anthology* (Penguin, Harmondsworth, 1971).

Clifford, J. L. and Landa, L. A., (eds) *Pope and His Contemporaries: Essays Presented to George Sherburn* (Clarendon Press, Oxford, 1949).

Dixon, P., (ed.) *Writers and their Background: Alexander Pope* (Bell, London, 1972).

Erskine-Hill, H. and Smith A., (eds) *The Art of Alexander Pope* (Vision Press, London, 1979).

Fairer, D., (ed.) *Pope: New Contexts* (Harvester Wheatsheaf, Brighton, 1990).

Guerinot, J. V., (ed.) *Pope*, Twentieth-Century Views (Prentice-Hall, New Jersey, 1972).

Mack, M., *Collected in Himself: Essays Critical, Biographical and Bibliographical on Pope and Some of His Contemporaries* (University of Delaware Press, Newark, Delaware, 1982).

Mack, M., (ed.) *Essential Articles for the Study of Alexander Pope* (Archon Books, Hamden, Connecticut, 1964).

Mack, M. and Winn, J. A., (eds) *Pope: Recent Essays by Several Hands* (The Harvester Press, Brighton, 1980).

Nicolson, C., (ed.) *Alexander Pope: Essays for the Tercentenary* (Aberdeen University Press, Aberdeen, 1988).

Rousseau, G. S. and Rogers, P., (eds) *The Enduring Legacy: Alexander Pope Tercentenary Essays* (Cambridge University Press, Cambridge, 1988).

General

Brower, R. A., *Alexander Pope: the Poetry of Allusion* (Clarendon Press, Oxford, 1959).

Damrosch, L., Jr, *The Imaginative World of Alexander Pope* (University of California Press, Berkeley, 1987).

Dixon, P., *The World of Pope's Satires* (Methuen, London, 1968).

Edwards, T. R., *This Dark Estate: A Reading of Pope* (University of California Press, Berkeley and Los Angeles, 1963).

Fairer, D., *Pope's Imagination* (Manchester University Press, Manchester, 1984).

Fairer, D., *The Poetry of Alexander Pope*, Penguin Critical Studies (Penguin, Harmondsworth, 1989).

Fraser, G. S., *Alexander Pope* (Routledge and Kegan Paul, London 1978).

Gurr, E., *Pope*, Writers and Critics (Oliver and Boyd, Edinburgh, 1981).

Hammond, B. S., *Pope*, Harvester New Readings (The Harvester Press, Brighton, 1986).

Jack, I., *Augustan Satire: Intention and Idiom in English Poetry, 1660–1750* (Clarendon Press, Oxford, 1952).

Leranbaum, M., *Alexander Pope's 'Opus Magnum', 1729–1744* (Clarendon Press, Oxford, 1977).

Mack, M., *The Garden and the City: Retirement and Politics in the Later Poetry of Pope, 1731–1743* (University of Toronto Press, Toronto, 1969).

Mack, M., *The Last and Greatest Art: Some Unpublished Poetical Manuscripts of Alexander Pope* (University of Delaware Press, Newark, 1984).

Nussbaum, F., *The Brink of All We Hate: English Satires on Women, 1660–1750*, (University Press of Kentucky, Lexington, 1984).

Pollak, E., *The Poetics of Sexual Myth: Gender and Ideology in the Verse of Swift and Pope* (University of Chicago Press, Chicago, 1985).

Rogers, P., *An Introduction to Pope* (Methuen, London, 1975).

269

Rogers, P., *Hacks and Dunces: Pope, Swift and Grub Street* (Methuen, London, 1980).

Tillotson, G., *On the Poetry of Pope* (Clarendon Press, Oxford, 1938; 1959).

Wasserman, E. R., *The Subtler Language: Critical Readings of Neoclassic and Romantic Poems* (Johns Hopkins Press, Baltimore, 1959).

Particular poems

Cunningham, J. S., *Pope: The Rape of the Lock* (Edward Arnold, London, 1961).

Erskine-Hill, H., *Pope: The Dunciad*, (Edward Arnold, London, 1972).

Halsband, R., *The Rape of the Lock and its Illustrations, 1714–1896* (Clarendon Press, Oxford, 1980).

Maresca, T. E., *Pope's Horatian Poems* (Ohio State University Press, Columbus, 1966).

Nuttal, A. D., *Pope's 'Essay on Man'*, Unwin Critical Library (George Allen and Unwin, London, 1984).

Sitter, J. E., *The Poetry of Pope's 'Dunciad'* (University of Minnesota Press, Minneapolis, 1971).

Stack, F., *Pope and Horace: Studies in Imitation* (Cambridge University Press, Cambridge, 1985).

Wasserman, E. R., *Pope's Epistle to Bathurst: A Critical Reading with an Edition of the Manuscripts* (Johns Hopkins University Press, Baltimore, 1960).

Williams, A., *Pope's Dunciad: A Study of Its Meaning* (Methuen, London, 1955).

Contextual studies

Intellectual history

Fussell, P., *The Rhetorical World of Augustan Humanism: Ethics and Imagery from Swift to Burke* (Clarendon Press, Oxford, 1965).

Hampson, N., *The Enlightenment*, The Pelican History of European Thought, Vol. 4 (Penguin, Harmondsworth, 1968).

Hipple, W., *The Beautiful, the Sublime and the Picturesque in Eighteenth-Century British Aesthetic Theory* (Carbondale, Illinois, 1957).

Hussey, C., *The Picturesque, Studies in a Point of View* (London, 1927).

Lovejoy, A. O., *Essays in the History of Ideas* (Johns Hopkins University Press, Baltimore, 1948).

Lovejoy, A. O., *The Great Chain of Being: A Study of the History of an Idea* (Harvard University Press, Cambridge, Mass., 1936).

Monk, S. H., *The Sublime: A Study of Critical Theories in XVIII-Century England* (1935; University of Michigan, Ann Arbor, 1960).

Nicolson, M. H., *Mountain Gloom and Mountain Glory: The Development of the Aesthetics of the Infinite* (1959; Norton, New York, 1963).

Sprat, T., *History of the Royal Society* (1667; ed. Jackson I. Cope and Harold Whitmore Jones, Washington University Studies, Saint Louis, Missouri, 1958).

Stephen, L., *History of English Thought in the Eighteenth Century*, 2 vols, (Smith, Elder and Co., London, 1876).

Weber, M., *The Protestant Ethic and the Spirit of Capitalism*, translated by T. Parsons (George Allen and Unwin, London, 1930).

Willey, B., *Eighteenth-Century Background*, (Chatto and Windus, London, 1940).

Social and political history

Bell, I. A., *Literature and Crime in Augustan England* (Routledge, London, 1991).

Besant, Sir W., *London in the Eighteenth Century* (Adam and Charles Black, London, 1902).

Castle, T., *Masquerade and Civilization: The Carnivalesque in Eighteenth-Century English Culture and Fiction* (Stanford University Press, Stanford, California, 1986).

George, D., *England in Transition* (1931; Penguin, Harmondsworth, 1953).

Holmes, G., *British Politics in the Age of Anne*, revised edition (Hambledon, London, 1987).

Humphreys, A. R., *The Augustan World* (Methuen, London, 1954).

Jarrett, D., *Britain 1688–1815* (Longman, London, 1965).

Kramnick, I., *Bolingbroke and his Circle* (Harvard University Press, Cambridge, Mass., 1968).

Plumb, J. H., *The Growth of Political Stability in England, 1675–1725* (1967; Penguin, Harmondsworth, 1969).

Rogers, P., *Grub Street: Studies in a Subculture* (Methuen, London, 1972).

Rudé, G., *Hanoverian London, 1714–1808* (Secker and Warburg, London, 1971).

Speck, W. A., *Stability and Strife: England, 1714–60* (Edward Arnold, London, 1977).

Stow, J., *A Survey of the Cities of London and Westminster* (1598, Corrected, Improved and very much enlarged by John Strype, in Six Books, London, 1720).

Summerson, J., *Georgian London* (1945; Penguin, Harmondsworth, 1962).

Trevelyan, G. M., *Illustrated English Social History: Volume Three; The Eighteenth Century* (1952; Penguin, Harmondsworth, 1964).

Turberville, A. S., *English Men and Manners in the Eighteenth Century* (Oxford University Press, Oxford, 1926; reprinted 1957).

Literary criticism

Atkins, J. W. H., *English Literary Criticism: Seventeenth and Eighteenth Centuries* (Methuen, London, 1951).

Elledge, S., (ed.) *Eighteenth-Century Critical Essays*, 2 vols (Cornell University Press, Ithaca, 1961).

Goldgar, B. A., (ed.), *Literary Criticism of Alexander Pope* (University of Nebraska Press, Lincoln, 1965).

Wimsatt, W. K. and Brooks C., *Literary Criticism: a short history* (Vintage Books, Alfred A. Knopf, New York, 1957).

The kindred arts

Brownell, M. R., *Alexander Pope and the Arts of Georgian England* (Clarendon Press, Oxford, 1978).

Hagstrum, J., *The Sister Arts* (University of Chicago Press, Chicago, 1958).

Hunt, J. D., *The Figure in the Landscape: Poetry, Painting and Gardening during the Eighteenth Century* (Johns Hopkins University Press, Baltimore, 1976).

Hussey, C., *English Gardens and Landscapes, 1700–1750* (Country Life Ltd, London, 1967).

Malins, E., *English Landscaping and Literature, 1660–1840* (Oxford University Press, Oxford, 1966).

Martin, P., *Pursuing Innocent Pleasures: The Gardening World of Alexander Pope* (Archon Books, Hamden, Connecticut, 1984).

Whinney, M., *Sculpture in Britain, 1530–1830*, Pelican History of Art (Penguin Books, Harmondsworth, 1964).

Wimsatt, W. K., *The Portraits of Alexander Pope* (Yale University Press, New Haven, 1965).

Index

Index to Pope's works